Social Work

PRACTICAL POLITICS

and Political Responsibility

MARYANN MAHAFFEY
and JOHN W. HANKS
editors

NATIONAL ASSOCIATION OF
SOCIAL WORKERS
Washington, DC

First Reprinting, May 1989

Second Reprinting, April 1993

Designed by Joan Stoliar

International Standard Book No.: 0-87101-099-2
                           0-87101-093-3 (paperback edition)
Library of Congress Catalog Card No.: 82-80273

Printed in U.S.A.

Political advocacy of "changes in policy and legislation to improve social conditions and to promote social justice" is a significant component of the revised Code of Ethics adopted in 1979 by the National Association of Social Workers (NASW). This formulation of the social worker's ethical responsibility was not the result of a sudden theoretical advance; nor did it represent an ideal remote from contemporary social work practice. Rather, it was merely the codification of principles and practices that had been developing since the early years of the profession.

Political awareness and involvement have been intensifying among social workers since the 1960s. Many had become aware that politicians usually determine who gets what services, and with this awareness came the recognition that few politicians well understand social issues, human needs, or the history of previous attempts to solve social problems—certainly not to the extent that professional social workers do. This perception, coupled with the profession's historic commitment to meeting human needs, was a powerful incentive for social workers to increase their participation in the political institutions that formulate social policy.

Many social workers confined their political activities to less conspicuous roles—as campaign workers, technical advisers, and political appointees—but increasing numbers began to assume leadership positions as candidates, heads of coalitions, and full-time lobbyists. More social workers held political office in the 1970s than ever before in United States history. The national professional association also assumed greater political responsibility in the 1970s: to be nearer the center of political power in this country, it moved its headquarters to Washington, D.C.; it established organizational channels to support candidates and influence legislation; and in 1976, it sponsored its first conference on social workers and politics.

The 1970s also saw the widespread development of curricula in social work education relating to political processes. The regressive social and political changes of the early 1980s seemed likely both to accelerate this trend in social work education and to spur even more social workers to increase their political involvement in order to preserve the integrity of social service agencies and services to clients.

It is not surprising that social workers, with their intense concern for community programs, intergroup relations, and social action, are often deeply involved in political causes and campaigns. What is surprising is that the literature of the profession should contain so little relating the values, objectives, and skills of social work to the political process. Relatively few articles have treated any aspect of the subject. This is the first book to do so.

Because *Practical Politics: Social Work and Political Responsibility* is a pioneering effort, we have included articles that address a broad range of questions: What are the historic precedents for the current political activism among social workers? What basic principles underlie the recognition of a political component in social work practice? What skills do social workers need to improve their effectiveness as legislative advocates or political candidates? How can holding elective office help a social worker achieve service goals?

Although the emphasis is decidedly on the practical—how to organize a campaign, how to testify, how to establish a coalition—this book bears little relation to the how-to handbooks of political parties or groups such as the Women's Education Fund. A major difference is that the contributors to this volume consistently relate the political technology they discuss to the objectives, values, and methods of social work. The aim is not to transform social workers into politicians but to help them become more effective in pursuing social work goals through political channels.

Social workers bring something of special importance to political life; it derives from their unique combination of experience and training. A personal observation of Congressman Ron Dellums of California suggests the importance of both:

> As a social worker, I have a perspective on the issues that tends to
> be humanistic rather than legalistic. A social worker knows misery
> and human needs from actual contact. Politicians normally deal
> only in the abstract and usually have been isolated from people who
> face despair and tragic living conditions.... Social work training
> allows me to deal with individuals on an individual basis, to be able
> to acknowledge their needs and problems, yet retain a professional
> demeanor in facing these problems.[1]

---

1. Personal communication to Maryann Mahaffey, Detroit, Michigan, 1978.

Dellums, like other social workers elected to office, has found that social work's traditional method of solving problems in therapeutic situations—diagnosing and defining the problem, setting goals and objectives, agreeing on a contract, developing strategies for intervention, and evaluating and correcting the interventive process—transfers readily to the political realm. Social workers no less than politicians rely on compromise and accommodation.

This book is a first step in explaining how the knowledge, experience, and skills of social work apply to the political process and how political participation can help social workers fulfill their professional responsibilities. We recognize that the book omits certain key aspects of social workers' contributions to politics—for example, the roles of the administrative aide and the technical expert and a chronicle of NASW's own distinguished contribution to national lobbying efforts—but the urgency we share with politically active social workers about bringing this subject into print and drawing the profession's attention to it supersedes our desire for comprehensiveness. We hope this volume both encourages and improves social workers' participation in politics and that it is soon followed by other books on the subject of social workers in politics.

A few acknowledgments are essential. We thank Chauncey Alexander for his broad vision of the role of social work—and hence for his leadership in identifying the political responsibilities of social workers, for his support of social workers in politics, and for his insistence that this book be completed and published. We deeply appreciate the attention that Beatrice Saunders gave this book during the busy months just before her retirement as the director of NASW's Publications Department. Bea guided us through early pitfalls, provided both constructive criticism and encouragement, and then placed our project in the capable hands of her successor, Jacqueline Atkins, and consulting editor Rick Langstaff. We are also grateful to Lemmie Blakemore of Maryann Mahaffey's staff for her calm efficiency in keeping all the parts of the book's manuscript flowing among its editors and authors.

MARYANN MAHAFFEY

JOHN W. HANKS

November 1981

Contents

MARYANN MAHAFFEY, *MSW, Member, Detroit City Council, and Professor, School of Social Work, Wayne State University, Detroit, Michigan.*
JOHN W. HANKS, *Ph.D., retired, Professor, Department of Social Work, University of Wyoming, Laramie.*

DONALD BRIELAND, *Ph.D., Dean, Jane Addams College of Social Work, University of Illinois, Chicago.*

PART I
POLITICAL ACTIVITY AND PROFESSIONAL GOALS

CHAUNCEY A. ALEXANDER, *MSW, Executive Director, National Association of Social Workers, Washington, D.C.*

ALLEN F. DAVIS, *Ph.D., Professor, Department of History, Temple University, Philadelphia, Pennsylvania.*

KATHARINE HOOPER BRIAR, *DSW, Assistant Professor, School of Social Work, University of Washington, Seattle.*
SCOTT BRIAR, *DSW, Dean and Professor, School of Social Work, University of Washington, Seattle.*

THE PROFESSIONAL ASSOCIATION AND POLITICAL ACTION

PART IV

Introduction

DONALD BRIELAND

ALTHOUGH the public policies that emerge from political processes often have direct impact on social work programs, many social workers are reluctant to involve themselves in political activities. Until the courts affirmed the civil rights of government employees, Hatch Act restrictions often discouraged political participation among social workers and other public employees. The act was commonly overinterpreted, however, particularly by the employees themselves.

Nor have legal restrictions, real or presumed, been the primary obstacle. Many social workers oppose political efforts as diverting attention from practice; others express reservations about their effectiveness in politics. Even those social workers who are interested in shaping social policy rarely work their way up in traditional political organizations to qualify for party support. Few have the time or money to run for political office. Consequently, social workers are often frustrated by the greater political influence of economists, business analysts, and lawyers, and they frequently watch from the sidelines as public administrators take over the management of state budgets and, occasionally, of public agencies.

Obstacles and reasons for pessimism surely exist, but that is only part of the picture. A recent study of members of the Michigan Chapter of the National Association of Social Workers (NASW) found that social workers are as politically active as other professionals and business executives.[1] At the same time, an increasing number of social workers—such as Ron Dellums of California and Barbara Mikulski of Maryland, who are members of Congress—hold political office, and the last decade has seen a steady increase in the involvement of social workers in political campaigns, lobbying efforts, and advisory roles to politicians and legislative committees.

In presenting samples of these and other forms of political activity by social workers, *Practical Politics: Social Work and Political Responsibility* aims to provide social workers with practical guidelines for gaining and exercising political influence. Although the book focuses on social work, it will be equally useful to members of other helping professions whose practice is also strongly affected by social policies. This volume presents organizational approaches, linkages between practice and politics, lobbying techniques, and examples and suggestions from practitioners involved in politics as campaign workers, candidates, officeholders, and executives of professional organizations.

The emphasis of the book is strongly on the practical, but several articles address the theoretical considerations that arise in assessing the political obligations and capabilities of social workers. Such considerations necessarily involve attention to historical precedents, and it will be useful, in this introductory overview, to sketch the historical backdrop to the current rise of social work involvement in elective and legislative processes.

Historical Developments

After the establishment of almshouses and asylums, four movements were important to the development of political action as a component of professional social work practice. Three of them originated in the second half of the nineteenth century, the fourth in the 1930s.

- The annual meetings of the National Conference of Charities and Correction, which was founded in the 1870s, brought practitioners together from institutions and neighborhood centers and stimulated pronouncements on urban problems and racial discrimination. These meetings also provided staff members with the impetus to enlist the help of politicians in addressing problems of poverty and injustice.

- In analyzing the causes of poverty, the charity organization societies originally emphasized a theory of personal failure, but later extended their analysis to include social policies that led to child labor, low wages, inadequate housing, and public health problems. They came to see these conditions as requiring political action. In its political efforts, this movement emphasized fact gathering and reporting, and data on welfare issues that it published in the magazine *Survey* were influential in policy decisions.

- The settlement movement successfully used both personal intervention with politicians and data based on a firsthand knowledge of the neighborhood to influence social policies. Settlement staff involved neighborhood residents in reform movements and served as advocates for women, children, and ethnic minorities. They also supported the development of labor unions. Although settlement workers did not usually become officeholders, they were often successful in dramatizing neighborhood problems to influential citizens. Community leaders, in turn, often served as board members of the settlements.

- Community organization developed as a field in the 1930s after social work had established itself as a profession. A report defining community organization was presented to the National Conference of Social Work in 1939. Because community organization was to involve social workers in neighborhood and other grass-roots activities, it attracted activist social workers and probably served initially to reduce the pressure on clinical social workers for political participation. Some social workers look back nostalgically to the dramatic approaches of such organizers as Saul Alinsky, but others regard them as unprofessional. Community organization techniques reached the most people through the antipoverty programs of President Lyndon Johnson.

Although all four movements could be reviewed in detail for their part in shaping the political patterns of social work, the settlement movement serves as an extended example in the article by Allen Davis. Davis emphasizes that the leaders of the movement at first operated with no political theory and with little interest in politics, but that they learned fast. He characterizes settlement workers in the Progressive Era at the turn of the century as tough-minded realists who understood how the American political system operated.

Political Linkages

After the development of community organization, clinical practitioners and workers oriented to social action vied for position in social work. This conflict was not yet resolved in 1955 when NASW was formed from seven constituent groups, but as Chauncey Alexander observes in his analysis of the political responsibilities of social workers, association-sponsored inquiries successfully demonstrated the organic relationship between service programs and social policy. This had the effect of making political activity an obligation of the professional social worker and of the professional association: "To ignore this vital component," Alexander states, "is to abandon professional accountability and pervert the primary service." In the 1970s, the national organizations of many professions, including social work, expanded their lobbying at the federal level, and most of them moved their offices to Washington, D.C., to have a base for political action.

Whereas the Alexander article emphasizes the broad conceptual issues behind the linkage of practitioner, policymaker, and political activist, Katharine Hooper Briar and Scott Briar focus on the reciprocal interactions of policy and practice as they manifest themselves in day-to-day clinical practice. They point out that social work interventions with individuals often constitute mini policy experiments and that the knowledge social workers derive from such experiments is vitally important to policymakers, who often lack information on policy impacts and deficits. The Briars emphasize that "simple statements of anticipated harms or benefits," rather than scientific rigor, are "acceptable first steps in creating an informed base for decision making."

Linkages between policies and practice have been most troublesome for radical social workers who strongly question how they can work in bureaucracies that not only take the existing social order for granted, but actually perpetuate it by maintaining dominant social norms. Paul Adams analyzes this dilemma and lays out the options the radical social worker must consider. He draws on firsthand experience in England, where radical social work is more visible than in America, and where practitioners' discontent over professional salaries and cuts in services led to the organization of the British Union of Social Workers and, in 1977–78, to widespread strikes by practitioners. Adams points out that social workers who look to the job itself—to work with clients—as a means of radical change risk distorting practice and doing a disservice to clients. Instead, he identifies worker-to-worker and worker-to-employer relationships, possibly through trade union efforts, as more appropriate and promising avenues for serious political activity.

The trade union issue is interesting as it relates to NASW. The association has never considered itself a union, but the possibilities for political action inherent in its structure make it more akin to the union model than the professional association model. NASW has a unified structure with a single membership and a dues structure covering local, state, and national activities. By contrast, the American Medical Association is organized similarly in some but not all states, and participation in the American Bar Association confers only national membership. The singularity in NASW's structure offers advantages both in facilitating a unified political focus and in training social workers for political activities at the local, state, and national levels.

Political Advocacy

Social workers become involved in political action in different ways. A few bring a broad range of political interests and activities with them from their student days, but most probably identify first with issues that affect social services for their clients. Direct service workers know their clients' needs firsthand and often represent their clients' interests by giving legislative testimony and by otherwise attempting to influence public policy. This is political advocacy. Recently, many social workers have also been attracted to lobbying for professional issues, such as licensing and third-party payments, and Richan has found that social workers are most likely to support a political issue if it involves both concern for the consumer and professional interests.[2] Most social workers are also interested in broad societal issues that concern all citizens and that are only indirectly related to social work or its clients. The articles in this book relate primarily to the advocacy role.

Lobbying, which may be defined as political activity in behalf of legislation, is the main technique of political advocacy.[3] In an article that is often quoted and that has been revised for this volume, Maryann Mahaffey identifies lobbying as a methodology for creating change, presents the elements of lobbying—struggle, confrontation, negotiation, compromise, coalition building, and the application of power—and sets forth the essentials of an effective lobbying program and the characteristics of a good lobbyist. Among the major tasks of lobbyists, Mahaffey cites technical assistance to legislators first. Her article also presents a realistic chronological model for the development of legislation.

George Sharwell reviews procedures for testifying before legislative committees and presents a detailed guide for preparing a written summary of the testimony. He also recommends using the summary for subsequent lobbying by the professional organization.

Based on their analysis of the characteristics of almost two hundred social and health service bills introduced in a single session of the Washington State legislature, Ronald Dear and Rino Patti suggest tactics to increase the chances of gaining favorable legislative outcomes. These tactics are likely to be familiar to experienced lobbyists, but Dear and Patti's intention is to "suggest tactics that can readily be used by part-time, single-issue advocates who make an occasional foray into the legislative arena to promote a bill of immediate interest to their agency or a client constituency." Dear and Patti's work is the first to establish an empirical base for such guidelines.

The framework for monitoring a bureaucracy is similar to that for successful lobbying. As the article by William Bell and Budd Bell makes clear, "monitoring the bureaucracy, the agency of legislative implementation, is a concomitant responsibility to legislative lobbying; it adds a measure of assurance that social change sought by legislation will take place." The two roles, monitoring and lobbying, complement one another. The Bells' article draws on Budd Bell's extensive experience monitoring Florida's Department of Health and Rehabilitative Services and presents four case examples that illustrate monitoring efforts to affect state budgeting, implement federal regulations regarding parental payments for day care, overcome resistance to community care for the aging, and reduce the incidence of involuntary commitments to state mental hospitals. The guidelines offered by the Bells at the end of their article should enhance the effectiveness of any state chapter's monitoring program.

Coalitions

As Mahaffey's and Dear and Patti's articles both point out, coalition building is often an important element of a lobbying program. Social work organizations have long used coalitions of professional and lay groups to gain support for social actions in behalf of clients. The Wyoming coalition described by William Whitaker rallied support from more than thirty organizations, including the Wyoming Chapter of NASW, for a supplemental food program for women, infants, and children. The legislative lobbying efforts of the coalition were under the direction of a social worker. Basing its campaign on the finding that every dollar the food program spent saved four dollars in medical costs, the coalition succeeded. As Whitaker notes, the Wyoming coalition offers "hope that progressive change is possible even in the face of heavy conservative opposition." Whitaker bases his analysis of the Wyoming coalition's structure and strategies on Roland Warren's six-dimension model of change efforts.

The ad hoc, single-issue, local coalition such as the Wyoming example is just one of several forms of successful coalitions in which social workers frequently participate. Stable coalitions offer distinct advantages in that they can both undertake a variety of prolonged political actions and perform legislative review functions. Coalitions of this kind are not easy to sustain, however, and many organizations prefer to affiliate only with short-term, ad hoc coalitions and to enter into such an arrangement only after rigorously defining the goals of their participation and the level and kind of support they are prepared to contribute.

At the national level, the 33 organizations that came together in 1973 in behalf of Title XX of the Social Security Act exemplify a particularly successful coalition that had a great effect on the development and passage of legislation.[4] In recent years, such national-level coalitions have become increasingly difficult to form and maintain because human service organizations that might otherwise join forces have found themselves competing for the same portions of a shrinking federal pie. However, the Reagan administration's doctrinaire approach in subordinating virtually all human service concerns to budget cuts had a galvanizing effect on many social welfare organizations and may have prepared the way for reviving national coalitions. Formed shortly after Reagan took office, the Illinois Coalition Against Reagan Economics (I CARE) drew support from the Illinois Chapter of NASW and 175 other organizations, indicating that a broad spectrum of groups can find common interests against an economic program of severe and general cutbacks.

Elective Process

Working in political campaigns is basic to a legislative action program because it can put candidates in office who will vote in accordance with the objectives of the organization. Social work organizations usually work to elect the choice of one major political party or the other, but, as noted earlier, increasing numbers of social workers are choosing to become candidates or, in other cases, to assume active roles in campaigns and other political functions. If the experiences related in this book are typical, social workers, both as candidates and as campaign workers, are frequently attracted to independent candidacy in primary elections. Victory in such candidacies means defeating the candidate who has party backing. If an independent candidate is successful in the primary, party support may come in the general election as it did for Mike Schwarzwalder, a candidate for a senate seat in Ohio, whose campaign staff included several social workers in key positions. In their article, William Whitaker and Jan Flory-Baker describe the social work influence as a key element in making the Schwarzwalder campaign responsive to the social and economic needs of the voters.

Social worker Cecilia Kleinkauf entered the race for the Alaska legislature much too late to develop an effective campaign organization, but the story of her campaign illustrates the role conflicts placed on candidates, particularly social work candidates, and offers useful information about how to understand and cope with them. Professionals considering running for office will see from Kleinkauf's experiences the need for a campaign manager, preferably one with extensive experience, and for an effective strategy to raise funds. The lack of help from social work colleagues was a sobering reality that Kleinkauf, like many social work candidates, had to face.

As a member of the Detroit City Council, Maryann Mahaffey undertook an extended effort to establish a means of dealing with the problem of family violence. Her objective was to involve both social workers and police in a program that could defuse incidents of violence and provide social services to the disputants. Persistence, timing, and political sophistication are all evident in Mahaffey's success in obtaining first a pilot project and then a grant for a larger effort. Fortuitous changes in the police department's political alignments contributed to the victory, but only because the program's supporters were continually alert to opportunities.

Ruth Messinger, a member of the New York City Council, emphasizes the importance of her social work background and training in shaping her administrative style and political objectives. A principal objective that grows directly out of her social work background is empowerment—helping constituents by showing them how they can get for themselves the assistance they need. Messinger, like the other social workers writing on their political experiences in this book, exhibits enthusiasm for and commitment to the elective process. Seeking and winning public office is clearly the most effective way to ensure that social welfare concerns are represented in legislatures. As larger numbers of social workers take active roles in political campaigns, more of them are acquiring expertise in political and legislative processes and are being sought as candidates. People with degrees in both social work and law make especially attractive candidates.

Mechanisms for Political Action

Alexander identifies the professional association as the medium for distilling professional knowledge and opinion and for bringing the collective wisdom of the association's members into the political arena. NASW has established two mechanisms for collective political action—the Education Legislative Action Network (ELAN) to pursue the association's legislative objectives through lobbying, and Political Action for Candidate Election (PACE), a political action committee that endorses and makes financial contributions to the campaigns of candidates who will support the association's programs. Although ELAN and PACE are still far from reaching their potential and remain undeveloped in many areas of the country, the unified structure of the national association has organizational and financial advantages that enhance the potential of both organizations. The final chapters of this book give state organizations helpful suggestions about how to establish ELAN and PACE.

In describing the development of ELAN in Washington State, David Dempsey characterizes ELAN as "a tightly knit communication system" for expressing "to congressional and other legislative leaders the various needs and interests of the social work profession and its clients." The basic resource of such a communications network is people—the NASW membership who are kept informed through a carefully organized telephone tree and who can be counted on to deliver the association's message to legislators from their district at precisely the right time.

PACE is different from ELAN. It has its own membership, it is organized and financed separately from the state chapter to comply with tax laws, and its purpose involves direct support of candidates. Raising money is a critical function of any political action committee, but it is a difficult task among social workers, who are not in the habit of supporting political candidates financially.

Harvey Abrams and Sheldon Goldstein describe the organization of PACE as part of a comprehensive political program by the Florida Chapter of NASW. They emphasize the importance of the state chapter's establishing definite legislative goals each year and then using a multifaceted program of lobbying, political action, education, and monitoring in which each element, including PACE, complements the others.

Political action programs for a professional organization, whether at the state or national level, require staff members who can prepare and publicize clear position statements on public issues, lobbyists to draft bills and promote social welfare legislation, and committed members to reinforce the stand of the organization with legislators, agency administrators, and other influential citizens. Continuing, sophisticated social action programs can serve the welfare of clients, the profession, and society at large. This book shows how it has been done and invites your participation in future efforts.

Notes and References

1. *See* James L. Wolk, "Are Social Workers Politically Active?" *Social Work,* 26 (July 1981), pp. 283–288.

2. Willard C. Richan, *Social Service Politics in the United States and Britain* (Philadelphia: Temple University Press, 1981), p. 24.

3. For a more detailed discussion of lobbying, *see* Donald Brieland and John Lemmon, *Social Work and the Law* (St. Paul, Minn.: West Publishing Co., 1977), p. 6.

4. *See* Paul E. Mott, *Meeting Human Needs: The Social and Political History of Title XX* (Columbus, Ohio: National Conference on Social Welfare, 1977).

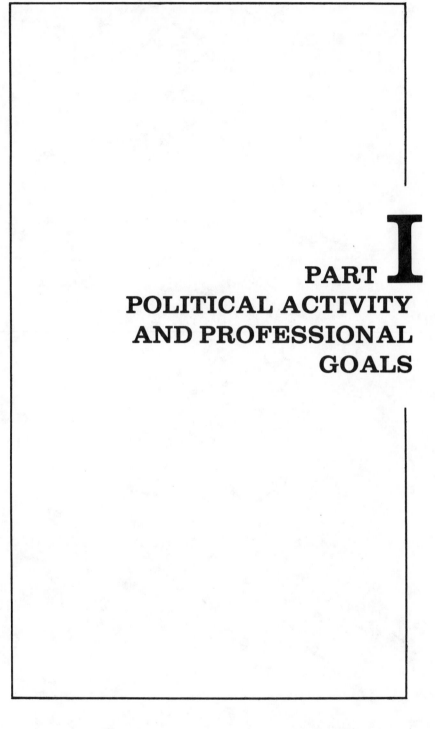

PART I
POLITICAL ACTIVITY
AND PROFESSIONAL
GOALS

Professional Social Workers and Political Responsibility

CHAUNCEY A. ALEXANDER

1

THE social work profession, from its inception, has had a love-hate relationship with politics. The range of sentiments regarding politics swings from the optimistic opinion that the humblest of the land,"when clad in the armor of a righteous cause, is stronger than all the hosts of error" (William Jennings Bryan) to the pessimistic view that "nowhere are prejudices more mistaken for the truth, passion for reason, and invective for documentation than in politics" (John Mason Brown).

Behind this ambivalence, which has intensified with the maturation of the profession, has been a fundamental conflict in establishing the recognized and accepted functions of the professional social worker—the struggle for primacy between individual intervention and social change to improve the quality of life. An examination of the relationship between the social worker's professional function and political responsibility suggests a resolution to this long-standing confusion and conflict—a resolution founded on the development of a conceptual base that locates the profession's obligations at points of dissonance between the individual and society.

ɔf Political Responsibility

of the conflict were sown in the origins of the social
᠁ssion in the social reform movements of the latter part
᠁ nineteenth century and then nurtured by the economic and
social forces in which the profession grew. The early child labor,
settlement house, workmen's compensation, and other movements
sought solutions to adverse social conditions through concerted
social action, including legislative lobbying and the mobilization of
political influence. The names of the pioneer leaders of those
movements—Jane Addams, Florence Kelley, Edith Abbott, Harry
Hopkins—are still invoked by advocates of greater political activity on the part of social workers.

During the same period, the necessity to provide a humane
counter to the poor-law–oriented institutional bureaucracies of the
state boards of charities and the need to end abuses by professional beggars resulted in the development of the charity organization societies. Committed as they were to "scientific philanthropy," these societies worked at developing the technology of
helping—the interview, the case conference, the referral, and the
coordination of services. That pioneer of professionalization, Mary
Richmond, symbolized this second stream of social welfare development with her emphasis on improving the functioning of the
personality and the family. It turns out, however, that she was
more sensitive to the relationship between improving an individual's condition and the broader aims of social reforms than many of
her professional descendants.

The struggle for primacy between social intervention and
individual or personal intervention was launched with these two
streams of activity. Political responsibility became a component of
those emphasizing social intervention. The chasm between the
two historical streams is illustrated by the observation Davis
makes in the next chapter of this book (p. 32):

> Settlement workers during the Progressive Era were probably more
> committed to political action than any other group of welfare
> workers before or since. Charity organization workers also cooper-
> ated on occasion in political reform projects, but Robert Hunter,
> the itinerant radical settlement worker and charity expert, was
> probably right in 1902, even if he exaggerated, when he decided
> that the settlement worker and the charity worker had basically
> different temperaments.

ALEXANDER

This genetic explanation for professional function and preference persists to the present time.

During the rapid growth of social work in the Progressive years from 1890 to 1920, settlement workers used the survey technique to link social conditions with economic factors and legislative action. These efforts were matched in the emphasis on specialized technical competence by such organizations as the American Association of Medical Social Workers and the National Association of School Social Workers.

EMPHASIS ON THE INDIVIDUAL

World War I and the 1920s brought a new era for social work, one in which a combination of social forces reduced the functional relationship of professionals to politics. The reactionary attacks on any progressive measures, in concert with the expansion of liberal capitalism and rational technology, created a climate in social work and throughout society that was conducive to individual enterprise and technological emphases and hostile to political reform. The development of business-sponsored community chests, the entry of the philanthropic foundations into social welfare financing, and the concentration of voluntary agencies on the refinement of their technical service capabilities influenced social workers to focus their concerns on finding solutions to individual dysfunction. This emphasis was heightened by the importation and promulgation of psychoanalytic theory, which gave an important ideological base to the techniques of helping people. This development has been discussed extensively in the social work literature.

The concentration on the technology of individual social casework culminated in two landmark clarifications that largely excluded political activity as a significant component of the social worker's function. In 1929, Lee made the distinction between social work as cause and function, supporting the tendency to concentrate on technical proficiency.[1] The Milford Conference defined generic social casework with only remote reference to legislative action as a community resource.[2]

The Great Depression of 1929 brought to the nation a decade of widespread social misery and a surge of political radicalism. Both had profound influence on the social welfare scene and social work. The massive unemployment problem and the "ill fed, the ill clad, and the ill housed" subjected social agencies and social workers to a wrenching adjustment in their outlook and responsibility. Private agency services gave way to large-scale government programs, which expanded into the present multibillion-dollar fragmented system.

ORGANIZATIONAL TRENDS

Although the main stock-in-trade of social work was casework, which formed much of the basic methodology of the large-scale programs, the move of social workers into organizational and administrative positions demanded new techniques of group work and community organization. The burgeoning of personnel stimulated the need for training and greatly expanded the number of schools of social work, with consequent impact on the breadth and theory of social work practice. These technological expansions were accompanied by a rapid politicization of workers and their practice ideology as a result of their experiences with the politics of government programs. The growth of trade unionism among social workers and the fervor of the various political movements oriented to social welfare increased the social worker's awareness of the need to become influential in governmental decisions.

The thrust of this period, amid heated debate, was toward an increased recognition that the social worker, as a professional with special knowledge of social conditions, had a responsibility to engage in political activity. However, that activity was not generally considered to be an inherent professional responsibility, but an aspect of the separate methodology of community organization, which was to be exercised in behalf of one's social agency, through one's trade union, or as a personal duty of citizenship to be carried out in special interest groups or political organizations. Attempts to assign political responsibility to any of the seven professional associations in existence at that time met with only transitory successes. Strong arguments for "professionalism"—adherence to the functions of improving practice and developing standards—tended to prevail.

World War II, with its focus on national unity and an all-out war effort, absorbed the political concerns of social workers. They concentrated on developing techniques for new settings, and this resulted in new knowledge, increased the attention to practice analysis, and maintained the professional identity of social work. Political operations as a professional function were not advocated except by a small group of progressive social workers. References to politics were usually in the framework of generalized "social action" programs, principally as the "promotion of constructive legislation." For example, a 1944 "call to action" by an ad hoc Social Workers Emergency Committee assigned the principal responsibility for the promotion of constructive legislation to organizations outside social work.[3] Similarly, the 1945 annual report of the American Association of Social Workers, which looked "to the future," did not contain any reference to political activity.[4]

An exception to these trends was Pray's seminal article on social workers and partisan politics. In it, he concluded that

> ...the individual social worker not only can, but must, reach a specific conclusion, on the basis of his own judgment not only as to the validity of programs and principles, but as to the relative importance of these and other issues in the political arena, and as to the most dependable instruments—in parties or candidates—for the attainment of these ends.[5]

However, Pray also placed limits on social workers' political responsibility. He thought that activities within the boundaries of the social agency should be confined to "the function to which [the agency] is dedicated," a viewpoint that was influential until the challenges of the 1960s, and he further argued that the political activities of the professional association should be limited to one basic purpose—"the advancement of professional standards of performance."[6]

ORGANIZATIONAL CONSOLIDATION

It would take the next fifteen years, punctuated by such 1950s deterrents as the McCarthy period, the House Un-American Activities Committee, the Korean War, and conservative federal administrations, for social workers to explore, learn, and implement the political process in social agencies, in professional associations, and in individual professional activities. During this period, the definition and scope of political interest continually expanded. The programs of social agencies developed from the analysis of problems and programs to expert testimony and from the dissemination of information to the mobilization of concerned constituents. However, this expansion took place principally within the methodological framework of community organizations, which simply applied techniques of organization to ever wider areas of professional and agency concerns.

In 1955 seven predecessor professional associations were combined into a single National Association of Social Workers (NASW), and a struggle, often bitter in tone, occurred within the new organization concerning the nature and degree of political activity appropriate for a professional association. The conflict also concerned the relationship between political activity and the professional obligation of social work practitioners to give attention to social policy factors in their work with clients. Initially, NASW saw the political responsibility of social workers as limited principally to legislative and administrative contacts and to testimony before legislative committees. It established a Commission of Social Policy and Action to guide these activities and, in 1956, employed a staff member to work with the commission. A 1960-63 review of the structure and function of the association reaffirmed this pattern of limited legislative activity as the means of fulfilling the profession's political responsibility, and the Social Policy and Action Division was established to develop this form of political activity as one of the three primary functions to be performed by the association.

CHALLENGES OF THE 1960s

In the 1960s, social workers' participation in the social welfare thrusts of John F. Kennedy's New Frontier and the Great Society programs of Lyndon B. Johnson's administration legitimated many political activities, particularly within agency structures, as appropriate functions of social work. The attempt of the profession to respond to the social challenges of the civil rights, student, and consumer movements of the 1960s also escalated the profession's political activities and eventually tended to authenticate certain political techniques as activities of social workers. For example, the technique of organizational confrontation, which was originally decried as a radical measure, became incorporated into the impedimenta of social work educators and practitioners. Unfortunately, the stresses of that period, often exacerbated by either well-intentioned or opportunistic rhetoric, resulted in a devastating polarization between ardent advocates of "clinical practice" and equally fervent proponents of "social policy and action," with both sides claiming to identify and own the exclusive functions of the social worker. The profession was left in ideological and organizational disarray.

CLARIFICATION OF FUNCTIONS

The 1970s brought a different challenge to the profession, one that required a political response and helped to mend the wounds of the 1960s. The Nixon administration initiated a general reduction and selective elimination of social welfare programs. This was accompanied by a systematic elimination of social workers from policy, planning, and decision-making positions in major programs. It was part of a political strategy to concentrate administrative power by reducing the influence of professional, scientific, and civic organizations.

NASW, recovering from the organizational, ideological, and financial excesses of the 1960s, reorganized to meet the challenges through a program to unify and balance the functions of the professional association, which were redefined as: the improvement of knowledge and practice, the advancement of professional standards, the promotion of social service programs and policies, and the provision of membership services. The clarification of the first three of these functions demonstrated the organic relationship between the technical service and the social policy within which the service is provided and thereby established political activity as a formal obligation of the professional association and increased the recognition of political responsibility as a component of the professional social worker's function. This recognition was reflected in the move of NASW's national office to the nation's capital in December 1972.

In 1971, in response to overt need and membership demand, NASW established a decentralized national legislative apparatus called the Educational Legislative Action Network (ELAN) to pursue the association's functions and program priorities in legislation. Direct and indirect communications to members and related organizations were utilized. Individual social workers were thus informed of the relationships among policy, financing, and services; they were also exposed to the political processes of legislative analysis, policy and program advocacy, and coalition building and other organizational techniques. The formal assumption by the association of increased political responsibility in behalf of the profession is documented in actions of the biennial Delegate Assemblies, in the formulation of standards for association endorsement of political candidates, and in the establishment of Political Action for Candidate Election (PACE) in 1975 to raise funds for the direct support of political candidates. The formation of PACE committed the profession to full political responsibility.

Conceptual Base

Paralleling these organizational developments were fresh explications of the conceptual frameworks of professional practice. The purpose of these association-sponsored inquiries, which were initiated by NASW's Committee on Publications in 1974, was to establish general agreement on the functions of social workers and to formulate a unitary conception of social work. The theoretical constructs that emerged supported the inclusion of political responsibility as a component of professional functioning. The participants in those inquiries substantially agreed that in helping individuals, groups, and communities in their psychosocial functioning, the professional's central responsibility is to improve the interaction between people and their societal institutions or social units.[7] Thus, the professional's obligation for this interaction is no longer weighted on the side of personal problem solving, clinical practice, and personality alteration or, conversely, on the side of social action, institutional modification, or environmental manipulation. Rather, it is focused on the points where the individual and society come together, where problems occur as a result of some dissonance between people and their societal institutions. This means that the professional social worker is responsible for a dialectical process—or a dual responsibility, as it is often stated—to aid in the mobilization of both the individual's inner capabilities and society's external resources. The profession is coming to understand that no social worker is thoroughly professional who ignores either side of the equation of life.

Such recognition of the social forces that influence the nature and conditions of the service to be provided must necessarily lead to the fountainhead of society's liability, the policies and the policymakers. To ignore this vital component is to abandon professional accountability and pervert the primary service.

PERSON-ENVIRONMENT INTERPLAY

This conception moves the profession away from the narrow polarization between clinical services and policymaking and

toward the unity of social work practice that draws on knowl[ ]
of both personal and social factors to assist in change. Social v[ ]
practice has thus been defined as "a professionally guided sys[ ]
that engages people and their social units in change activities to
alter their psychosocial functioning for the purpose of improving
the quality of life."[8] Further, this conception, along with the
present scope and distribution of practice, demonstrates the
validity of professional social work as a service operative in all the
primary institutions of society—health, education, work, justice,
government, religion, recreation, and the family. Such a service is
not just oriented to rehabilitation but encompasses a duty for
preventive and developmental activities. This recognition that the
social work mandate is no longer confined to the residual
problems and dysfunctional structures of society provides new
dimensions to the profession's accountability for the political
process.

Moreover, a careful examination of the elements that in
constellation make up practice or the professional service system—values, purpose, sanction, knowledge, and methods—underscores the profession's increasing recognition of the interplay
between the individual and the social environment, and particularly the impact of social policy.[9] Thus, although there is pres-
ently no official taxonomy of values, certain values appear univer-
sally in the literature and demonstrate that the experience of
professional practice has broadened the understanding and application of the values underlying the social work process. For
example, the right of self-determination has long been extolled as
fundamental. Social workers learned to respect and use this concept to control their own need to take over the client's problem
and thus gave clients the opportunity to use the social worker's
service to obtain their own solutions to problems and build their
own capacities.

Although at first considered absolute, the concept of self-
determination was later recognized as being subject to its antithe-
sis, the responsibility to others, or the reality of compelling social
forces that no one can ignore. The profession thus learned that the
individual cannot be expected to stand alone, armed only with self-
determination, to combat the often overwhelming demands of
society. The right of self-determination can only be exercised posi-
tively in the face of society's reciprocal responsibility to respect
the individual.

RECIPROCITY OF VALUES

Another basic value that the profession has found must underpin its practice relates to the uniqueness of each person. Understanding the complexity of the biological, psychological, and anthropological makeup of the human provides the basis for recognizing the uniqueness of the individual. At the same time, an examination of the conglomerate of individuals reveals similarities of biology, psychology, and culture and again underscores the extent to which the individual is interlocked with the social. The profession therefore recognizes that its value regarding the interdependence of people has to be linked to a parallel commitment to the value of equality of opportunity for the individual. This is an instance that requires reciprocity between basic and potentially conflicting values.

What is suggested here is that social work values are not just arbitrary statements of preference formulated from the exclusive standpoint of either the individual or the society, but principles of human relationship that have been found to work in practice. Perhaps more rigorous definitions can state these values in full recognition of the fundamental reciprocity between the individual and the society. Regardless of any present limitations in the definitions, however, it is evident that the value base of the profession, with its recognition of the interaction between the individual and the social, underpins the functions of social work. It also readily supports the view that a knowledge of politics, of the art and science of governance, is an inherent requirement for professional performance.

In addition, these values have been used in the development of the methods and techniques of social work and, over the years, have, to some degree, been translated into public policy. With their origins in Judeo-Christian ethics, many of the profession's values are emotionally accepted by the general population. However, their acceptance and implementation have occurred only in proportion to the intensity of the profession's and others' struggle for their achievement. The profession attempts to implement these values and, in doing so, often comes in conflict with the special interests that operate by another code. Social workers and their professional association are thus faced with a constant responsibility to close the gap between purpose and performance, between policy and program, between the

ALEXANDER

implementation of certain social values and the reality of individual and societal deviations from them. The acceptance of this responsibility and role, underpinned by expert knowledge and skill in dealing with the products of the collision between the individual and society, has brought legitimacy to the concept of professional advocacy. This perception of the responsibility to champion corrections for dysfunctional policies and behaviors also reinforces the recognition of the need for political involvement.

A similar examination of the knowledge, methods, and other elements that make up social work practice would show that none of them can be defined or analyzed without attention to both individual and social factors. The overall purpose of social work, to improve the quality of life, must be accomplished in the context of a social environment. Although social work knowledge is not as well organized or standardized as it should be, the 86 graduate and 226 undergraduate schools of social work whose curricula meet general academic criteria draw not just from the body of literature regarding the individual, but also from the wide range of findings on social systems, organizations, social processes, and politics.

The social work method—the responsible, conscious, disciplined use of self in a relationship with an individual or group—finds its application in situations involving people's personal, group, and community problems. For many years, the profession defined its teaching and practice techniques in terms of those three streams of activity, although many professionals were convinced that the social work method was universal in application. Now, that unity of method and process is being approached. Social work has matured precisely by becoming proficient in treating those human problems located at the interchange of the individual and the social. The profession is thus coming to verbalize the dialectical nature of a process it has long used from practical experience. It is also coming to understand that the true professional cannot ignore that interrelationship.

Sources of Confusion

No analysis of the relationship between the functions of the social worker and political responsibility would be complete without attention to several areas of confusion in social workers' attitudes toward political responsibility. A distracting array of demands and loyalties have influenced the viewpoints and practices of the individual social worker. That inspired invention, the social agency, has been the primary source of confusion in understanding the relationship between professional function and political responsibility. As the society's expression of responsibility for individual and social problems, the social agency (governmental, voluntary, or private) reflects the combined results of professional and lay understanding of social problems and the resources that society is willing to expend in response to those problems.

The social worker must function within the purpose, policy, function, and structure of the agency. Immense investments of time and intellect were involved over the years as professionals learned the positive and negative uses and the limits of the agency. The secret of the professional social worker's expertise is the understanding of the impact the agency service has on the person seeking or requiring help, a fact that many inside and outside the profession disregard in their criticisms of the methodology and accountability of the profession. This identification with the agency has been of immense strength to social work in developing technical competence in the delivery of services. Social workers, in turn, transformed social agencies from warehouses to charitable benefactors, to humane service providers, and to service advocates. Although social workers have exerted leadership in bringing agencies to adapt to economic and social demands, establishing a political role for the agency has been most difficult.

Agency Interests

The intimate dependence on the agency has impeded social work in its climb from apprenticeship to professional status and narrowed social workers' perception of their broader professional responsibilities. This identification with the agency has always interfered with social workers' assuming their independent responsibilities as professionals, particularly when that role has brought them in conflict with the agency's leadership or interests. The agency, with its internal and external limitations, inevitably creates a barrier to the professional's ability to respond fully to the recognized needs of clients or communities. This confusion created a defensive posture among many social workers when minorities and students challenged social agencies and other institutions during the 1960s.

Ignoring the strength of independent professional identification, some social workers have used the formal agency limits as an excuse for their own lack of initiative in behalf of clients. Others have succumbed to the fear that to deal with certain problems might threaten their positions. The specter that a problem might be political has probably been the greatest deterrent of all.

Nevertheless, understanding the role of the agency as part of the social service system and the independent role and responsibility of the professional has enabled many social workers to aid agency policymakers and leaders in making creative use of the agency's resources. The accumulation of experiences, the documenting of need, the analysis of the number and nature of problems, the interpretations before boards and legislators, the formulation of alternative policies and programs, and the guidance of plans through political thickets have become part of the armamentarium of the professional social worker.

Such broad duties are not just the responsibility of the social work administrator, they begin with the direct service worker. The worker may, for example, recognize a special problem in a pregnant adolescent and inquire, by word of mouth or memorandum, among colleagues for similar observations regarding other pregnant teenagers. The collection of information, and eventually of data, may lead to a simple request to the agency administration for policy and service clarifications, and this is often stimulus enough to initiate agency changes. The agency can organize or expand to provide the service and may, by continued experience, become convinced that more extensive service in the community is needed. The agency leadership can, by representation to the appropriate administrative or legislative resource—and often by acting in concert with the professional association—broaden the range of services the agency offers. Obviously, the way an individual social worker deals with such a matter depends on many factors, including the extent of the worker's professional socialization and commitment, the worker's position in the agency structure, the degree of freedom in the agency's administration, and the strength of the local professional association. Evident in this scenario is the extent to which political responsibility is a necessary component of the social worker's function.

Role of the Professional Association

Another source of confusion regarding the exercise of political responsibility concerns the role of the professional association, the collective expression of social workers. At the present time, the single national professional association, NASW, executes the functions of improving knowledge and practice, developing and implementing standards, promoting social service policies and programs, and providing certain membership services. These functions are performed through drawing on the expertise of members and staff and through subjecting the association's policies to the representative decision making of the members.

In return for the special status society allots to professional associations, the association is expected to provide society with the collective expertise of its members. The association can and should pursue its purposes and functions in every legitimate arena, including the political realm. Therefore, to withhold professional expertise and viewpoints from that process is, in some degree, to limit or defeat the political process—to cheat the society that has invested in the profession.

The limitations put on the professional association during its development may have been justified by the need to consolidate the technology of an unfolding profession, or they may have been dictated by the conditions of the times. However, intensive study and debate and testing and argument have brought the community of social workers into strong support of political expression at this stage in the life of the profession.

The professional association provides a medium for the distillation of professional knowledge and opinion and for the support and clarification of practice methodologies and standards. It also provides the social worker with some freedom from the confining boundaries of agencies and the opportunity to increase the utilization of the results of practice experience. Through its Code of Ethics, its standards and policies, and its representation of collective wisdom, the association gives guidance and support to the individual worker. By identifying with the profession formally through membership, by participating in the development of standards and policies, and by supporting collective action, the individual social worker extends a professional commitment and increases the association's power in the pursuit of its stated functions.

Another area of disagreement and confusion about the role and functions of the professional association concerns the problems that periodically arise for social workers as a result of differences between the policies of their agency and those of the professional association. The association usually has more progressive standards than the agency, and in certain conflicts of policy, the worker could even be faced with the bread-and-butter decision over continuance with the agency.

Does this mean that the social worker is tightly bound by the strictures of the profession? Unfortunately, this is an area that often is not clear because policies and standards are evolving. For example, NASW members are morally and legally bound by the Code of Ethics, which they sign on entering membership. However, there is wide latitude in the area of political activity because the association undertakes to represent the will of the majority of its members.

Obviously, not every member agrees with every public policy of the association, such as those on abortion or immigration. In this respect, the association must be seen as an arena for debating viewpoints and positions in order to provide creative ideas or change. Nevertheless, two principles should prevail: (1) the association leadership has the responsibility to carry out the will of the majority, and (2) individual social workers in disagreement with a public policy of the association cannot represent any more than their own individual viewpoints and should act within the democratic processes of the association to obtain support for their convictions.

Expertise and Conviction

A third important area of confusion between professional function and political responsibility concerns the distinction between the role of the social worker and that of the lay citizen. Characteristically, on matters of a political nature, lines have been drawn narrowly as to the subjects on which a social worker is considered to have a professional viewpoint. Wide differences have been and are still expressed as to whether a professional social worker should express any views at all, speak just on restricted technical matters, address any subject to which some social work expertise can be brought to bear, or speak on anything under the sun.

Most of the objections to engaging in the political process have been based on the argument that social workers are not knowledgeable in areas other than specific social services. Yet social workers are well aware of the impact on people of energy shortages (real or imagined), war (threatened or actual), economic fluctuations (genuine or contrived), military versus social expenditures, and other issues more esoteric.

With the widespread penetration of social workers into all facets of society, the acquisition of expertise is becoming much broader, and the range of subjects raised for political consideration among social workers is multiplying geometrically. Therefore, there is little reality to the narrow construction of the political responsibility of the social worker.

Because, by definition, the professional is someone whose judgments are arrived at through scientific analysis and through thinking in concert with his or her peers, it is evident that the individual social worker should be guided by the association's confirmed experience and knowledge. The right to draw from professional experience to express professional views must also be recognized. However, drawing on lay knowledge and personal bias and presenting this as professional knowledge, which it is easy to do in political matters, could only be considered unethical. Nevertheless, the profession must always respect the social worker's right to express opinions as an individual citizen, informed or otherwise.

Political Potential of the Profession

Historically, the social work profession has created a discipline of knowledge and practice out of social experience; it has shaped a scientific and artful reality that is distinct from the unstructured impressions and social helpfulness of lay persons. Recognizing the human needs that have been created by industrialization and, subsequently, by the service society, social workers have learned the complex professional role that is inherent in their purpose and function. Although they have swung between responding to individual cries for help and advocating changes in the social structures that impinge adversely on people, they have strengthened their understanding of what it means to serve as the agent for dealing with the conflicts that arise between people and institutions. That understanding has shown the organic relationship

ALEXANDER

between professional function and political responsibility.

Mastering the social work role and responsibility to enhance the interaction between the individual and society, including that portion of this role which involves the political process, promises to produce a quantum leap forward in the impact the profession has and in the recognition it receives. Intelligent advocacy, based on objective policies of the profession, will bring social workers into legislative and decision-making bodies as constituents, consultants, and elected participants, and it will optimize their efforts to obtain more humane and cost-effective social services and programs.

Notes and References

1. Porter R. Lee, "Social Work as Cause and Function," in *Proceedings of the National Conference of Social Work, 1929* (Chicago: University of Chicago Press, 1930), pp. 3–20.

2. *Social Case Work: Generic and Specific: A Report of the Milford Conference* (Washington, D.C.: National Association of Social Workers, 1974, reprint of 1929 ed.), p. 26.

3. "To Social Workers: A Call to Action," *Compass*, 25 (April 1944), pp. 25–28.

4. Joseph P. Anderson, "The Social Work Profession Looks to the Future: A Report to the Membership," *Compass*, 26 (September 1945), pp. 23–27.

5. Kenneth L.M. Pray, "Social Workers and Partisan Politics," *Compass*, 26 (June 1945), p. 5.

6. Ibid.

7. "Special Issues on Conceptual Frameworks," *Social Work* (entire issues), 22 and 26 (September 1977 and January 1981); "The Nature of Clinical Social Work," report of the National Association of Social Workers' Task Force on Clinical Social Work Practice (Washington, D.C.: National Association of Social Workers, 1979); and National Association of Social Workers–Council on Social Work Education Joint Task Force on Specialization, "Specialization in the Social Work Profession," *NASW News*, 24 (April 1979), p. 20.

8. Chauncey A. Alexander, "Social Work Practice: A Unitary Conception," *Social Work*, 22 (September 1977), p. 413.

9. Subcommittee on the Working Definition of Social Work Practice for the Commission on Social Work Practice, National Association of Social Workers, "Working Definition of Social Work Practice," as printed in Harriett M. Bartlett, "Toward Clarification and Improvement of Social Work Practice," *Social Work*, 3 (April 1958), pp. 5–9.

Settlement Workers in Politics, 1890-1914

ALLEN F. DAVIS

2

S ETTLEMENT workers during the Progressive Era were probably more committed to political action than any other group
of welfare workers before or since. Charity organization workers
also cooperated on occasion in political reform projects, but Robert
Hunter, the itinerant radical settlement worker and charity expert,
was probably right in 1902, even if he exaggerated, when he decided that the settlement worker and the charity worker had basically different temperaments. The charity worker was hesitant to
get involved with reform, Hunter decided; he had a philosophy of
"don't, don't" and was constantly troubled by the fear that his
relief would destroy independence. The settlement worker, on the
other hand, was more often the victim of unbounded enthusiasm
than of moral questioning. "He is constantly doing, urging; he is
constantly pressing forward, occasionally tilting at wind mills, at
times making mistakes, often perhaps doing injury, but filled with
enthusiasm, warmth and purpose, without much question."[1]

Settlement workers were usually activists. The pioneer settlement workers in the United States had enthusiasm and purpose
as well as a few doubts, but they had no political theory in mind
when they established their outposts in the slums. Indeed they had

From Review of Politics, *26:4 (October 1964), pp. 505- 517.*
© *1964,* Review of Politics. *Reprinted with permission.*

little interest in politics. Influenced largely by the British settlement and university extension movements, young men and women like Stanton Coit, Jane Robbins, Robert Woods, Ellen Gates Starr, and Jane Addams set out to solve the problems of industrial America by living in an urban working-class district. They sought to re-create a feeling of neighborhood in the sprawling, crowded city. They wanted to share their lives and their learning with those less fortunate, but beyond that they were not sure. They were reformers, but not political reformers in the beginning.[2]

The early settlement workers, however, soon discovered that they had invaded a political world. When Jane Robbins, Jean Fine, and the other well-dressed, young Smith College graduates began the New York College Settlement on the Lower East Side in 1889, their first visitor was a local policeman who thought they were opening another house of prostitution. He stopped by to let them know that he would not disturb them as long as they made a regular monthly contribution to his income. The young settlement workers may have been shocked, but at least they learned that they could not reform the neighborhood without clashing with the existing political structure.[3]

Nearly every activity begun by the settlement workers was interpreted in political terms by the men and women in the neighborhood. Even the picture and art exhibitions that they fancied were bringing meaning and beauty into the drab lives of the workingmen seemed to one New York politician, "a cleverly disguised trick on the part of the eminent mugwumps in the University Settlement Society to get a grip on the district in the ante-election months." When the settlement workers moved from picture exhibitions and classes in Dante to attempts to improve the living and working conditions in their neighborhood, they became even more aware of the political structure and of political realities. Jane Addams and the other residents of Hull House started a campaign to clean up the streets of the nineteenth ward soon after they moved to the area. At first they thought that it was a lack of knowledge about the spread of disease and a dearth of pride in the neighborhood among the citizens that caused the filthy streets. Jane Addams began a campaign of education, but then an investigation by Edward Burchard, the first male resident of Hull House, revealed that Johnny Powers, the shrewd and powerful ward boss, used the position of garbage collector as a political plum. One of his henchmen collected the money, but little of the garbage. Jane

Addams's attempt to promote cleaner streets caused her to submit a bid for the collection of garbage in the ward, resulted in the mayor appointing her a garbage inspector, and led her eventually into two unsuccessful attempts to unseat Powers from his position as alderman from the nineteenth ward. In this instance of Jane Addams the settlement idea led inevitably to political action.[4]

Other settlement workers discovered as they tried to "recreate a feeling of neighborhood" in the industrial city that the precinct and the ward already provided one form of neighborhood organization. But not all settlement workers could agree with Jane Addams that they had "no right to meddle in all aspects of a community's life and ignore politics." Mary K. Simkhovitch of Greenwich House in New York argued that political parties did not express, in any vital way, the real interest of the citizens of the neighborhood, and that the settlement therefore ought to remain aloof from partisan politics. Robert Woods, the tall and taciturn head resident of South End House in Boston, agreed basically with Mrs. Simkhovitch. He argued that the settlement lost more than it gained by a partisan stand in local politics. He maintained that it was better to cooperate with the ward boss than to try to defeat him. Of course, the situation in Boston's ninth ward was somewhat unusual; James Donovan, the affable Irish boss, in part because he was badly in need of allies, seemed willing to cooperate with the settlement workers in making the ward a better place in which to live. Despite their statements, however, both Woods and Mrs. Simkhovitch on occasion took part in reform campaigns when evidently they felt the public's interest was being expressed by a political organization.[5]

More successful than Hull House, South End House, or Greenwich House in influencing the politics in their ward was Chicago Commons, founded in 1894 by Graham Taylor. After preliminary and unsuccessful attempts to cooperate with the boss in the ward the settlement men's club managed to defeat him, and then for nearly two decades the settlement effectively controlled elections for alderman in the ward. Instead of running an independent candidate, the settlement concentrated on getting good candidates nominated from the major parties. The settlement workers controlled enough votes so that their endorsement was tantamount to election. The Commons had the advantage of being located in a ward where the local political boss had little real power. But Taylor alone could not have made his settlement into a successful political machine. He was aided by a group of young, politically oriented social workers who, unlike the settlement pioneers, consciously sought to make the settlement a base for political reform in the ward and the city. Such men as Allen T. Burns, who came to the settlement after graduate work at the University of Chicago, and Raymond Robins, who wandered into Chicago Commons in 1901 after he had been a coal miner, a fruit grower, a lawyer, and a minister, became experts at managing political campaigns. They made surveys, filed reports, checked for voting frauds, organized political rallies and torch parades, and distributed posters and handbills. Most important, they became acquainted with the people and the politicians in the ward and the city. For Burns and Robins, Chicago Commons and the seventeenth ward provided practical lessons in political reform that they utilized for years after they left the settlement.[6]

Chicago had no monopoly on politically active settlement workers. James B. Reynolds, an ordained Congregational minister, gave up his work for the YMCA in 1893 to become head resident of University Settlement in New York. As early as 1896 he urged a group of social workers to "Go into politics." "Be earnest, be practical, be active," he advised, "political reform is the great moral opportunity of our day." To Henry Moskowitz politics was more than a moral opportunity; it was a way of life. Unlike most of the settlement workers, Moskowitz, a Rumanian Jew, had grown up in a tenement on the Lower East Side. He was inspired by classes at Neighborhood Guild and eventually became a settlement worker himself at Madison House. He battled the boss in the ward, fought for better city government, and dreamed of the day when there would be a settlement in every neighborhood in the city to counteract the influence of the political machines. Like Raymond Robins, James B. Reynolds, and Graham Taylor, he believed the settlement could become the antidote to boss rule in ward politics and the base for political reform in the city.[7]

The politically minded settlement workers, whether they took an active part in local politics or not, learned a great deal about the nature of politics in the downtown wards of the great industrial cities. Many of them, especially Roberts Woods and Jane Addams, contributed to a better understanding of city politics through their writings. They discovered, for example, that often the political machine depended on an elaborate structure of boys' gangs that duplicated in miniature the political organization of the city. It was from these gangs that the ward heelers as well as the bosses got their leadership experience. The political boss often remained in power, they learned, through a combination of ruthlessness and genuine neighborliness. There was an element of truth in Johnny Powers's bald statement: "The trouble with Miss Addams," he announced on one occasion, "is that she is jealous of my charitable work in the ward." He was a friendly visitor all right; he gave away turkeys at Christmas time, provided free passes on the railroad, bailed men out of jail, and got the unemployed jobs. There was no charge, no forms to fill out (as there always were at the Charity Organization Society). The only thing expected in return was a vote cast in the proper way on election day. Despite the obvious corruption of the boss, no matter how he robbed the ward, he was known for his philanthropy rather than for his dishonesty. The settlement workers, however, learned from the politicians. Although they soon discovered they could not compete in handing out favors, they could emulate the politician's real concern for the problems of his constituents. They could be a little less critical of the present situation, talk less about their elaborate plans for the future, and concentrate, as the bosses did, on making their reforms "concrete and human."[8]

In part because of their vantage point in a working-class neighborhood and their close observation of local politics, settlement workers often put less emphasis than some reformers on the revision of a charter or the defeat of a corrupt politician. They could appreciate the usefulness of the boss even as they were in despair at his lack of civic pride. Jane Addams decided it was not worthwhile to oppose Powers after he had twice defeated her candidate. Most settlement workers soon realized that, even if it were possible to defeat the local boss, it was impossible to accomplish much in one ward. For this reason they were often active, though somewhat cautious, participants in a variety of municipal reform campaigns, especially in Boston, New York, and Chicago.[9]

Settlement workers seldom ran for political office in the city, rather they served as campaign managers, advisers on policy, statistics gatherers, and "brain trusters" for reform administrations. In Boston in the 1890s Mayor Josiah Quincy often depended on the advice and aid of Robert Woods in attempting to provide the city with public bathhouses, gymnasiums, and playgrounds. In Boston as in other cities, the settlements contributed to municipal reform by demonstrating the need for action, by initiating kindergartens, playgrounds, and bathhouses, and by then convincing the municipal authorities that it was was the city's responsibility to take them over and expand their usefulness. In the first decade of the twentieth century, Boston settlement workers played important roles in the nearly futile campaigns of the Good Government Association to bring honesty and reform into the city government. In the reform campaign of 1909-10, four young men closely associated with South End House virtually ran the unsuccessful campaign of James J. Storrow. One served as his campaign manager, another as his assistant campaign manager, a third as his personal secretary, and a fourth as the secretary of the Good Government Association. In the long run, the settlements' most important contribution to a better city government may have been through their education of a generation of young men in the tactics of municipal reform and the training of a group of experts in city administration.[10]

In New York, James B. Reynolds was a prominent member of the Citizens Union, and he was in part responsible for drafting Seth Low, the president of Columbia University and a member of the University Settlement Council, to run for mayor in 1901. Reynolds worked behind the scenes to manage Low's campaign and enlisted the support of his settlement friends, especially Lillian Wald of Henry Street Settlement, Henry Moskowitz of Madison House, and Elizabeth Williams of College Settlement, in the campaign. When Low was elected, Reynolds became his personal secretary and closest adviser. For two years the settlement workers, having a direct line to the mayor, used it to promote better housing laws, more playgrounds, and a city-supported system of visiting nurses in the public schools. Lillian Wald and the others at Henry Street Settlement were primarily responsible for the latter innovation. They had been troubled for some time by the number of children prevented from going to school because they had eczema, hookworm, or some other disease. Doctors had been inspecting the students in the city for several years, but no one made any attempt to treat the ill children. Low's reform administration only complicated a difficult situation, for it made the inspection more rigorous but did nothing to treat the rejects. Because she knew Mayor Low and many other officials in his administration, Lillian Wald was able to suggest a solution. She offered to supply visiting nurses who could work with the doctors and treat the sick children. Before she began, however, she made the city officials promise that, if the experiment proved successful, they would maintain it with city funds. After only one month the Board of Estimate appropriated the money to hire school nurses and soon the experiment was being copied in other cities. Lillian Wald and other settlement workers often accomplished much because they were respected and listened to by at least some of the politicians who occupied positions of power in city hall and the state capital.[11]

Sometimes the settlement worker's entry into the arena of municipal politics was concerned with opposition to a proposed measure rather than with a positive suggestion for reform. This was the case in 1905 when the settlements on the Lower East Side banded together to defeat a proposed elevated loop that would have connected the Brooklyn and Williamsburg Bridges. The settlement workers feared that the loop would cause needless blight and more congestion in one of the most crowded areas in the city. They favored a subway and suggested making Delancey Street into a boulevard. Lillian Wald, Florence Kelley, and Charles Stover, with help from housing reformer Lawrence Veiller, led the campaign that helped to defeat the measure. Stover, who had spent a lifetime fighting for more playgrounds in New York, called the first meeting and enlisted the support of many organizations on the Lower East Side. Sometimes the settlement workers had a difficult time convincing their immigrant neighbors of the need for opposing a ward boss or for supporting a reform bill, but this time it was easy to win their cooperation. The settlement workers organized mass meetings, sent out letters to influential people, persuaded newspapermen to present their point of view, and bombarded the city council with letters and petitions. Henry Street, College, and University Settlements handled most of the clerical work, gathered most of the names for the petitions, and helped arouse their members and supporters to protest the measure. They had a lot of help during the campaign. One source of aid they never suspected. Only after the measure was defeated did they learn that an unknown businessman, who feared the elevated loop would ruin his business, had spent fifty thousand dollars to oppose the measure. Whether it was bribe money or the aroused social conscience of the Lower East Side that caused the defeat of the elevated loop, the campaign illustrates how settlement workers could organize neighborhood opinion and bring that opinion to bear on public officials.[12]

In Chicago, Graham Taylor, Raymond Robins, and an energetic group of young settlement workers, who became experts at ferreting out the records of candidates, worked closely with the Municipal Voters' League and had some success in electing honest and well-qualified aldermen to the city council. Early in the twentieth century Hull House, which Henry Demarest Lloyd liked to call the best club in Chicago, served as the headquarters for a well-organized but futile attempt to promote the municipal ownership of street railways. The settlement at its best became a clearinghouse for reform and a meeting place for reformers.[13]

Settlement workers played important roles in several kinds of municipal reform campaigns. Many would have agreed with Jane Robbins. When asked why she was so interested in politics, she replied, "I never go into a tenement without longing for a better city government."[14] Most settlement workers, however, soon learned that to improve the tenements and the working and living conditions in the city, it was necessary to go beyond city hall to the state capital and even to Washington. Much more important, in the long run, than the settlement workers' attempts to defeat the ward boss or elect a reform mayor was their influence on state and national reform legislation.

Robert Bremner notes the important role that social workers played in communicating to the public the great need for reform. This of course they did, but they also played a large part in the practical task of getting bills passed at Springfield, Albany, or Washington. Arthur Schlesinger, Jr., describes the "subtle and persistent saintliness of the social workers." "Theirs," he says, "was the implacability of gentleness."[15] But behind the gentleness many settlement workers were tough-minded realists who understood the way the American political system operated. It is true, of course, that they were also idealists who sometimes came perilously close to believing that, if they gathered enough statistics and found out enough information about the social evils in America, the solution would follow naturally. Yet a large number of settlement workers became experts not only at collecting statistics, but also at using them to influence public opinion and elected officials. They had learned their politics in the precinct and the ward, not from a textbook, and their experience served them well in Springfield and Washington.

The passage of a series of amendments to the child labor law in 1897 in Illinois may serve as a case in point. The amendments were drafted by Florence Kelley who, more than anyone else, led the crusade against child labor. There was little publicity or fanfare in the beginning. Florence Kelley remarked to Henry Demarest Lloyd: "We want to get them out of committee before the editorial column raises its voice in defense of the infant newsboys and the toddling 'cash' who will both come under its provisions." Persuasion was more important than publicity in the beginning. Jane Addams led a contingent of social workers, labor leaders, and enlightened businessmen to the state capital to testify before the Senate Committee on Labor, to display impressive statistics, and to tell human stories about the results of child labor. Alzina Stevens, a Hull House resident and also a member of a labor union, got workingmen and women to write to the members of the Senate committee. George Hooker, a settlement worker and ordained minister, got the support of various members of the clergy in Chicago. When the amendments were reported out of committee, the settlement workers made sure they got the proper publicity in the newspapers. They also prepared pamphlets and scrapbooks filled with clippings demonstrating the need for better child labor laws and sent them to every member of the state legislature. The amendments passed; they did not end the problem of child labor by any means, but their passage illustrates the way settlement workers operated realistically in state politics.[16]

In New York a committee of settlement workers led by Robert Hunter organized in 1902 to protest against the incredible conditions of labor among children in the city. Florence Kelley, now in New York as general secretary of the National Consumers' League and a resident of Henry Street Settlement, along with young men and women like William English Walling, Ernest Poole, and Lillian Wald, took on the task of collecting information, arousing public opinion, and lobbying for better laws at Albany. J.G. Phelps Stokes, a wealthy young Yale graduate and resident of University Settlement, used the staff in his father's uptown office to turn out propaganda in favor of more effective child labor laws. The New York Child Labor Committee played an important part in the passage of a better child labor bill for New York in 1903; it also became the nucleus of the National Child Labor Committee.[17]

Just as the child labor reformers in New York began to realize in the first decade of the twentieth century that reform to be effective would have to be organized on the national level, so settlement workers in several cities began to devote more and more time to national organizations and national legislation. In addition to the National Child Labor Committee, they helped to organize the National Women's Trade Union League, the National Association for the Advancement of Colored People, a national investigation of women and children in industry, and a national Industrial Relations Commission.[18] Men like William English Walling, Henry Moskowitz, and Paul Kellogg became experts at bringing the right people together and getting a program of reform organized. They worked behind the scenes and so have never received the attention from historians that they deserve. They used much the same tactics on the national level that they had perfected in the ward, the city, and the state. They gathered statistics, collected information, and then used their knowledge and influence to exert pressure on elected officials.

In 1906 when James Reynolds was in Washington lobbying for the passage of a bill that would provide for federal inspection of meat packing plants, he wrote to Jane Addams asking her to "secure a strong expression of public sentiment in Chicago favoring passage of the Beveridge Amendment." Sometimes public sentiment could be effective, but often more direct tactics were needed. The next year Mary McDowell was in Washington lobbying for a bill to provide a federal investigation of women and children in industry. She wrote to Anita McCormick Blaine, the daughter of Cyrus McCormick, asking her to get letters from "conservative employers who have good conditions and are willing to have this significant subject of women in industry freed from confusion." Again in 1912 when Allen T. Burns and Graham Taylor, Jr., were coordinating a social work campaign for the passage of a bill in Congress providing for an Industrial Relations Commission, they asked the settlement workers to get pointed letters addressed to members of the congressional committee from labor leaders and businessmen as well as from social workers and university professors.[19]

Despite the realistic political tactics on the local, state, and national level, most settlement workers were disturbed by the slow and halting nature of their attempts to humanize the industrial city. Reform administrations were rarely reelected, and reform bills were often bypassed or ignored. They talked sometimes of the need of a great cause to unite all local efforts. In 1912 when Roosevelt bolted the Republican convention, a group of social workers led by Paul Kellogg and Henry Moskowitz were ready with a platform of industrial minimums. When the Progressive party adopted their platform, they convinced themselves that this was the great cause for which they had been waiting. Primarily because of the Progressive platform, Jane Addams, Raymond Robins, Henry Moskowitz, and many other young social workers flocked to the new party and threw themselves into the political campaign. They contributed to the religious enthusiasm; they also helped in the realistic task of organizing a new party.[20] Edward T. Devine of the New York Charity Organization Society could warn that it was "the first political duty of social workers to be persistently and aggressively non-partisan, to maintain such relations with men of social good will in all parties as will insure their cooperation in specific measures for the promoting of the common good." But Jane Addams felt differently. "When the ideas and measures we have long been advocating become part of a political campaign...would we not be the victims of a curious self-consciousness if we failed to follow them there?" she asked.[21] To Jane Addams the settlement idea led inevitably to political action even on the national level, and there were a large number of settlement workers who agreed with her.

Of course the Progressive campaign of 1912 seemed in some ways more like a crusade than like politics, and the collapse of the Progressive party and the outbreak of World War I altered, if it did not end, the political interests of the settlement workers. After 1914 there was a little less optimism, a little less confidence that evils could be righted by gathering statistics. It was perhaps more important that after 1914 settlement workers and other reformers became more interested in international affairs and a little less concerned with domestic reform and politics. In the twenties it was not so easy for settlement workers to have confidence in reform, and a new kind of social worker emerged who seemed to be more concerned with professional status than with political action. Something of the settlement workers' interest in political reform, something of their realistic tactics remained, of course, in the twenties and thirties, and something of that tradition survives even today, but it was in the Progressive Era that settlement workers were most concerned with political action—it was a concern that developed from their experience.[22] They could not always agree among themselves, but if they took the settlement idea seriously, they became involved one way or another in politics, first in the ward, then in the city, the state, and the nation.

Notes and References

1. Robert Hunter, "The Relation Between Social Settlements and Charity Organizations," *Journal of Political Economy,* 11 (1902), pp. 75–88; and *Proceedings of the National Conference of Charities and Correction,* 1902, pp. 302–314.

2. Robert Woods, "The University Settlement Idea," in *Philanthropy and Social Progress* (New York, 1893), pp. 57–97; Cannon Barnett, *Practicable Socialism* (London, 1915); and Jane Addams, "The Objective Value of the Social Settlement," in *Philanthropy and Social Progress,* pp. 27–56.

3. Helen Rand Thayer, "Blazing the Settlement Trail," *Smith Alumnae Quarterly* (April 1911), pp. 130–137; and Jane Robbins, "The First Year at the College Settlement," *Survey,* 27 (February 24, 1912), p. 1,802.

4. A.C. Bernheim, "Results of Picture Exhibition on Lower East Side," *Forum,* 19 (July 1895), p. 612. *See also* Allen F. Davis, "Jane Addams vs. the Ward Boss," *Journal of the Illinois State Historical Society,* 53 (Autumn 1960), pp. 247–265.

5. "Are Social Settlers Debarred from Political Work?" handwritten MSS, undated, Mary K. Simkhovitch MSS, Radcliffe Women's Archives, Cambridge, Mass.; and Robert Woods, "Settlement Houses and City Politics," *Municipal Affairs,* 4 (June 1900), pp. 396–397.

6. "Minutes of the Seventeenth Ward Council of the Civic Federation, 1895-97," Graham Taylor MSS, Newberry Library, Chicago, Ill. *See also* Allen F. Davis, "Raymond Robins: The Settlement Worker as Municipal Reformer," *Social Service Review,* 33 (June 1959), pp. 131–141.

7. James B. Reynolds, "The Settlement and Municipal Reform," in *Proceedings of the National Conference of Charities and Correction,* 1896, pp. 140–142; J. Salwyn Schapiro, "Henry Moskowitz: A Social Reformer in Politics," *Outlook,* 102 (October 26, 1912), pp. 446–449; and Henry Moskowitz, "A Settlement Followup," *Survey,* 25 (December 10, 1910), pp. 439–440.

8. *See especially* Jane Addams, "Ethical Survivals in Municipal Corruption," *International Journal of Ethics,* 8 (April 1898), pp. 273–291; Robert Woods, "The Roots of Political Power," in *City Wilderness: A Settlement Study* (Boston, 1898), pp. 114–147 (probably written by William Clark); and "Traffic in Citizenship," in *Americans in Process* (Boston, 1902), pp. 147–149.

9. Jane Addams, interview in the *Chicago Tribune,* February 19, 1900; and Addams, "Ethical Survivals."

10. Eleanor Woods, *Robert A. Woods* (Boston, 1929), pp. 119–123; George E. Hooker, "Mayor Quincy of Boston," *Review of Reviews,* 19 (May 1899), pp. 575–578; and *South End House Report,* 1910, p. 6.

11. "Reformatory Influence of Social Service Upon City Politics," *Commons,* 6 (March 1902), pp. 3–4; Lillian Wald, *House on Henry Street* (New York, 1915), pp. 46–53; and Wald to Dr. Abbott E. Kitteredge, October 29, 1903, Wald MSS, New York Public Library, New York, New York.

12. James H. Hamilton, "The Winning of the Boulevard," *University Settlement*

Studies Quarterly, 2 (December 1906), pp. 24-26; and Lillian Wald, "The East Side in Danger," *Commons,* 10 (April 1905), p. 222.

13. Edwin Burritt Smith, "Council Reform in Chicago," Work of the Municipal Voters' League, *Municipal Affairs,* 4 (June 1900), pp. 347-362; and John Commons to Henry Demarest Lloyd, July 27, 1903, George Hooker to Lloyd, July 5 and 13, 1903, and Lloyd to Edward Bemis, July 30, 1903, Henry Demarest Lloyd MSS, Wisconsin State Historical Society, Madison, Wisc.

14. Jane Robbins, "The Settlement and the Immigrant," *College Settlement Association Quarterly,* 1 (June 1916), p. 7.

15. Robert H. Bremner, *From the Depths: The Discovery of Poverty in the United States* (New York: New York University Press, 1956), pp. 201-203; and Arthur Schlesinger, Jr., *The Crisis of the Old Order* (Boston: Houghton Mifflin Co., 1957), p. 25.

16. The quotation is from Florence Kelley to Lloyd, March 2, 1895, Lloyd MSS, and actually refers to the campaign of that year for child labor laws in Illinois. The campaign was not successful and was renewed with similar tactics two years later. Jane Addams to Lloyd, March 16, 1897.

17. Helen Marot, "The Child Labor Movement in New York," *Commons,* 8 (April 1903), pp. 5-6; and J.G. Phelps Stokes, interview, January 22, 1959.

18. Alice Henry, *Women and the Labor Movement* (New York, 1930), p. 109; Mary McDowell, "The Need of a National Investigation," *Charities and the Commons,* 17 (January 5, 1907), pp. 634-636; William English Walling, "The Founding of the NAACP," *The Crisis,* 36 (July 1929), p. 226; and "Movement Under Way For an Industrial Commission," *Survey,* 27 (March 2, 1912), pp. 1,821-1,822.

19. Reynolds to Jane Addams, June 7, 1906, Addams MSS, Peace Collection, Swarthmore College, Swarthmore, Pa.; McDowell to Mrs. Emmons Blaine, February 9, 1907, Blaine MSS, McCormick Collection, Wisconsin State Historical Society, Madison, Wisc.; and Graham Taylor to Graham R. Taylor, March 10, 1912, Taylor MSS.

20. Jane Addams, "The Steps By Which I Became a Progressive," syndicated article, 1912, Addams MSS; Paul Kellogg, "The Industrial Platform," *Survey,* 28 (August 24, 1912); pp. 668-670; "Jane Addams Tells Why," *New York Evening Post,* August 8, 1912, clipping, Addams MSS; and Henry Moskowitz to Lillian Wald, August 2, 1912, Wald MSS. *See also* Allen F. Davis, "The Social Workers and The Progressive Party, 1910-1916," *American Historical Review,* (April 1964).

21. Edward T. Devine, "Politics and Social Work," *Survey,* 29 (October 5, 1912), p. 9; and Jane Addams, "Pragmatism in Politics," *Survey,* 29 (October 5, 1912), p. 12.

22. *See* John Haynes Holmes, "War and the Social Movement," *Survey,* 32 (September 26, 1914), pp. 629-630; Edward T. Devine, "Civilization's Peril," *Survey,* 33 (February 6, 1915), pp. 518-519; and Paul Kellogg, "To the Unfinished Work," *Survey,* 42 (July 5, 1919), pp. 513-514. *See also* Clarke A. Chambers, "Creative Effort in an Age of Normalcy, 1918-33," *Social Welfare Forum, 1961* (New York: Columbia University Press, 1961), pp. 252-271.

Clinical Social Work and Public Policies

KATHARINE HOOPER BRIAR
SCOTT BRIAR

3

IN recent decades, the expansion of public policies and programs in social welfare has made social work practice inextricably dependent on policy decisions. Because social workers have special knowledge of how public policies affect individuals and populations, this trend places on practitioners a responsibility to introduce their knowledge into the policymaking process. For a variety of reasons, however, the link between practice and public policy has received little attention in the profession. This oversight has kept practitioners from examining the policy-related context of their practice and from recognizing the major opportunities they have for improving policy.

Social workers are not alone in lacking clarity about the link between public policy and practice. Members of the other helping professions also tend to focus primarily on the jobs they have to do without considering the broader context that shapes both clients' needs and the responses available. Instead, every helping profession should have a dual focus—on the way policies shape practice and on the way practice can inform policy decisions and improve outcomes. This requires an awareness of the political context in which practice occurs.

The same trial-and-error problem-solving process used in clinical practice occurs in the development of social policies. A major difference between the two is the magnitude of the decisions. Whereas decisions in clinical practice affect at most several people, policy decisions may affect thousands and even millions of people.

Policy-Related Assessment

The purpose of this article is to explore the varied effects of public policy on clinical practice—on such basic components of practice as assessment and service delivery and on the forms of service specialization, the locus of practice, and even which clients are served by which service. The article also identifies avenues for social workers to participate in the development of policy, suggesting how the information base that is available to social workers in their clinical practice can be used to inform and improve policy. Throughout, public or social policies are defined as decisions made in governmental or quasi-governmental arenas that influence or respond to human needs, rights, or problems. The failure to develop an explicit policy to deal with a certain issue or need often constitutes collective neglect, which is also a form of social policy.

Because most aspects of practice are affected by policy, either an explicit policy or a policy deficit, it is important that assessment be informed by an awareness of policy. In clinical practice, an assessment process that includes a policy perspective becomes, in part, a form of impact analysis, which specifies cause and effect. Such an assessment pinpoints the link between the client's presenting problems and broad policy defects or deficits. That a battered spouse is homeless because no shelter or housing is available is an example of a policy deficit; it is not just an isolated problem of an individual client. A requirement that battered women file for divorce before they can obtain a restraining order through legal services is an example of how social policies can also be misdirected.

Policy-related assessment also includes an analysis of who owns the problem. Although telling the battered spouse of the need for service innovation and policy development does not directly help her with her immediate need for housing, her knowledge of this need may, at some future time, make her a source of support and help in fostering such an innovation. Such empowering of clients must include explicit pinpointing of the link between their problems and public policies.

Policy-related assessment further entails the understanding that the problems brought to social workers are often direct results of the need for preventive services and policy innovations. The depression of the 64-year-old male, unemployed welder facing involuntary retirement should not be viewed solely as his personal problem; it may also reflect a policy and service issue. The depression could indicate the need for job guarantees for older workers, for employer-sponsored retirement planning services, and for reconsideration of the appropriateness of mandatory retirement policies. Clinicians thus have the responsibility to help clients see the connection between their plight and policy deficits or service gaps.

The practitioner's tendency to define the presenting problem primarily in terms of the help available often obscures the connection between public policy and the problem of an individual client. Research on social workers' responses to unemployed people seeking help in finding work showed that the clients' problems were redefined to fit the services the worker was prepared to muster. Thus, a client's joblessness might be recast as an interpersonal or psychodynamic problem, rather than as the outcome of a public policy to maintain high rates of unemployment.[1]

Policy and Clinical Intervention

Public policies do not just affect assessment, they affect practice decisions as well. Interventions and even measures of treatment success are shaped both by what policies provide and by what they omit. In the case of the depressed welder facing retirement, the problem-solving process may include an inventory of the income supports and related services that directly result from public policies. Social security, public service employment for senior citizens, and senior centers help determine the interventions to be considered in helping the client plan for retirement.

Practitioners are in a unique position to discern the impact of policies both on clients' problems and on their own practice effectiveness, but many are reluctant to make such connections explicit to their clients. This hesitancy reinforces the status quo and abdicates responsibilities to clients, to the profession, and to effective practice. If practitioners explicitly recognized the impact of policies on clients' problems and on practice, they might better understand the sources of their own burnout, of unsuccessful treatment, and of clients' dissatisfaction with treatment.[2] The tendency, moreover, to reinforce clients' perceptions of their problems as being solely of their own making is a risk inherent in direct service. Helping clients deal with their problems by modifying their behavior tends to shift attention away from external factors. A worker's failure to discern imbalances between personal and systemic responsibility for human problems and to point out the policy links to personal discomfort can be viewed as acquiescence in victim-blaming methodologies.[3] The practice of social work is fraught with compromises, and much of it involves workers' dealing with problems that are the inevitable result of the value base of the political and economic system. In fact, much of social work practice is a collective attempt to counter ideologies that hold individuals culpable for their problems.

Impact of Deficits

Social policies are often the result of compromises between competing values, and they frequently involve the fusion of conflicting values. Although the contradictions inherent in a policy may be the handwork of well-intentioned leaders, the negative impact of these contradictions compounds the difficulty of practicing social work. Moreover, some policies that are known to create human suffering are often supported because the information needed to counter them effectively is unavailable. For example, policies to control inflation are partly responsible for the millions without work and thereby for the consequences that accompany unemployment—suicide, mental illness, health problems, crime, and divorce. These consequences are not always obvious to policymakers, and when these effects are brought to their attention, they often cite unemployment benefits, public assistance, and other programs as providing safety nets.

Another obvious concern of the profession over the years, and a direct consequence of policy, has been the remedial, residual cast to most social services. Social policies are problem-solving tools that often emerge to remedy a problem once it has developed, rather than to prevent its evolution in the first place. Many policies in the areas of housing, health care, and income maintenance are clear examples of this remedial approach.

In countries where social policies evolve from philosophies that support preventive social services, the practice of social work is remarkably different. Instead of emphasizing clinical therapy, social workers in such countries function as social brokers, case managers, and client advocates. Social workers visiting the United States from western European countries frequently chide American social workers for emphasizing the refinement of clinical methods at the expense of policy development. In the United States, clients' problems are frequently addressed within a therapy-oriented focus, a tradition that has evolved from ideologies about individual rather than systemic responsibility for human needs.

Pathways of Care

Even the locus of social work practice is often determined by social policy. This has always been the case. Until the twentieth century, social service interventions centered around the workhouse and the asylum, reflecting public policies that identified these sites as the appropriate locus for the limited social welfare services provided in that period. In this century, the proliferation of voluntary and public agencies has promoted multiple and varied avenues of care for those who are troubled. However, this multiplicity can be confusing to the person seeking help. For example, the stressed parent and child may wonder whether to seek help for their conflict through a mental health center, a family counseling agency, or a child welfare agency.

In recent years, policies of deinstitutionalization were a dramatic effort to shift the locus of practice. As the mentally ill and developmentally disabled were returned to the community from life in institutions, social work practice was also to shift to community-based service delivery. The trend toward deinstitutionalization should have occasioned the creation of new pathways of community-based care to replace the traditional means of access eliminated by the policy shift. That in many instances these new services were not created is another instance of policy oversights and deficits. Similarly, changes in the juvenile code removing dependent and neglected children from institutions seem to be progressive and to offer opportunities for earlier interventions by social workers, but in the absence of adequate policy and service alternatives, hopes for such outcomes may be frustrated.

Policy oversights no less than well-considered policy decisions are apt to determine the sites for the delivery of social work services. For example, as jails and prisons overflow with people, some of whom have "fallen through the cracks" of the social service system, social workers are faced with growing demands to take their practice into the criminal justice system. Despite declines in federal funding for human services, many local and state policies foster increased social work involvement in such initiatives as police social work teams, victim and witness programs, and various kinds of pretrial jail, prison, parole, and probation work.

Similarly, the growth in employment and training programs during the 1970s challenged some social work practitioners to recast client problems as employment and training issues. Thus, social workers associated with the implementation of various titles of the Comprehensive Employment and Training Act (CETA) program found themselves responding to stringent measurements of service that focused solely on job placement rather than service outcomes. Practicing in such a context forced social workers to compromise client-centered practice and to emphasize instead meeting the predetermined objectives and quotas of the U.S. Department of Labor.

In both the public and private sectors of the economy, growing concern about the productivity of the American worker is likely to reinforce social workers' roles in promoting workplace democracy and industrial social services. Although the workplace is an obvious site for offering social work skills to people who have had difficulty making use of traditional social services, the development of policies that support such interventions will undoubtedly increase the use of the workplace as the locus of social services.

Service Specializations

Policy emphases shift frequently, giving recognition to the unmet needs of different segments of the population. This forces social workers to change their focus continually to keep pace with developing policies. Although such changing emphases often open new avenues in which social workers can exercise leadership in service design, they also tend to define human needs narrowly and to take categorical, restrictive approaches to solutions. Increasingly, social work practice is forced to fit specialized definitions of human needs and to find ways of accommodating practice only to those deemed eligible for service. For instance, no matter how centrally concerned the profession may be with such goals as strengthening family life, it nevertheless must fit practice into service patterns that sometimes run counter to these values. An example of this is that the practice of child welfare has, until recently, been child rather than family centered; this meant that instead of eliminating specific conditions that were harmful to a child, the emphasis was on removing the child from what was harmful in the family.

The piecemeal nature of policies and their categorical responses to human needs force practice to fit into narrow service specializations. This pattern often constrains practitioners to force clients' problems to fit the service specialization, rather than the reverse. For example, a depressed, seasonally employed construction worker who frequents bars with growing regularity may receive treatment for depression at a mental health agency, interventions for alcohol problems at an alcoholism agency, and career reassessment services at an employment agency. Moreover, the pattern of practitioners' referring clients from one agency to another is usually not an abdication of the profession's commitment to treatment but simply reflects policies that categorically segregate clients' needs into specialized definitions of problems, eligibility criteria, and service responses. Practice innovations that foster service integration are bold attempts by the profession to counteract the proliferation of fragmented services.

Politics and Policy

Given the pervasive and multiple effects of social policies on practice, it is understandable that many practitioners try to shield themselves from these intrusive influences by emphasizing a psychological perspective on clients' problems. Sometimes it is not until the harmful effects of this approach are recognized that practitioners seek ways to promote improved service responses.

Some practitioners assume that by not becoming involved in politics they are escaping compromises. They hope that by avoiding policy issues, they will keep their practice more pure than that of a social worker embroiled in political activity. Not only is such a dichotomy artificial, but a failure to examine the effects public policies have on practice, client problems, and the solutions practitioners can offer is a submission to norms reinforcing the view that clients are the perpetrators of their own plight. Some practitioners feel that human needs are apolitical and thus find noxious the political content of practice. Although this view has merits, it should not move clinicians to shun political activities but to promote a nonpartisan view of clients' needs.

There are several avenues by which social workers can use their special knowledge and skills to make public policy more responsive to human needs. Social workers serving as elected officials often comment on their frequent use of social work skills both in responding to immediate personal problems of constituents and in analyzing and developing social policies. This was noted by Phyllis Erickson, a social worker serving as a representative in the Washington State legislature and as an elected council member in Pierce County, Washington. Detroit City Council member Maryann Mahaffey and Congresswoman Barbara Mikulski of Baltimore, both social workers, frequently identify connections between individual stresses and policy oversights or impacts. Social workers' involvement in politics as officeholders has increased in recent years, as has their participation in the profession's lobbying and political action organizations.

Social workers have a long tradition of giving policymakers the benefit of their expertise and perspective through testifying before legislative and other bodies. A relatively new form for this kind of political participation is impact analysis. Actually, impact analysis, which attempts to predict the various consequences of a policy decision, is neither a new nor an esoteric discipline. Most day-to-day, moment-to-moment personal and professional decisions are attempts to predict the outcomes of alternative courses of action. Although impact analysis in policymaking is most widely associated with ecological impact statements, most legislative testimony offers numerous examples of this kind of analysis.

A recent mandate for using impact analysis in social policy decisions grew out of the 1980 White House Conference on Families, in which participants selected family impact analysis as a major vehicle for examining and eliminating the harmful effects that policies of the public and private sector had on families. A framework for using impact analysis to predict the outcomes of social policies was pioneered by Sidney Johnson, a social worker, and his staff, Hubbell, Bohen and Viveros-Long, and Ooms, at the Family Impact Seminar at George Washington University.[4] The work of the seminar included studies of foster care and families, work and family life, and teenage pregnancy and families. The analytical contributions of the seminar prompted citizens' groups, professional associations, and agencies to use impact analysis to improve their understanding of how various legislative actions might affect families.

An important contribution of the Family Impact Seminar has been its demonstration that the requirement of scientific rigor in predicting the impact of public policy decisions is often unrealistic and unnecessary. Instead, simple statements of anticipated harms or benefits to those the policy will affect are acceptable first steps in creating an informed base for decision making. This finding has been corroborated by similar efforts elsewhere, and it points also to the possibility of using clinical observations as an information base in the development of policy. Strategies for using this information to assess the impact of social policies are likely to involve social workers in collaboration with practitioners of other professions and with agency directors.

Social workers have long been astute in specifying the impact that agency policies have on clients and on their own practice. They have also been effective in curbing the negative effects of agency policies and in promoting service innovations to increase the responsiveness of agencies to clients' needs. These same assessment and policy development skills that were effective in agencies need to be systematically targeted at public and private policymaking bodies.

Mini Policy Experiments

It is important that clinical social workers recognize they may be in a uniquely advantageous position to predict the consequences of social policies. One of the best ways of determining the impact of a policy is to conduct an experiment in which the policy is implemented and its effects described and measured. Obviously, when such experiments are carried out on a large scale, they are extremely costly. However, when a policy is implemented, its effects on the life of any one person are specific, every bit as specific as the effects of a direct service practitioner's intervention. This comparison works both ways—that is, the social worker's interventions at the case level, especially when they involve intervention in the environment, may be thought of as mini policy experiments. Incorporated into a program for thousands of people, these same interventions become a social policy. This suggests the opportunity the clinical practitioner has to collect invaluable information about the effects of current policies, policy deficits, and potential policies. Moreover, precisely because the practitioner's information is tied to specific people and situations, it sometimes has a more dramatic impact on policymakers than an array of abstract information.

Social workers are currently being exhorted to become more active politically. This admonition is important, but it should be balanced by an awareness of the significant contributions social work practitioners can make to the policy development process. Direct service practitioners are in a position to be the eyes and ears of policymakers, whose decisions typically are made in places remote from their impact. The consequences of these policy decisions are often visible in the lives of clients the practitioner sees daily, and policymakers have a right and a responsibility to obtain systematic information about the effects of the policies they generate. It is time to develop formal and informal mechanisms for introducing into the policy development process the invaluable information about policy impacts and deficits that comes to social workers in the course of their daily practice.

Notes and References

1. Katharine Hooper Briar, "Helping the Unemployed Client," *Journal of Sociology and Social Welfare,* 8 (November 1980), pp. 895–906.

2. John F. Longres, "Alienation among Social Service Workers: An Empirical Exploration from a Marxist Perspective." Paper presented at the Seventh Professional Symposium of the National Association of Social Workers, Philadelphia, Pa., November 21, 1981.

3. *See* William Ryan, *Blaming the Victim* (New York: Random House, 1971).

4. *See* Ruth Hubbell, *Foster Care and Families;* Halcyone H. Bohen and Anamaria Viveros-Long, *Balancing Jobs and Family Life;* and Theodora Ooms, ed., *Teenage Pregnancy in a Family Context* (Philadelphia: Temple University Press, all three 1981).

Politics and Social Work Practice: A Radical Dilemma

PAUL ADAMS

4

'**S** OCIAL work is political, but politically it is conservative.' This position, expressed both by social workers and by those outside the profession, is based on the assumption that the class position, professional training, and occupational roles of social workers predispose them to define problems and concepts in a way that takes the existing social order for granted. A quarter of a century ago, Mills argued that the "activities and mental outlook [of social workers] are set within the existent norms of society.... In their professional work they tend to have an occupationally trained incapacity to rise above series of 'cases.'" Mills saw this training as being reinforced by a "similarity of origin and the probable lack of any continuous 'class experience,'" factors that "decrease [workers'] chances to see social structures rather than a scatter of situations."[1]

Marcuse, focusing on industrial sociology, motivational research, and "human relations in industry" rather than social work, provided a valuable analysis of the ideological nature of applied social sciences, which work in "the service of exploring and improving the existing social conditions, within the existing societal institutions."[2] He showed how issues of exploitation and poverty become translated into individual problems defined in terms that enable them to be handled within the agency setting and with available professional skills. Marcuse also showed in examples from the famous Hawthorne experiments how general complaints are defined in a way that makes them amenable to remedy within the limits of the personnel management system. The translation robs the complaint of its generalizable, critical significance and makes it instead a treatable and tractable incident. "The therapeutic and operational concept becomes false," he argued, "to the extent to which it insulates and atomizes the facts, stabilizes them within the repressive whole, or accepts the terms of this whole as the terms of the analysis."[3] Social casework, no less than personnel management in industry, may be seen as a managerial ideology that accepts, under the banner of practicality and realism, the given form of social relations as the ultimate frame of reference for theory and practice. Other components of social work, such as social planning and administration, exhibit even more clearly than casework the "managerial mode of thought and research" that Marcuse identified.[4]

Many writers have discussed the "therapy" or "treatment" administered by social workers and members of other "helping professions" as a mechanism of social control.[5] Social workers contribute to the defining and processing of deviant behavior, and so to the maintenance of dominant societal norms, all in the name of helping the individual client. Some political scientists, notably Edelman, have emphasized not only the highly coercive character of this professional help, but also its political significance. What Mills called the "professional ideology of social pathologists," Edelman sees as a symbolic language of pathology and therapy that disguises coercion and political repression. "The helping professions are the most effective agents of social conformity and isolation," he concludes. "In playing this political role they undergird the entire political structure, yet are largely spared from self-criticism, from political criticism, and even from political observation through a special language."[6] From this perspective, social work and other helping professions play a vital role in the maintenance of Western capitalism.

Radical Social Work?

Such critiques of social work's inherent conservatism and repressiveness have, of course, influenced radicals within the profession. They face a dilemma. If social workers are indeed agents of social control who help reinforce the labor market and maintain capitalism while translating the problems of poverty, oppression, and exploitation into the language of pathology and treatment, how can one be a radical or socialist and a social worker at the same time? If, however, social work can also provide a genuinely helpful service to the client, as many believe, is it sensible to abandon the profession to the forces of conservatism and dismiss it as hopelessly reactionary?

One response to this dilemma has been the attempt to develop a specifically radical way of doing social work. Such models of radical practice generally eschew diagnosis and treatment in favor of a kind of mutual consciousness raising engaged in by client and worker together. Instead of "individualizing" clients' problems in the manner of traditional casework and of human relations in industry, radical social workers may seek to generalize from the particular case, break down its isolation, and relate it to a pathogenic socioeconomic structure.[7]

"ANTIDOTE TO BOLSHEVISM"

Consciousness raising between worker and client may well have therapeutic value, but does it constitute an effective political strategy, one that contributes significantly to societal transformation? Gil, for one, seems to believe so when he suggests that practitioners must choose between antithetical modes of practice. On one side, he argues, are

> status-quo-preserving, symptom-ameliorating practice models—the models of service organizations which operate within the sanctions and resources of the prevailing social order. Alternatively, practitioners may reject these models, challenge the ideology of existing service organizations, and choose to participate in the development of radical, innovative, system-transforming practice.[8]

Most social workers, radical or not, work in "existing service organizations" that accept the "prevailing social order." How would a clinical social worker (or a grass-roots community organizer, for that matter) who wanted to use Gil's model go about developing a practice that would be "system-transforming"? Who would employ him or her? It would seem the worker must either operate subversively in a "status-quo-preserving" agency, like a Bolshevik in the Czarist army, or work for some private "alternative" employer, funded perhaps by wealthy radical philanthropists. The latter option, quite apart from the question of its strategic utility, is available to only a handful of social workers.

The former, subversive approach is clearly more realistic, but Gil seems to rule it out by calling for practitioners to be open and accountable for their politics. Objections to mixing politics and practice are invalid, he claims, since all practice has political implications, even if the worker is unaware of them. He draws the following conclusion: "To replace prevailing, unintentional, covert political aspects of practice with conscious, overt ones and to hold practitioners responsible for the political perspective of their practice, would seem a more honest, and hence more appropriate, course in ethical and professional terms."[9]

Two points need to be made about this issue. One is that liberals who are inherently conservative supporters of capitalism are not always unaware of or silent about the political aspects of practice. Indeed, it was once authoritatively claimed that "the only real antidote to Bolshevism is good casework."[10] Social workers and casework-oriented probation officers have long argued in court for the greater efficacy of their "treatment" methods compared with more punitive methods in inducing conformity. A more serious question is, who would "hold practitioners responsible for the political perspective of their practice"? Under West German law, upheld by the Federal Constitutional Court in 1975, the state holds employees of the government bureaucracy and public educational institutions responsible for their political perspectives, whether evident in their practice or not. The result has been the mass firing of radicals.

IN A CLASS SOCIETY

Attempts to develop a radical social work always run the risk of falling into utopianism, a mode of thinking tending to ignore the power structures of a class society and divert attention from the real struggles that alone have the potential to transform systems. Too often, academicians develop a paradigm for radical practice that workers in the field find of little strategic relevance to the

ADAMS

conflicts and struggles they face on the job.[11] Radicals need both to develop ways of practicing social work under capitalism in as humane and nonrepressive a manner as the job allows and to develop effective political strategies. These two needs are related but distinct. A model of practice applicable only in a future socialist society does not meet either need.

Radical analyses of the conservative political functions of social work point to the conclusion—not always drawn by the analysts themselves—that a truly radical social work can never be institutionalized under capitalism, except perhaps briefly by accident or oversight. The possibilities for subverting or resisting the coercive aspect of one's job and of genuinely improving the client's situation depend on what, in Marxist shorthand, might be called the balance of class forces, in society and at the workplace. Thus, the kind of counseling available depends much less on developments in social work than on the political strength and ideological coherence of oppositional movements in the wider society. Milligan describes an interdependence of nonrepressive counseling and political action for gays that has obvious parallels with other oppressed groups:

> The purpose of political action is to defend and extend the freedom of homosexual people to enjoy their sexuality. On the other hand, the object of counselling must be to render individuals capable of living, loving and working in a hostile environment. Political struggle and counselling depend on each other. An isolated gay person is unlikely to develop the pride and self-confidence necessary to live openly without the sort of individual help offered by counselling and befriending agencies.
>
> However, these agencies owe their existence directly to the political action of gay people themselves. The counselling of gay people was not seriously considered until homosexual people began to struggle for social as well as legal change. Recognition of the need for counselling has grown as a result of political struggle. More importantly the activity of gay people has created new ideas and attitudes to counter our oppression. Without these alternative ideas counselling would exist only in the form of support for repressive psychotherapy and clinical "treatment."[12]

Milligan shows how a radical movement can both highlight the need for individual counseling and redefine the problem and thus the kind of treatment considered appropriate.

What is possible in any particular work situation also depends on the strength of union organization and the ability to resist victimization. The more a radical social worker's day-to-day practice departs from the norm, the more he or she needs the backing of organized fellow workers inside and beyond the workplace. The more a group of workers pursues policies in conflict with basic capitalist norms and priorities, the more they need the backing of a strong, politically advanced labor movement. Social workers, however radical, contribute little to the forces of social transformation if they get fired or lose their funding without putting up an effective fight.

Locus of Radicalism

A strategy for radical social workers needs to link the possibilities for action in the worker's immediate situation to the long-term goal of social transformation. It needs to be based on an analysis of the structure, dynamics, and contradictions—and hence the tendencies to fundamental change—of capitalism. It needs to take account of the social weight, oppositional potential, and strategic significance of different classes, strata, and occupational groups. Such an analysis is beyond the scope of the present essay, but to approach the matter in this way is at once to call into question the assumption of the profession's importance widely shared by conservative, liberal, and radical social workers and critics of social work.

To show that all social work is political is not to show that it is essential to the survival of capitalism or that it has the potential to play a major role in its overthrow. Social work is neither an effective antidote to Bolshevism nor an adequate substitute for it. It is more political in character than work on an automobile assembly line—one can be a radical auto worker, but it is not possible to do radical auto work. But auto workers, like other industrial workers, are central to the capitalist economy. The political and economic leverage inherent in their capacity to strike is beyond comparison with that of social workers.[13]

Social workers play an important role as ideological servants of the state, both by controlling the deviance of individual clients and by fostering the belief that complex problems directly caused by capitalism are amenable to social work solutions. (One objection to utopian schemes for radical practice is precisely that they encourage belief in the ideology that social work has the capacity to solve these problems.) It is just because industrial workers are essential to the daily reproduction of capitalism that they are so well positioned to be its gravediggers. By the same token, social workers, as part of the state's apparatus of repression and ideological hegemony, have the capacity, when they are radicalized and act collectively, to undermine the legitimacy of the system they represent. However, the locus of their radicalism is not, insofar as it amounts to anything, the client-worker relationship, but that of the employer and employee. That is, it is primarily as workers, as part of the labor movement, that social workers have the potential to be effective agents of social change.

British Example

Radical social workers in Britain, such as those who were associated with the journal *Case Con* in the first half of the 1970s, have been able on a small scale to challenge the repressiveness of social welfare bureaucracies and to undermine traditional social work ideology. This is because they organized social workers into the National and Local Government Officers Association, one of the largest white-collar unions in the world, and because they became part of the militant rank and file of that union and of the larger labor movement.

Case Con, a revolutionary magazine for social workers, first appeared in London in 1970 and soon spawned a national movement with wide support.[14] Despite some opposition from those who advocated dropping out of conventional social work employment, the group associated with the magazine rapidly came to see as their central task the organizing of rank-and-file social workers in public agencies as part of the labor movement. There was no lack of awareness on their part of the bureaucratic and class-collaborationist character of the union leadership. They rejected, however, the prevalent tendency of middle-class radicals to dismiss the unions as hopelessly conservative and apolitical, arguing instead that unions were essential to the defense of workers' conditions and living standards, both on the job and in defending political rights and the benefits of the welfare state. Rank-and-file workers, they maintained, had to take control of their unions, democratize them, and make them effective instruments of class struggle.[15] Social workers had a special duty to raise political, social policy issues in the union and to "stress the importance of increased social provision for the deprived sector of the community that makes up the bulk of [their] clients."[16]

In London and many other large cities, *Case Con* supporters undertook a wide range of militant activities, involving concerns about pay and work load, refusal to carry out repressive agency policies, support of and collaboration with clients in fighting their local government (which was the social workers' employer) over issues such as housing, and resistance to the victimization of individual workers. All these activities demanded—and were most likely to succeed with—the backing of an effective trade union and alliance with other groups of workers.

This orientation was criticized in *Case Con*'s pages and elsewhere for being a kind of after-hours radicalism that left the day-to-day routine of radical social workers largely indistinguishable from that of their conventional colleagues. What was needed, the critics argued, was some way of doing radical social work and of relating to clients, as well as to courts and other authorities, in a radical manner. The charge of after-hours radicalism—that is, of supporting tenants and welfare rights groups by night while functioning as usual by day—was both unfounded and misguided. Many of the actions undertaken by *Case Con* supporters involved on-the-job conflict over agency policy and the subversion of or open refusal to implement that policy.

Behind the charge, however, was a belief in the capacity of radical social work, by virtue of its political character, to substitute for political activity. The social worker was seen as a political organizer, and clients were expected to replace the working class of orthodox revolutionary theories. But social work clients are even less central than social workers themselves to the struggle for social transformation. They tend to be the least organized and organizable elements of the working class. Those outside or on the fringes of the work force, recipients of Aid to Families with Dependent Children, the old, the sick and disabled, the unemployed, and the isolated are relatively powerless, no matter how radical they may be. When mobilized apart from the labor movement, the poor have achieved little and sustained less.[17]

Appropriate Allies?

Those who see the client-worker relationship rather than that of social work employee to employer as the key locus of radicalism find themselves advocating a rigorous client selection process. Clients are seen as political allies, and priority is given those most capable of accepting this role.[18] Once a more modest view is adopted of what a radical can do in the performance of his or her job, however, the notion of selecting clients on the basis of what can be achieved politically with them can be discarded. Even the idea that a job should be chosen on the basis of the political possibilities it affords is erroneous if those political opportunities are seen as located in the client-worker relationship. A social worker might conceivably find himself or herself in the position of choosing between a job involving grass-roots community organizing for a private philanthropic agency and one involving work with the terminally ill or with alcoholic vagrants. If the second job has no serious possibilities of radicalizing clients but is in a large public agency whose workers are organized or organizable, then, in political terms, it is a more promising choice. If the worker has a special interest and skill in the area of work with the terminally ill, the job, qua job, is likely to prove more satisfying and useful even though this group is unlikely to be mobilized for the revolution. The same is true of more common types of social work, such as adoption and foster care work. Some jobs, for example, parole officer, are so purely repressive that, in general, no radical should take them.

In many ways the position of social workers is analogous to that of teachers. Both have ideologies and social control functions. Both groups have professional aspirations, but many have been drawn in the direction of union and political militancy—although teachers are far more conscious of the importance of trade unions than are social workers. It is especially in the large city schools and agencies—where the possibilities of radical, alternative education or social work may be highly constricted—that militancy has flourished. The radical teacher who practices in a utopian alternative school may thereby be cutting himself or herself off from the real struggles in the public education system, the struggles that help to build the power to transform society.

The social worker's job is political, and although the politics are usually conservative, there are radical possibilities inherent in the job itself. Many of those possibilities have been discussed by Galper and other suggestions have been offered by Piven and Cloward.[19] Social work can be done in a less conservative and repressive way than it usually is, but one should not look to the job itself, or to social work in general, as a means of changing society. To do so is likely to prove a disservice to one's clients without offering a viable strategy for radical social change. Although political in nature, social work is no substitute for serious political activity.

Notes and References

1. C. Wright Mills, "The Professional Ideology of Social Pathologists," *American Journal of Sociology*, 49 (September 1943-44), p. 171.

2. Herbert Marcuse, *One Dimensional Man: Studies in the Ideology of Advanced Industrial Society* (Boston: Beacon Press, 1964), p. 107.

3. Ibid., pp. 107–108. For the discussion of the Hawthorne studies, *see* pp. 108–114.

4. Ibid., p. 111.

5. *See*, for example, the writings of Howard Becker, Erving Goffman, David Matza, Thomas Scheff, and Thomas Szasz.

6. Murray Edelman, "The Political Language of the Helping Professions," *Politics and Society*, 4 (May 1974), p. 310.

7. *See* Jeffry H. Galper, *The Politics of Social Services* (Englewood Cliffs, N.J.: Prentice-Hall, 1975), pp. 208–212; and Paul Corrigan and Peter Leonard, *Social Work Practice under Capitalism: A Marxist Approach* (London: Macmillan & Co., 1978), pp. 106–123, 136–137.

8. David G. Gil, "Clinical Practice and the Politics of Human Liberation," *Catalyst*, 1 (1978), p. 68.

9. Ibid., p. 62.

10. *Fifty-eighth Annual Report* (London, England: Charity Organization Society, 1927), p. 1, cited by Kathleen Woodroofe, *From Charity to Social Work in England and the United States* (Toronto, Ont., Canada: University of Toronto Press, 1962), p. 55.

11. *See*, for example, Ian Taylor, "Client Refusal: A Political Strategy for Radical Social Work," *Case Con*, 7 (April 1972), pp. 5–10.

12. Don Milligan, "Homosexuality: Sexual Needs and Social Problems," in Roy Bailey and Mike Brake, eds., *Radical Social Work* (New York: Pantheon Books, 1976), p. 110.

13. For a fuller discussion of this point, *see* Paul Adams and Gary Freeman, "On the Political Character of Social Service Work." To be published in a forthcoming issue of *Social Service Review*.

14. Material on *Case Con* is drawn from the journal and from the author's own experience as assistant editor in the early 1970s.

15. *Case Con* supporters were urged to join both the National and Local Government Officers Association (NALGO) and its rank-and-file opposition group, NALGO Action, which aimed to make the union more democratic, militant, and politically progressive. NALGO Action's program and purposes were similar to those of such rank-and-file groups in American unions as the Teamsters for a Democratic Union or the United National Caucus in the United Auto Workers.

16. Celia Deacon, "Social Worker Trade Unionist?" *Case Con*, 1 (June 1970), p. 11. *See also* David Wagner and Marcia B. Cohen, "Social Workers, Class, and Professionalism," *Catalyst*, 1 (1978), pp. 25–53; and Milton Tambor, "Unions and Voluntary Agencies," *Social Work*, 18 (July 1973), pp. 41–47.

17. On the relationship of the poor to the organized working class, *see* the exchange that took place between Roach and Roach and Piven and Cloward in the following articles: Jack L. Roach and Janet K. Roach, "Mobilizing the Poor: Road to a Dead End," *Social Problems*, 26 (December 1978), pp. 160–171; Frances Fox Piven and Richard A. Cloward, "Social Movements and Societal Conditions: A Response to Roach and Roach," *Social Problems,* 26 (December 1978), pp. 172–178; and Roach and Roach, "Disunity and Unity of the Working Class: Reply to Piven and Cloward," *Social Problems*, 26 (February 1979), pp. 267–270. In this exchange, Roach and Roach argued convincingly that the "basic task of activists who are concerned about poverty is the promotion of socialist consciousness among the rank and file in the trade unions."

18. Galper, op. cit., pp. 213–215.

19. Ibid., pp. 188–227; and Frances Fox Piven and Richard A. Cloward, "Notes toward a Radical Social Work," in Bailey and Brake, *Radical Social Work*, pp. vii–xlviii.

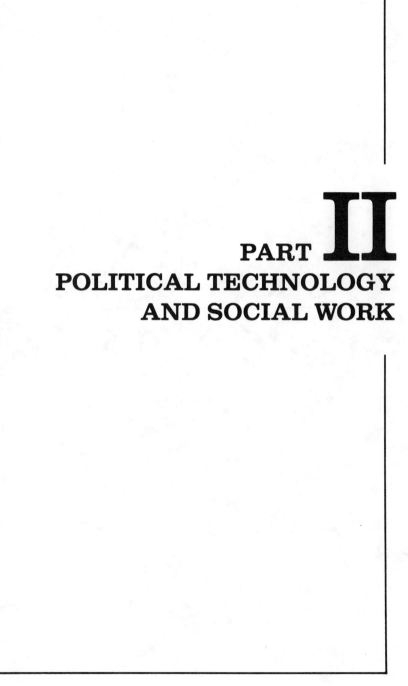

PART **II**
POLITICAL TECHNOLOGY
AND SOCIAL WORK

Lobbying and Social Work

MARYANN MAHAFFEY

5

THE specific and immediate goals of the social work profession vary widely in the different fields of practice, but, in general, social workers consistently seek to expand and improve social and rehabilitative services for those who are powerless, discriminated against, shackled by circumstances, and deprived of opportunities to achieve their maximum individual potential. In recognition of societal and environmental effects on personal well-being, social workers also seek to change the environment. The extent to which the social work professional is able to achieve these objectives, particularly those related to environmental and social change, depends at least in part on social policy and, consequently, on the principal forces in the formation of social policy—politics and government.

Despite the importance of government's legislative and administrative processes to the profession's objectives, the literature of social work (and other human service professions as well) is virtually devoid of materials delineating the discrete sequence of actions necessary to achieve political goals. The purpose of this article is to describe how social workers can advance their professional goals by undertaking political activities and, in particular, by lobbying to influence the legislative process.

An earlier version of this article ran in Social Work, *17:1 (January 1972), pp. 3-11.* © *1972, National Association of Social Workers, Inc.*

69

Political Strategies

Politics has been variously termed the art or science of government, the art of balancing, the art of compromise, the art of the possible, the art of dissimulation, and the exercise of power. In a governmental system that involves widely disparate groups, interests, and forces in the checks and balances of multiple decision centers, those active in the political process are inevitably concerned with dialectics—with opposing forces that are dying or coming to life and with the new problems created by solving old ones. Politics and government therefore involve participants in such strategies and tactics as struggle, confrontation, negotiation, compromise, building coalitions, and utilizing power. It is useful to review how some of these strategies apply to the political process.

STRUGGLE

Through struggle and striving for reform, people learn to identify their self-interest and distinguish friends from enemies. They begin to understand what the real issues are and to avoid secondary concerns that deplete their energies and deflect them from major goals. They learn to work together and build power based on numbers that can counteract other kinds and levels of power, such as money or position. For example, those participating in various liberation struggles, such as women, blacks, Chicanos, American Indians, and other oppressed minorities, are learning that by working together they can exert power to reduce the exploitation of any group or individual. Struggle often requires confronting the opposition and demands a willingness to fight for rights as well as privileges.

NEGOTIATION

Lobbying, and other forms of political activity as well, can be compared to union negotiating. Both union negotiator and lobbyist have to come to terms with the boss—the owner, manager, decision maker, or legislator—in a small group meeting, and both must continually remember the fundamental interests of their constituents or employing organization. Negotiators or lobbyists who forget the power of their supporters and the thrust of their goals cannot be effective; they can even sell out their constituents. Nor can negotiators be effective unless they understand the interests and power of the opposition. They must know the realm of the possible and continuously probe to expand its limits. They must struggle for definition and clarity and for agreement or closure on specific terms.

COOPERATION

Perhaps the most telling political axiom is "Union gives strength." Little can be done alone, and the cooperation of others is essential to most political and lobbying activities. Colleagues must be enlisted to expedite certain measures, and coalitions and alliances must be formed deliberately to serve organizational ends.

COMPROMISE

Lobbyists must be prepared to fight for as much as they can get and often be willing to forfeit one objective to obtain another. Compromise should lead to long-term gains rather than losses. Negotiations to achieve the best that is possible at the moment may involve accepting unfavorable conditions for the sake of advancing the major objective. For example, a lobbyist might support a family assistance plan because it established the principle of federal responsibility for ensuring a minimum income for families. Securing this principle might require accepting family allowances that were grossly inadequate, but the lobbyist might draw the line on supporting the measure if it included forced work and a means test. Before negotiating a compromise, the lobbyist should resolve three key questions: What principles are basic? Where is the line drawn between establishing a principle and selling out? What is acceptable to the sponsoring group? In addition, the positions must be clear and argued out before the compromise is struck, for attempting to avoid resistance by settling before positions have been firmed is to ask for trouble later.

STEP-BY-STEP PROGRESS

Once a principle is established by a legislative measure, there is always hope that the measure can be improved in the future. Amendments may relate, for instance, to expanding coverage, broadening services, or revising disadvantageous provisions. Small as well as big victories in the negotiating process strengthen massive demonstrations and protest movements. It is difficult to sustain a massive effort without periodic concrete achievements. Small victories build people's faith both in their ability to create change and in their change agent. The challenge lies in helping people see that the immediate success is a step along the way to the larger victory and to recognize that step-by-step progress is a way of building power.

USE OF POWER

The political process inevitably involves strategies for using power. These range from simple persuasion to bargaining and exchanging and to manipulation, dissimulation, and coercion. It is the wise lobbyist who uses power in such a way that friends and retained while objectives are achieved.

Sometimes those engaged in the political process become enthralled with the game, the means, and the power, developing an inflated pride in their own cleverness and skill with words and facts. It is a cardinal rule that lobbyists must never lose sight of their objectives. They must always remember that lobbying occurs within a system of political processes and is a methodology for creating change. Lobbying is not an end in itself.

Barriers to Interaction

Social workers have many illusions and misconceptions about the political process and politicians. These misapprehensions, coupled with the public stereotypes of social workers, form barriers to effective relationships between social workers and politicians. Such barriers must be broken down if social workers are to achieve credibility and influence as lobbyists.

Many social workers have a limited knowledge of government structures and even of the basic principles of civics and economics. Too few understand that a bill goes through a series of steps before it is voted on and that, in consequence, few bills can survive the legislative process in their original form. While a bill is in process, the sponsoring legislators prove they are on the job by proposing, supporting, or opposing—often in concert with colleagues—various deletions, revisions, and additions, taking what-

MAHAFFEY

ever actions seem most appropriate to protect their own and their constituents' interests.

It is important for social workers to recognize that politicians serving as ombudsmen for constituents continually deal with the messes that powerful interests, bureaucracies, and politicians themselves create and that result in constituents' being cheated or harassed by complicated regulations and inefficient administrators. Politicians are thus under constant pressure to find immediate solutions to these and other difficult problems. Moreover, politicians know that all issues are strongly linked to feelings, including their colleagues' competitiveness for position.

All too often social workers look on the political process with disdain and aversion. Many consider politicians reactionary, venal old men who make deals and sell out their principles. These generalizations may sweep the social worker off course and deter actions dictated by social work training. The social worker's responsibility is to diagnose the politician's concerns and relationships, locate people who can be helpful allies or supporters, and search for areas of common interest and consequent influence.

Social workers also tend to become impatient with the prolonged time involved in creating change, and some lack the staying power to survive the compromises and twists and turns of the political process. They forget that the larger the system, the more complex and difficult it is to change. Many social workers consider that their rights of self-determination and individual decision making are eroded by the disciplined group effort necessary to remain in the political mainstream, keep track of the complex interplay of forces, and maintain effective coalitions.

Illusions

Much has been written about politicians' tendency to react to crises of the moment, but the notion that all politicians lack values and long-range goals is an illusion. One state senator in Michigan, for example, measures every bill and governmental action by its effect on the poor blacks who make up his constit-uency. He is a supporter of government as the employer of last resort. He thinks the government subsidizes the rich and penalizes the poor, and he wants to reverse that. Believing in accountability to those who elected him, he holds an annual legislative conference and monthly public sessions with constituents. He works assiduously to build support in his district.

Another state senator in Michigan has introduced legislation to establish subsidized adoption and increase the assets elderly citizens can have and still qualify for old age assistance. Nevertheless, he also introduced legislation to reduce the allotment under Aid to Families with Dependent Children called for by the state's governor. He is a businessman from a rural area, concerned with preserving free enterprise, limiting the central government's powers, and, if possible, reducing governmental expenditures.

Some social workers' naiveté about politicians and the political process leads them to believe that politicians are so powerful that they are unapproachable. They forget that politicians usually want to get reelected, move to higher office, or increase their power and influence. Politicians, therefore, are vulnerable to voter pressure, especially pressure from those in their own districts. Social workers forget, too, that politicians are not always consistent and that some politicians, by virtue of their work to maintain bases in their districts, have been able to take advanced positions and continue in office. The support of national health care by Congressman Ron Dellums of California is an example.

Social workers who view themselves as morally and ethically superior and who rely on individual moral suasion to influence politicians are not being realistic. Legislators know that however strongly they may believe in a moral principle, they cannot use morality to sway colleagues who may be trying, for example, to avoid raising taxes. Politicians have long memories about casualties at the polls and recall all too vividly those who were defeated because they sponsored tax increases at the wrong time, although for altruistic reasons.

Social workers are just one of many lobbyist groups trying to influence politicians, and they are not generally in a favorable position at the outset. Politicians often believe that the social worker lacks political sophistication. They think social workers avoid conflict they cannot control and consequently lack the will to join in long-term struggles on controversial positions. Also, some politicians distrust intellectual professionals. Because of such negative attitudes, social worker-lobbyists do not always receive prompt and warm receptions. The need, therefore, is for the worker-lobbyist to maintain a delicate balance—to avoid oversensitivity, keep long-range goals in mind, and remain sensitive to

MAHAFFEY

the legislator's feelings while being alert to the issues at hand.

The social worker's position is also potentially advantageous. The social worker can be perceived not as a suppliant, but as the supplier of life-giving skills and coveted information. Politicians are perpetually concerned about getting feedback from varied sources to check their facts and impressions. They are constantly searching for reliable information about conditions and relationships in communities they represent. Social worker–lobbyists, who have training in social relationships and specific knowledge about people's needs and the services existing to meet needs, should be perennially helpful. It is necessary to be persistent, however, and to prove the value of the social worker's expertise.

Many politicians believe that change could be accelerated and people helped more if social workers showed less concern for self-protection and greater eagerness to help clean up politics, including a willingness to run for public office. Because the elected governing bodies of the nation are major sites for potential change, the stakes are high. They are especially high if social worker-lobbyists are ready to engage in the long, arduous, and time-consuming task of educating people to their self-interest and organizing them to influence the political process. It is essential that social workers be elected to public office and that others support them with time and money.

Lobbyists' Functions and Skills

The lobbyist is a person paid to represent an organization officially with governmental officeholders and agencies. Most lobbying focuses on legislation relating to special interests. It is pursued with legislative and administrative leaders and does not ordinarily receive public attention. In recent years, citizens' groups concerned with specific issues have been on the increase.

The responsibility of the social worker–lobbyist is to protect the employing organization's interests in legislatures and with administrative units. Endeavoring to present a personal image of tact, integrity, and discretion, social worker–lobbyists establish governmental contacts for the professional organization, ascertaining the limits of action and apprising the organization's leaders of findings so they can determine an appropriate course.

Effective lobbyists have varied skills and they can be depended on by both the employing organization and by legislators. They are friendly, outgoing, articulate, and persuasive. They can work independently, following the organization's general directives, and they must be flexible and willing to maintain irregular work hours if necessary. A good lobbyist has the maturity to argue vociferously on one issue, be a friendly partner on another, and ignore personal rebuffs by either friend or foe. Above all, the lobbyist knows when to talk and when to listen. The effective lobbyist also knows how to wait. It is unnecessary to buy lunches, but politicians remember who supports them at election time and who contributes money to their campaigns. Campaigns are expensive, and politicians hate fund raising.

The social worker–lobbyist should be skilled and experienced in the strategies and tactics of politics and have a sophisticated sense of timing and appropriateness. For example, if there is to be a demonstration, the lobbyist should be able to recommend astutely when and where it might be held, how many might participate, and what the target should be. If the time and place are wrong, if few or too many take part, or if the target is poorly chosen, the results may be psychologically damaging for participants and may weaken the cause itself.

Lobbyists must be familiar with parliamentary procedure, with the structure of the legislature and other governmental bodies, and with the concerns and circumstances of incumbent officeholders and legislators. They must develop the skills needed to glamorize a specific issue and keep it alive with legislators who are inundated with issues. Lobbyists must know how and when to seize the initiative and put the pressure on through telephone and letter campaigns and meetings with constituents. It is important to remember that most legislation is modified and defeated in committee and that many times it is easier to defeat a bill than to pass it.

Good lobbyists develop the ability to diagnose the motivation of individuals and groups; they know how to analyze forces operative in the field and probe for areas of compromise. It is also important for lobbyists to become aware of the stresses and strains between the houses of the legislature, among various levels and branches of government, and among parties, factions, and individual officeholders. Lobbyists learn about the power of those who chair a committee and those who are committee members, and they acquaint themselves with secretaries and aides, who are

MAHAFFEY

sometimes the key to reaching officeholders. Aides should be cultivated, for the politician is often too busy to go into detail on many issues and must rely on aides to analyze and summarize them and recommend actions and strategies. This is particularly true of administrators. Because a major portion of the politician's work is to respond to the complaints of constituents, it is important that the lobbyist gear discussions to the needs of each politician's constituents.

A lobbyist may discover that the person who chairs a powerful committee is unshakable on certain issues but willing to compromise on others. The head of another committee may lack leadership ability and be unable to twist arms, trade on bills, or get legislation through. If a legislator is tough and a good diagnostician, is willing to take political risks for the sake of crucial issues, has clearly defined political and legislative goals, and wields power through control over the agenda and skillful use of the gavel, he or she may be the key to achieving the organization's objectives.

Major Tasks

The major tasks of the social worker–lobbyist may therefore be summarized as follows:

- Offering the expertise of the social work profession to legislators, who find it impossible to study and understand all the numerous bills they must consider. The lobbyist volunteers to give support and information and, in turn, seeks support and data helpful to the employing organization. The lobbyist offers technical assistance at the appropriate moment on one bill, provides research results before a crisis is reached on another, and organizes and exerts constituent pressure on still another, maintaining bipartisan relationships on all bills. Sometimes the lobbyist organizes support for the politician, enabling the politician to go out on a limb.

- Keeping track of all pertinent legislation, regardless of whether it is sponsored or opposed by the employing organization. The lobbyist finds out who would best support certain legislation and works closely with that lawmaker, discovering who wants to amend the bill and checking on the positions of administrative departments, the chief executive's office, and others concerned. Amendments agreed to by the employing organization are offered to legislators.

- Paying special attention to committee votes. These votes are not publicized and are often difficult to ascertain, but they are vital in targeting organizational influence. The lobbyist also seeks to know what is happening in party caucuses because positions are hammered out and deals often made in these important meetings.

- Developing relationships with other lobbyists, sharing information with them, looking for common goals, and sounding out possibilities for coalitions.

- Developing liaisons between the employing organization and the legislative body. The lobbyist pins down votes and follows up on why legislators voted the way they did. This information is fed back to the client organization and its members. Lobbyists may also be helpful in contacting the press, setting up press conferences, and working with the organization's public relations director or committee.

- Assisting the employing organization in training and organizing its members to influence the political process. This includes working with the organization and planning and coordinating delegations, demonstrations, and members' appearances at committee hearings and at sessions when votes are taken.

Employing Organization

Political power develops when people are organized, united, and active. Social work organizations should organize their members and be able to mobilize them as necessary. Having a lobbyist may stimulate such action. In employing one, the organization clearly indicates the lobbyist's responsibilities and the person to whom he or she answers. The organization itself remains primarily responsible for organizing its members, educating them on issues, keeping them informed about events, and unearthing those, including board members of social agencies, who know and have influence with legislators. However, it may be part of the lobbyist's job to assist in all this work.

The organization is also responsible for keeping issues alive

MAHAFFEY

among its members, which involves the constant struggle of competing with countless other demands on members' time, attention, and finances. A piece of legislation can take five years or more to pass, and in the prolonged process, members can forget reasons for early compromises and priorities. When an organization is splintered at a crucial moment, it can lose the legislation because legislators will say, "If you're not together, we're not going to bother with the bill and your position on it." Alerting members to progress on major issues is vital. This can be done through newsletters or special bulletins, which should cover questions raised, arguments used, and key opposition or support gained or lost. Telephone trees and networks, such as the Educational Legislative Action Network of the National Association of Social Workers, are essential.

The social work organization should train its members in working with politicians so that they can take on the tasks needed to push legislation ahead. If members are organized, they can be mobilized when a critical point in the legislative process is reached. Appropriate actions might include the use of such tactics as carefully timed telephone campaigns with messages left with politicians' secretaries or aides; contacts in meetings; handwritten, one-paragraph letters; presence in numbers (sometimes with signs) at hearings; testimony at hearings; visible presence when the vote on a bill is taken; and, after the voting, thank-you letters or acknowledgments regardless of the results.

In all this, it is important that the organization establish priorities and stick to them. A lobbyist can work well on only a limited number of bills. An organization's members can devote time and enthusiasm to a limited number of issues. The organization might be wise to concentrate on a few significant legislative measures that have some likelihood of passage, rather than scatter its efforts on a dozen or more minor measures or waste time on provisions that are perennially defeated. At the same time, it must always be ready to mobilize forces to defeat or change legislation that may not be on its priority list, but that suddenly develops strength in the legislative body.

Expert Knowledge

As noted earlier, elected officials often rely on social workers for expertise in specific fields. They look to social workers to provide supporting data for bills related to social work concerns, give requested advice, analyze bills, and draft legislative proposals or amendments. Those who are experienced in preparing such information for legislators know that a premium is placed on brevity, and they learn to prepare one-page summaries that begin with a one-sentence statement of the problem and that document needs, state pros and cons, and furnish precedents and costs. It is important to deal with just a few issues at a time, or, preferably, just one, and to be willing to talk to the legislator's aides, who often read the summaries aloud to the legislator. Above all, the materials provided must be honest.

At times, the outstanding expertise, authority, or influence of a specific social worker—perhaps the director of an agency or a board member—may be called for. For example, influential social workers may affect the committee assignment of bills, thus helping to save favored legislation.

Appearances at hearings by members of the social work organization should be coordinated through the lobbyist and the designated organizational chairman or chairwoman. In general, members should be prepared to testify before committees. The lobbyist should hold an orientation session with them, telling them what to expect, pointing out the elements of an impressive presentation, and warning of pitfalls. Role playing is helpful. Common faults that create hazards for the testifying social worker are issuing moral arguments without concrete accompanying proposals, making statements that are not backed by adequate research and documentation, and using confrontational tactics that can alienate the politician. Attacks may win an audience, but they turn off legislators. It is also important to be concise in presentations.

Unfortunately, some public hearings merely seek to document positions already determined. Realizing this, some legislators are not influenced by hearings. Nevertheless, hearings serve several useful purposes. They provide opportunities to (1) spotlight issues, (2) educate the public and arouse public opinion, (3) publicize the positions and proposed solutions of those testifying, (4) educate committee members, and (5) permit legislators to test public reactions to their positions. Although the publicity arising out of hearings may be useful to politicians, it is often essential to groups that are unable to draw media coverage unless a politician is willing to share the spotlight with them in a hearing.

Model for Legislative Action

Assuming a January session of a state legislature as the target date, the following is a model for a legislative action program by a social work organization. The model identifies only the tasks that need doing, without specifying whether they are to be made the responsibility of the lobbyist, the organization's board of directors, or other agents of the organization.

PREVIOUS SPRING

Discuss with key members of the organization the specific legislative propositions to be worked on in the following session, including areas of agreement with the proposed measure and items that can be compromised if need be.

PREVIOUS SUMMER

Form an organizational steering committee and select a coordinator to work with the lobbyist in planning and carrying out the following activities:

- Collect evidence providing a rationale for the proposed legislation.
- Draft a petition for social workers and community residents. The petition should be addressed to legislators and signed according to legislative districts. (Social workers' refusal to sign may indicate opposition within the organization.)
- Arrange for the organization's members to form district delegations and name a chairman or chairwoman for each delegation. Each district delegation should then hold meetings with its lawmakers to explore support. If it is an election year, there should be meetings with all candidates to ascertain their position on issues. Two members of the organization who are constituents of the appropriate district should be assigned to get to know each legislator and to maintain a relationship before and during the session. These members should make appointments with the legislators they have been assigned and prepare for the meetings by outlining in writing the issues (no more than three) they wish to discuss. These visits should be short and the presentations succinct.

PREVIOUS FALL

Form a small committee representing a cross section of the membership. These people should have the enthusiasm and the time to be part of periodic delegations to the government halls. Their work during the fall is exploratory; demands and pressure come later:

- Arrange for an official visit with the chief executive by the committee to ascertain the executive's viewpoint. After the meeting, the committee should leave a brief written account of the points it wants to make, including solutions and documentation.
- Meet with appropriate leaders of the organization to report findings and to select and order priorities.
- If it is not an election year, select legislators to sponsor new bills and meet with them. Tie each issue to their constituents' interests.
- If it is an election year, arrange delegation meetings in each legislative district to meet with primary winners and assess their support on issues of high priority. After the election, arrange for the committee to meet with the winners and obtain commitments.
- Obtain commitments from allies and from coalitions when possible.
- Discuss legislation with key administrators, ascertaining their level of support or opposition and the changes they may favor.

JANUARY SESSION

Because all important contacts have already been made, the beginning of the legislative session is a time for consolidating positions with lawmakers, exerting preliminary pressure regarding major measures, and offering social work expertise on bills under consideration:

- Arrange for a committee delegation to visit the chief executive and his or her aides to obtain active support for targeted legislation. The delegation should present letters from the organization's members favoring the legislation. Similar visits might also be arranged with key lawmakers and their aides.

- Present each legislator with a list of bills the organization supports and opposes.
- Continue to collect and analyze background information about lawmakers. Records should be kept of all political contacts and actions.
- Report to the organization's members via newsletter.

THROUGHOUT THE SESSION

After the legislative bodies have chosen their officers and their committee heads and members—about mid-January—the work goes forward and continues until the session:

- Make sure of promised support.
- Work with legislators on the introduction of measures.
- Visit lawmakers to enlist allies and assess strength.
- Send newsletters regularly, perhaps weekly, to key members of the organization, including the chairmen and chairwomen of the district delegations.
- Send monthly letters reporting on the effects of the legislative efforts to the organization's total membership.
- Hold organizational steering committee meetings regularly to decide compromises, arrange members' visits to legislators, discuss coalitions, and so on. This feedback system is crucial to success in influencing the political process.
- Thank legislators, administrators, and all others who provided support.

Summary

Lawmakers are always influenced by a variety of people and organizations, and social workers should increasingly be among those who exert influence. However, if social workers are to serve effectively as lobbyists, they must have training in the political process and increase their political sophistication. The profession as a whole must grow in the ability to use conflict, develop power, be decisive, and take risks while at the same time pursuing the art of compromise. Lobbying demands that social workers use to the fullest their diagnostic and organizational skills. It may well prove easier to train a social worker to be a lobbyist than to train a lobbyist to understand and represent social work goals.

The social worker–lobbyist must marry social action with practice. To achieve change, the lobbyist must have the experience, skills, and knowledge to be authoritative in providing lawmakers with the information they need. The lobbyist can maintain a commitment to the philosophy and values of social work only by clearly defining objectives, relating means to ends, and establishing proximate and middle-range goals that are consonant with and directed toward long-range goals. Compromise can establish a principle to be developed in future legislation, but the lobbyist must be willing to continue the fight to expand the principle and be clear about where to draw the line so that a sell-out is avoided.

The knowledge and skills of social workers are appropriate to gaining and using political influence. The very principles social work has isolated as useful in clinical practice and policy development are integral to the political process; the problem-solving process as social workers use it in working with individuals, groups, and communities is crucial to lobbying. Both the politician and the lobbyist must be sensitive to individuals, understand group process and complex organizations, and know what to do to effect change.

Fortunately, social workers are becoming more active politically as elected officials, lobbyists, campaign workers, and members of commissions and of politicians' staffs. The stakes are high. Elected officials ultimately determine policy, including the implementation of programs. Among the issues they will determine during the next decade is whether social security and Medicare will continue as public programs or be absorbed by the private sector, forcing people to buy protection from private insurers.

How to Testify Before a Legislative Committee

GEORGE R. SHARWELL

6

T HE need for social workers to address legislative issues has never been greater. This is true, in part, because legislation is reaching into the lives of more people and institutions every day. In part this is true because issues have arisen in recent years that are of concern both to social workers and legislators; child abuse and neglect and licensure of social workers are perhaps the best examples of such issues. In addition, legislative concern over the best use of the taxpayer's dollar and the recent legislative disenchantment with social welfare programs generally have forced social workers to defend many existing programs and to advocate more creative programs to take the place of those that have been ineffective. Finally, social workers have increasingly recognized their responsibility to speak out on a variety of issues in regard to which they have special information and insight.

It is obvious that if social workers are to be effective advocates in the Congress and in the statehouses throughout the nation, they must possess a knowledge of legislative behavior and principles of advocacy, be aware of the relevant values that guide social workers' actions, and attain skill in the application of that knowledge in a manner consistent with social work values.

Reprinted from Toward Human Dignity, *John W. Hanks, ed., pp. 87-98.*
© *1978, National Association of Social Workers, Inc.*

Unfortunately, few social workers have been exposed to the knowledge-value-skill trilogy during the course of their professional education. Moreover, the literature has largely ignored close examination of legislative advocacy. Mahaffey, an experienced legislative advocate and past president of the National Association of Social Workers (NASW), is one of a number of social workers who have noticed this gap in the literature. As she writes, "How does a social worker influence the legislative and administrative process to achieve the profession's social policy objectives? The literature on social work—and other human service professions as well—is virtually devoid of materials delineating the discrete sequence of actions necessary."[1]

The purpose of this article is to address part of this literature gap by delineating the discrete actions necessary for competent testimony before legislative committees and subcommittees. The principles and mechanics discussed in this article apply equally well to administrative bodies and to local legislative bodies, such as county or city councils. One assumption is that the advocate speaks in a representative capacity for a professional association, such as an NASW chapter, or for a human service organization, such as United Way or a family service agency. This assumption is made for two reasons: (1) it is probably more commonplace for a social worker to speak in a representative capacity than it is for a social worker to express individual views as a constituent-citizen or as one with expert knowledge on a specific topic of legislation and (2) the process involved in speaking in a representative capacity is much more complex than the process involved when one speaks only for oneself—but the skills involved in speaking only for oneself are identical in all important respects to the skills involved in testifying in a representative capacity.

Preliminary Points

Before the mechanics of testimony before legislative committees are addressed, two important preliminary points must be made: (1) ineffective advocacy does not merely fail; it undermines the very cause it seeks to advance and (2) it can damage future efforts of both the advocate and the organization the advocate represents. It is better to stay out of the legislative arena entirely than to enter it and display incompetence or lack of professional responsibility to deal with facts fully, fairly, and skillfully. One must recognize a distinction between ordinary citizen groups and professional associations, a distinction that legislators make. The citizen group's justification for speaking out is purely political—that is, the group communicates to legislators the wishes of a group of persons who are constituents; their strength is tied to their right to cast votes, not to their claimed ability to give sound advice on matters of public policy. In contrast, the professional association both claims special expertise and is expected by legislators to make a sound contribution to the development of public policy. Although there is a political dimension to the clout that professional organizations can develop, the political side is secondary to the claim of expertise. Thus, while a citizen group is often free to be intemperate in its actions, inaccurate in its facts, and unreasonable in its demands—and to do so with impunity—the professional association is not. Every advocate must be aware of this legislative double standard. The trite admonition that anything worth doing is worth doing well is nowhere more true than with respect to legislative advocacy.

Inept advocacy depletes resources of time, energy, and money without a positive return, and it tends to demoralize the advocate, the organization the advocate represents, and their partners in a given legislative matter. Moreover, because timing and circumstances often are important in legislative matters, failure to advance a legislative objective in a specific legislative session often means that another effort to achieve that objective cannot be mounted for a long time; a missed opportunity may be lost forever. In addition, legislative memories can be excellent. An advocate's ineptness or lapse in judgment can tarnish the image of the advocate and of the organization that person represents for many years to come and thus can affect the outcome of issues not yet even imagined. Fortunately, the reverse is also true. Competent advocacy not only advances a current legislative objective but enhances the ability of the advocate and of the organization represented to further future legislative objectives. Thus, the advocate has a responsibility to prepare sufficiently and approach legislative tasks in no less a professional manner than that person approaches clinical practice or other social work responsibilities.

DEMONSTRATING COMPETENCE

In addition to the specific legislative objectives that an advocate will attempt to accomplish, the advocate needs to further one global goal. This goal is to demonstrate by words and actions that the advocate and the organization represented are competent and characterized by integrity. The full scope and nuances of competence and integrity cannot be captured in the abstract. Generally, though, competence is demonstrated through awareness of the issues involved in a proposed piece of legislation, ability to express the issues clearly and succinctly, awareness of alternate routes that legislation might take to resolve the issues, advocacy of a *specific* route that legislation should take, and the cataloging of the defects in each of the alternative proposals.[2] Throughout all of this, the advocate must demonstrate awareness of relevant facts and political realities and express ideas in a convincing manner.[3] The key to all of this is obviously that the advocate must check factual matters and the prevailing political winds as well as agonize over the choice of words, so that the advocate's statements are both factually accurate and convincingly expressed.

CONVEYING INTEGRITY

Integrity is conveyed by accurately and fully disclosing all information that is relevant to the legislative issues and never misleading or being untruthful. To do otherwise courts disaster. Legislative advocacy takes place in a largely adversary arena—a setting in which opponents will seize on any improper or incorrect statement and expose it. Diligence and honesty may not always be rewarded in the legislative arena or anywhere else, but inaccuracy or dishonesty in a legislative forum is almost certain to have adverse consequences.

Need for a Written Statement

Legislative committees generally prefer to be furnished with a written statement of an advocate's positions on proposed legislation either at the time that oral testimony is given or, preferably, prior to that time. The oral presentation at a hearing can then consist of either reading the text of the written statement (if it is not too lengthy) or paraphrasing or summarizing the written statement. The advantages of providing a committee with a written statement in addition to oral testimony are numerous and important:

- It demonstrates professionalism.

- It shows a more than casual, impetuous interest in the legislative matter.

- It ensures that the committee record of the testimony will be accurate.

- It can make the oral presentation to the committee more effective, because some of the committee members and the committee staff will read the written statement in addition to listening to the testimony.

- It permits the advocate to say all he or she wants to say in the written statement while still being able to meet the time restraints often imposed on oral testimony.

- It gives flexibility in that the advocate can cover all the issues in the written statement but can highlight points in the oral portion that are especially responsive to points raised at a hearing by the opponents.

- It provides greater assurance of coverage in the media, because copies of the written statement can be provided to media representatives prior to the testimony.

- It provides greater assurance that media coverage of the testimony will be fuller and more accurate, because media representatives can work from the written statement rather than from hastily penciled notes.

- It enables the advocate to inform members of the organization represented and other persons and organizations as well of the content of the testimony.

- It provides a better record for the advocate's own organization than will notes from memory.

- It can be used as a model from which to draw in the future.

- It forces thorough preparation prior to testimony, and this preparation in itself should lead to a more competent performance before a legislative committee.

- It generally minimizes faulty communication within and outside the organization represented.

Figure 1 suggests the format and contents of a cover page for the prepared statement. While it may seem that some of the information contained on the cover sheet is not necessary (telephone number or descriptive information regarding the organization, for example), experience suggests that it is helpful, because the statement should be circulated and read widely—by representatives of the media, committee staff members, and various other people and organizations.

Fig. 1. Illustrative Copy of a Cover Page

Testimony Regarding
H. 2069—CHILD PROTECTION ACT OF 1977

Before the
JUDICIARY COMMITTEE
X STATE SENATE
March 27, 1977

Presented by
Jane Roe
Executive Director, *Y*

In Behalf of
Z Association[a]
0000 Nth Avenue
City, State 00000
Telephone (000) 000-0000

---

[a] If desired, include a brief description of the organization, giving membership size.

Fig. 2. Structure of the Prepared Statement

A. Introductory Remarks

This should be a brief introductory paragraph—usually requiring fewer than seventy-five words—in which the advocate identifies the organization represented, describes the organization briefly—including the number of the organization's members—and thanks the committee for the opportunity to be heard.

B. Body

1. a. Most important point
   b. Rationale
   c. Flaws in opponents' arguments

2. a. Least important point
   b. Rationale
   c. Flaws in opponents' arguments

3. a. Second most important point
   b. Rationale
   c. Flaws in opponents' arguments

The body consists principally of a series of specific recommendations, each supported by one or more reasons, and includes arguments to counter recommendations made by opponents of the advocate's position. The body is organized with the most important points coming at either the beginning or the end, while the less important points are placed in the middle portion.

C. Closing Remarks

This should be a brief paragraph—usually requiring fewer than fifty words—in which the advocate thanks the committee for the opportunity to testify, stating that she or he will be available at any time to provide additional information for the committee and is willing to answer questions of the committee at this time.

Figure 2 suggests the structure of the prepared statement. The body of the statement—which is bookended by brief introductory remarks and brief closing remarks—consists of a series of points, recommendations, or arguments.[4] Each point is supported by a rationale—factual, logical, or ideological. And each affirmative point that is made and justified should also be followed with arguments to refute the arguments advanced by those who oppose the advocate's point. This final nicety—the refutation of opposing positions—is a powerful weapon that is seldom used by neophyte advocates. By refuting opposing positions, one's own arguments are strengthened in comparison. Moreover, attacks on opposing positions can put opponents on the defensive, with the result that they cannot advance their own arguments because it is difficult to attack and defend simultaneously. Any advocate who develops arguments along the tripartite dimensions of affirmative argument, justification, and refutation—the three dimensions used by lawyers in developing their arguments—is certain to have a strong case to present to a committee.

It should be noted that Figure 2 suggests that the body of the prepared statement be organized so that the most important points are presented either early in the presentation or near its end, while the least important points are placed toward the middle of the statement. Experience proves that a strong start combined with a strong finish produces a favorable overall impression. Beyond this, lawyers have learned in the courtroom, and psychologists have learned during the course of the investigation of human memory, that people tend to remember best that which comes either first or last in a presentation and that they tend to retain least well information that comes in the middle portion.[5] This tendency of the human mind to remember best the first and final portions of a presentation is sometimes called the primacy-recency rule. This rule explains not only the placement of arguments within the body of the presentation, but it also explains why introductory remarks and closing remarks should be brief.[6]

The primacy-recency rule also gives counsel as to the length of a presentation—it should be no more lengthy than necessary. As a general rule, a prepared statement should not be longer than 2,500 words—and preferably not more than about 1,500 words. Quality, of course, should not be sacrificed to brevity, but most presentations can be shortened considerably without sacrificing substantive content or persuasiveness. If a presentation is lengthy, this sometimes is because it contains much technical information. In such a case, it is often desirable to append one or more documents to the presentation so that the presentation itself is largely devoid of technical matters, but the technical material will be available for those who may wish to consult it.[7]

ANTICIPATING ISSUES AND ATTACKS

It has been said that it is not possible to know beforehand what specific issues and arguments will be advanced in regard to a specific legislative proposal, but this is seldom true. Investigations made prior to preparation of a written statement of positions on a bill can forewarn one of many of the issues involved, enable one to anticipate many of the arguments that will be used to attack one's positions, and may even uncover arguments that can be used both to further one's affirmative points and to counter arguments that are hurled against one.

In order to identify issues, an advocate should obtain each bill introduced in the legislature that deals with the subject matter of present concern, go back several years, and then trace changes in the bills. Each change usually signals some issue. The available committee reports and the recorded debate on the bills on the floor of the legislature should be checked. These committee reports and records of legislative debate will identify not only issues but arguments as well, pro and con. If there is federal legislation related to the subject matter, the advocate should try to uncover similar information on bills, committee reports, and debate. Congressional committee reports tend to be especially full and to illuminate issues and arguments.

It is often helpful to follow the bills, committee reports, and legislative debate in a state other than one's own. California and New York tend to address most legislative issues before other states and to have such large and diverse populations as to ensure thorough discussion of issues on any important legislative topic.

It is helpful to consult the professional literature—and the advocate should not neglect legal publications. Law review articles tend to identify issues thoroughly and to argue them exhaustively; they can lay the intellectual groundwork for one's testimony thoroughly.[8] Moreover, because many legislators and legislative advocates are either lawyers or frequently consult such literature, law reviews can be invaluable aids not only in avoiding embarrassment but in identifying arguments and counterarguments. Other sources of information also can be helpful: local newspapers, contacts with people and organizations that are concerned with the specific piece of proposed legislation, experts in the subject matter of the bill, and friendly legislators.

PREPARING THE WRITTEN STATEMENT

The advocate should begin to draft the written statement as soon as research has been completed. Then the advocate should circulate the draft among key members of the organization represented, among those people and organizations that are allied with the organization represented in regard to the bill at hand, and among people who are experts on the subject matter of the bill. The advocate should begin to write the statement early so that there will be time both to get feedback and clearances from the organization represented and to modify the draft prior to testifying. It can be helpful to examine the testimony given by a variety of advocates. Copies of testimony in behalf of NASW are routinely provided to state chapter offices, and the *Congressional Record* contains many fine examples of testimony given by experienced advocates.[9]

The following guidelines may be helpful in preparing a written statement:

- Write the statement so that it stands on its own and can be understood by any reasonably literate adult.
- Do not use jargon, except in appended materials.
- Prefer the specific to the general.
- Do not preach—argue on the basis of facts and logic.
- Beware of humor; it can detract from serious argument and often appears tasteless or ghoulish. (There is little that is humorous in rape, malnutrition, child abuse, or most other topics on which social workers testify.)
- Avoid hostility in any form.
- Focus testimony directly on the proposed legislation at hand; do not use the opportunity to be heard to state views on a wide variety of problems. Problems are solved, if at all, one at a time, not in bunches.

Being Heard by the Committee

As soon as a bill is referred to a legislative committee, the chair and the committee staff person should be contacted. Normally it is desirable to telephone committee staff members to advise them of the advocate's name, the name of the organization represented, a brief description of the organization, and the advocate's general position on the bill. Staff members should be advised that the advocate wishes to testify in behalf of the organization and that the advocate wants to be notified of the time, date, and place of any hearings that will be held on the bill. This discussion should be followed up with a letter on the organization's letterhead addressed to the chair.[10]

The advocate should try to get a commitment that he or she will be heard and will be placed on an agenda if there is one. It is desirable to be placed on an agenda, if possible, not only because it gives some status and recognition to the organization, but also because the media may give more attention to those organizations that are scheduled to testify. A representative of an organization on the agenda also is likely to testify prior to organizations that are not on the agenda, and additional time restraints or pressures often are placed on those who testify later. Moreover, media representatives sometimes attend only part of a hearing; testifying early may permit an advocate to testify before some reporters leave.

Attracting the Attention of the Media

Other things being equal, the fact that an advocate can provide the media with a statement of testimony gives greater assurance of coverage in the media than if there is no prepared statement. Representatives of the media do read prepared statements, and if an advocate gets to a hearing room early so that copies of the testimony can be given out early, many representatives may read it while waiting for the hearing to begin. This reading reinforces the impact of later testimony.

Moreover, a prepared statement makes the media representatives' jobs safer and easier. A typewritten statement is easier and more trustworthy than a reporter's own hastily written summary of remarks. And a media representative need fear no accusation of misstatement if she or he quotes directly from a prepared statement. It is also easier for a harried reporter to bracket portions of a written statement on which to report than it is to write out excerpts from oral testimony. A copy of an advocate's testimony should be put into the hands of the media representatives before the testimony is given.

Presenting Testimony

If the advocate has prepared thoroughly in advance and has a written statement, he or she should have little difficulty presenting the testimony. Preparation is the key. The advocate can, of course, read a prepared statement to the committee. However, this is not generally advisable. Normally it is better to summarize the major points of a prepared statement and then stand ready to answer any questions that the members of the committee may want to put. If the advocate cannot answer a question fully, it is advisable to indicate to the committee that an answer will be provided at a later time or to suggest that someone else who is present in the hearing room can answer the question capably.

The style of the advocate's presentation should be natural. It is the quality of the material and the argument that is important, not the advocate's delivery. Role playing beforehand may help give an advocate assurance, however, and it may also help to talk with the chairperson or committee staff prior to the hearing to learn the format of the hearing.

Post-Testimony Activities

Immediately following the presentation of the testimony, the advocate should do three things: (1) start planning the next steps, which would include lining up legislative support on the bill once it is reported from the committee, (2) communicate his or her activity on the bill to the membership of the organization represented (it is recommended that the entire text of the testimony be communicated to the membership in a newsletter or otherwise[11]), and (3) place one or more copies of the statement in the files of the organization represented, for use not only for historical purposes but, more important, to build a file that will be of use in the future. Professionalism depends to a large extent on the preservation of materials for future use. Files are no less important for the legislative advocate than they are for the clinical practitioner or administrator. It is largely through the preservation of the experience of an advocate that an organization can become increasingly influential.

At some point, too, the advocate should prepare letters of appreciation to be mailed to legislators and others who have allied with or helped the advocate and the organization in relation to the bill. The end of the legislative session is one time to write these letters; clear victory or loss is another time to do so. Such letters are important, and they distinguish the professional from the inept advocate—because legislators know that most of the letters they receive are letters of complaint, not letters of appreciation.

Conclusion

The real key to effective legislative advocacy is preparation. Unfortunately, thorough preparation takes time and work, but there is no adequate substitute. Fortunately, however, the time and energy expended in preparing for legislative testimony lead to success. The successes are never total, and they are sometimes temporary, but they make the time and energy well spent. And beyond this, today's success makes tomorrow's victories more certain.

Notes and References

1. Maryann Mahaffey, "Lobbying and Social Work," *Social Work*, 17 (January 1972), p. 3. Mahaffey discussed the entire range of actions in which a legislative advocate might engage. The present article focuses directly on a narrower range of actions—those related to testimony before a legislative committee. [For a revised version of Mahaffey's article, *see* p. 69 of this book.]

2. Inexperienced advocates often fail to attack the positions of their opponents. This is unfortunate because it is sometimes easier to win a point by demonstrating the weaknesses of opposing positions than it is to advance a specific affirmative point.

3. Social workers often look with disdain on political dimensions of issues and focus on substantive issues only. On many issues, however, legislators cannot act counter to the wishes of their constituents—no matter how ill-informed their constituents may be—if they are to remain legislators past the next election. The object is therefore to help legislators find some alternative that will not displease their constituents and that does not represent poor public policy.

4. Some illustrations of opening remarks are as follows:
   "Mr. Chairman and distinguished members of this committee: My name is Robert Cohen. I am Senior Staff Associate for the National Association of Social Workers, the largest organization of professional social workers in the world. I am here in behalf of the association, although I would note that I have resided in Montgomery County, Maryland, since 1963. NASW represents over 70,000 members, located in chapters throughout the 50 states, the District of Columbia, Puerto Rico, the Virgin Islands, and Europe. In Maryland over 2,500 social workers are currently active in the national association." Testimony of Robert H. Cohen before the Economic Affairs Committee of the Maryland State Senate on January 25, 1977. Note that Mr. Cohen identified himself as a Maryland resident as well as a representative of NASW.

"Mr. Chairman, members of the committee, ladies, and gentlemen. My name is George Sharwell. I represent the South Carolina State Chapter of the National Association of Social Workers, the only body of professionally educated social workers in South Carolina. There are more than 450 members in this chapter." Testimony by George R. Sharwell before the Medical, Military, Public, and Municipal Affairs Committee of the South Carolina House of Representatives, March 9, 1977.

The following are illustrations of concluding remarks:

"We appreciate the opportunity to testify before this committee and will be pleased to answer any questions the members may have." Testimony of Robert H. Cohen in behalf of NASW before the Economic Affairs Committee of the Maryland State Senate on January 25, 1977.

"In conclusion, may I thank you for permitting me to testify and urge you to support the passage of H.B. 5984, an act concerning the licensure of social work." Testimony of Sondra K. Match in behalf of NASW before the Public Health and Safety Committee of the Connecticut State Legislature on March 25, 1977.

5. Bernard Berelson and Gary A. Steiner, *Human Behavior: An Inventory of Scientific Findings* (New York: Harcourt, Brace & World, 1964), pp. 164–165.

6. The rule also is sometimes termed the "serial-position effect." *See* ibid.

7. Committee staff members or those drafting bills may be interested in technical information, while committee members may be less interested in such information.

8. Law review articles can be located by consulting *The Index to Legal Periodicals.*

9. One of the most instructive examples of testimony before a legislative committee is the testimony of Senator Hubert H. Humphrey reported in the *Congressional Record* of June 27, 1974, p. S11697 (daily edition). His testimony is especially noteworthy because although Senator Humphrey had a reputation for being verbose, his testimony was given in fewer than 700 words!

10. The body of such a letter might read somewhat as follows:

"I am writing to inform you that X wants to present its view on H. 2069 before the House Judiciary Committee.

"I have been informed by Y, Secretary to the Judiciary Committee, that hearings on H. 2069 have not yet been scheduled. I request that the Judiciary Committee provide X with an opportunity to be heard on this bill when a hearing is scheduled, and that I be notified of the time, date, and place of the hearing when it is scheduled.

"For purposes of planning, it may be helpful for your committee to know that our association will provide the committee with a written statement containing the views of our association's nearly —— members and that oral presentation will be limited to a summary of the written statement. It is anticipated that our position will be essentially supportive of H. 2069."

11. The full text is the best communication to provide to the membership. A summary is never adequate and, in any event, members deserve to be informed. A summarized statement is sometimes defended on the ground that members will not read a full statement. This is not necessarily true. But beyond this, members deserve to have the fullest possible information made available to them.

Legislative Advocacy: Seven Effective Tactics

RONALD B. DEAR
RINO J. PATTI

IT is often said that the legislative system is more effective in defeating bad bills than in enacting good ones. Indeed, the legislative process can be characterized as a series of obstacles that collectively constitute a formidable barrier to the passage of legislation, good or bad. The most telling evidence in this regard is that roughly one in five bills introduced in state and federal legislatures becomes public law.[1] For some this may be a source of comfort, but for the human service professional seeking enactment of a bill that will have a positive impact on the health and welfare of a population, these are poor odds.

The purpose of this article is to present tactics that will increase the advocate's chances of obtaining a favorable outcome on legislation as demonstrated by empirical evidence assembled by the authors and others. The tactics fall short of a complete model of legislative advocacy. Omitted from consideration are such efforts as involvement in political campaigns, the use of community pressure, coalition building, and the wielding of interpersonal influence. Although these and other tactics are potentially important to a fully articulated model of advocacy and have received some

Reprinted from Social Work, *26:4 (July 1981), pp. 289-296.*
© *1981, National Association of Social Workers, Inc.*

attention in the literature, there is yet little empirical evidence that systematically links them with legislative outcomes.[2]

The primary concern in what follows is to suggest tactics that can readily be used by part-time, single-issue advocates who make an occasional foray into the legislative arena to promote a bill of immediate interest to their agency or a client constituency. Such people are generally not immersed in the legislative culture or aware of the nuances and subtleties of the legislative process. They seldom have the opportunity to develop the resources, skills, and credibility that are the stock-in-trade of the seasoned lobbyist. Notwithstanding these limitations, part-time advocates can play a crucial role in promoting constructive social legislation if they focus on using time and energy appropriately. The seven tactical guidelines presented in this article are reasonably concrete steps that increase the probability of obtaining favorable legislative outcomes. In general, the tactics suggested are those that may be implemented by advocates with limited power and resources.

Background

The authors' research, which provides much of the basis for this discussion, involved an analysis of all 183 social and health services bills introduced in the forty-fourth session (1975-77) of the Washington State legislature and subsequently referred to the Social and Health Services Committees of the house and senate. The data collected on each bill included legislative outcome; process characteristics, such as source of request, date of introduction, number of sponsors, nature of sponsorship, committee deliberations, and number and magnitude of amendments; characteristics of sponsors, such as the prime sponsor's party, the number of terms served, committee membership, positions of leadership, occupation, age, and sex; and substantive characteristics, such as subject matter, magnitude of change proposed, nature of change proposed, and fiscal impact. The data were aggregated and analyzed to determine the relationships, if any, between the outcome of each bill and its process, sponsor, and substantive characteristics.

For purposes of this study, outcomes were defined in terms of whether a bill remained in, or was reported out of, the Social and Health Services Committee to which it was originally referred. It was necessary to resort to this restricted definition because the number of bills in the sample that ultimately became public law was so small as to preclude meaningful analysis. In addition, since a committee's decision in the house of origin is by far the most critical obstacle a bill must traverse, this criterion arose as the best surrogate measure of a bill's success or failure. The authors also conducted a pilot study on social and health services bills in the forty-third session (1973-75) of the Washington State legislature. This article also reports some findings from that study. When it was possible to equate the data obtained from the two studies, this was done. The seven suggested tactics follow and are accompanied by a discussion of the empirical findings on which they are based.

Empirically Based Tactics

1. Introduce the bill early in the session or, ideally, before the session has begun. Any politician, lobbyist, political scientist, or careful observer of government readily acknowledges that the legislative process—the trail from idea to enactment—is a tortuous one beset with an incredible number of stumbling blocks, hurdles, and pitfalls.[3] To make matters worse, the constitution in most states permits the legislature to be in session only sixty to ninety days, often in alternate years, and the bill cutoff date—the last day a regular bill may be introduced—is usually about halfway into the session. This is why some political scientists contend that "no single factor has a greater effect on the legislative environment than the constitutional restriction on the length of session."[4]

In spite of short sessions and early cutoff dates, in the 1975 and 1976 sessions approximately 200,000 bills were introduced into the fifty state legislatures in this country. For most states the number of new bills averaged between 2,500 and 4,000, although the number ranged from under 1,000 in several states to an astonishing 34,000 in New York.[5] Clearly, there is no way each piece of this bewildering volume of legislation can be considered with equal seriousness, especially by part-time citizen-legislators buffeted by constant and conflicting storms of special interests.

Given these constraints, it has been suggested that introducing a bill early in the session, or even before the session begins (prefiling the bill), increases the chances of favorable consideration. There are a number of reasons why this is considered a good tactic.

First, bills that are introduced early in the session frequently are better pieces of legislation because the sponsor or sponsoring group has had the time to do the necessary research and a greater opportunity to see that the measure is well drafted. A striking example of the value of careful drafting can be seen in the success rate of bills drafted by the Legislative Council, the former research office of the Washington State legislature. An astounding 93 percent of all measures drafted by the council were passed into law. All these bills were drafted prior to the beginning of the session.[6]

Second, the early introduction of bills allows the advocate more time to lobby legislators and committee staff about the positive features of the bill and to press for hearings, muster community support, counter potential opposition, and negotiate changes. Third, early bill introduction is one of the best ways to avoid the last-minute legislative logjam. In the frantic rush of the closing days of a session, many bills are voted down after being given scant consideration.

The authors' research clearly supports the desirability of early bill introduction. For example, of eighty-one bills introduced into the House and Senate Social and Health Services Committees of the forty-fourth biennium of the Washington State legislature during the first four weeks, 61 percent were reported out of committee, whereas only 51 percent of the bills introduced thereafter were reported out of committee. Moreover, a bill's chance of becoming law deteriorated rather markedly as the session progressed. That is, the chances were better if the bill was introduced in the first ten days of the session, dwindled somewhat in the second ten days, and were worse yet after the legislature had been in session more than twenty days. The authors' pilot study of the forty-third session uncovered a similar pattern: bills introduced early in the regular session had a fifty-fifty chance of being reported out, whereas only one in three of the bills introduced later were reported out. At least one other study offers further empirical support for early bill introduction.[7] It should be noted that measures can be introduced late in the session and still move through all phases of the legislative process and pass into law. In such instances, though, there is usually a majority in support of the measure at the start or a powerful sponsor who sees that significant opposition is overcome.

2. It is advisable to have more than one legislator sponsor a bill. Bills with multiple sponsorship tend to have a better chance of making their way through the legislative obstacle course than those with a single sponsor. This is what one might expect. Additional sponsors increase the likelihood that a bill will be heard. Since the volume of legislation is so great, legislators can read only a small portion of the hundreds of bills introduced into each of their committees and are likely to be knowledgeable about only a tiny fraction of the thousands of bills active in the legislature in any one session. Naturally, they must rely on their colleagues to advise them on the great bulk of bills they have neither the time nor interest to read. In this context, multiple sponsors serve two important functions: they are likely to make the bill more visible, and they multiply the power that can be applied to push the bill past crucial legislative obstacles. In essence, then, multiple sponsors not only tend to give a stamp of credibility to a measure, they can also become all-important advocates who can be called on to muster collegial support within the legislature, press for hearings, make the necessary trades and compromises to move a bill out of committee, push to get it scheduled by the rules committee, and apply pressure to get it passed by both houses.

The value of multiple sponsors tends to be enhanced even further when at least one of the sponsors is a member or a chair of the substantive committee or the Rules Committee. Such legislators can be particularly effective, because one common practice used to determine which bill will be given a hearing is to allow each member of the committee (usually by rotation) to select the measure they want heard that day. Additional sponsors in the legislative chamber can thus use their individual and collective influence to have a bill reported out of the substantive committee and also out of the Rules Committee and onto the floor of the chamber for a vote. Finally, the more sponsors a bill has, the more legislators to whom the advocate will have access and the opportunity to influence.

Data obtained in the authors' study support the proposition that bills with more than two sponsors are more likely to be reported out of committee. In the forty-fourth biennium, there were 183 bills introduced into the Social and Health Services Committees. Seventy-three bills had two or fewer sponsors, and the remaining 110 bills had three or more sponsors. Less than one-half (48 percent) of the bills with one or two sponsors were reported out of committee, as opposed to 60 percent of the bills with three or more sponsors.

Analysis of all bills that successfully passed the Washington State legislature during one entire biennium (this includes all bills, not just those dealing with health and welfare matters) strikingly illustrates the efficacy of multiple sponsorship. There was a total of 465 successful bills; 225 were originally sponsored in the house, and the other 240 in the senate. Table 1 leaves little doubt that the more sponsors a bill has, the better its chance of passage.

This table warrants serious attention by advocates who may question whether it is really worth the effort to seek more than one sponsor on a pet measure. Of the 225 successful house bills,

Table 1. Number of Original Sponsors of 225 Successful House Bills in the Washington State Legislature, Forty-Fifth Biennial Session, 1977-79

Number of Original Sponsors[a]	Bills[b]		Total Number of Sponsors
	Number	Percent	
1	25	11	25
2	27	12	54
3	47	21	141
4-5	55	24	238
6 or more	71	32	807
Total	225	100	1,265

SOURCE: Compiled from data in *Legislative Report, 1977: Final Edition, Forty-fifth Regular and Extraordinary Sessions* (Olympia, Washington: House and Senate Research Center, July 1977).

[a] The table shows only the number of original sponsors. By definition, committee bills always have the sponsorship of the majority of the members of the committee. Such bills almost always gain more sponsors than they had when originally introduced.

[b] The total of 225 successful bills includes all committee legislation and special request legislation—legislation requested by governmental agencies or by the governor. Almost one-half (47.5 percent) of the 225 bills became committee bills, and over one-fifth (21 percent) were special request legislation.

200 originally had more than one sponsor. Thus, an astonishing 89 percent of all house bills that were initially reported out of committee (the authors' criterion of success in their analysis), passed both houses, and were signed into law had multiple sponsorship. Moreover, one-third of all successful bills had six or more sponsors. Conversely, only 25 of the 225 successful house bills—a mere 11 percent—originally had a single sponsor, and of those 25 bills, 14 later gained additional sponsors. Thus, only 11 bills, or less than 5 percent of all the bills that passed the house, had a single sponsor. This means the chances a bill that retains a single sponsor has of becoming law is about one in twenty—even worse odds than one would expect from chance alone, which would be about one in five. Further analysis of the data in Table 1 indicates that the modal number of sponsors on successful bills was three, and the mean number of sponsors was between five and six.

A similar picture emerges from analysis of the 240 successful Washington State senate bills, although the data are less striking, possibly because the senate is a smaller body tending to consist of a higher proportion of senior legislators. Of the 240 bills signed into law, less than 10 percent had a single sponsor. Both the mean and modal number of sponsors on successful bills was three.

3. The advocate of social legislation should seek to obtain the sponsorship of the majority party, especially when the majority is Democratic. It is even more beneficial to obtain meaningful bipartisan sponsorship with the primary sponsor a member of the Democratic majority. It is sometimes said that political parties are not as influential as they were at one time.[8] In spite of what may be a lessening of party influence and control, the fact remains that 96 out of 99 state legislative chambers in the United States are elected on a partisan ballot.[9] Wise advocates tailor their tactics to the reality of partisan politics.

A study of Democratic and Republican votes in Washington State on selected key human service issues, such as social services and income maintenance, points to the partisan nature of voting on social legislation.[10] Only contested votes were chosen for this study because they were the ones that were thought to reflect genuine party differences most accurately. There were twenty-four contested votes in the house and eleven in the senate. Every legislator was given a score based on his or her voting record on these key human service measures. A "perfect" score would be 100 percent and would indicate that the legislator had voted in favor of all contested social legislation.

In the senate, the scores for Republicans ranged from a low of 11 percent (presumably the most conservative) to a high of 91 percent, with a mean score for all Republican senators of 65 percent. Senate Democrats ranged from a low of 64 percent (again, the most conservative or anti-human service Democratic legislator) to a high of 100 percent, with a mean percentage of 89. Fifteen Democratic senators voted in favor of all contested social legislation and were given scores of 100 percent.

In the house, the voting records of its ninety-eight members were assessed in regard to twenty-four contested human service votes. The lower chamber was evenly divided with forty-nine Democrats and forty-nine Republicans, a most unusual and awkward political phenomenon. As might be anticipated under such circumstances, the partisan flavor of the legislature was even more striking, especially as it pertained to social legislation. The forty-nine Republican representatives had a mean percentage of forty-five, meaning that they voted against more than half of all key human service legislation. Scores ranged from a low of 9 percent to a high of 79 percent. Democrats had a mean percentage of 93, with a range from 71 to 100. Only one Republican scored higher than the lowest Democrat.

These findings are consistent with those of other research that links party affiliation with voting behavior. However, it is not clear whether the tendency of Democrats to support social welfare policy is attributable to these legislators' urban bases with low-income and minority constituencies or to their party affiliation. Regardless of the reason for Democratic support of welfare policies, it is enough of a reality for Rothman to advise that "in keeping with popular views on the subject, Democrats are natural allies for programs necessitating government intervention.... Working through Democratic legislators ... would appear to be a useful strategy for furthering many human service objectives."[11] Advocates would be well advised to adjust to and develop tactics that recognize the partisan characteristics of the legislature they wish to influence.

Although conventional wisdom buttressed by the empirical data recorded here might well lead the advocate to think that partisan support is sufficient, this is not the whole story. Additional evidence indicates that, in some instances, bipartisan sponsorship

DEAR and PATTI

may improve the chances of passage. The study of the forty-fourth legislative session indicates that social and health legislation with bipartisan sponsorship does just as well, and at times much better, than measures with only partisan support. Data from this research show that equal percentages of partisan and bipartisan bills were reported out of committee. The pilot study of the forty-third session found that 40 percent of the bipartisan bills were reported out of committee, whereas only 20 percent of partisan bills left the committee of their origin. Neither study found that partisan sponsorship (even of the majority party) was an advantage over bipartisan sponsorship.

Successful legislation is based on compromise, forming coalitions, gaining support, and nullifying opposition. It is important to gain the support of those normally seen as allies as well as those with whom one may not be in ideological agreement. Too often, those advocating a measure, particularly in social legislation, tend to write off the other party (usually the Republican party) as too conservative. This could be a fatal error for the advocate. In short, bipartisan sponsorship is a way of extending the influence of the majority party by making the measure more acceptable to a broad range of legislators.

4. Whenever possible, the advocate should obtain the support of the governor and of relevant state agencies. No bill becomes law unless it is signed by the chief executive. During a recent biennium, the governor of Washington State vetoed or partially vetoed 6 percent of all legislation passed by both houses. If for no other reason than to avoid the possibility of a veto, it is wise to gain executive support.

Since state agencies also have a significant influence over the fate of legislation, it is a good idea not to have opposition from them, although at times it is not possible to avoid such conflict. This is especially true when agencies perceive the legislation as working against their interests, a not uncommon occurrence in social welfare. Moreover, the position taken by representatives of relevant state agencies is usually listened to most seriously by legislators. This is understandable when one considers that people in state agencies are usually viewed by legislators as the experts in the substantive area of legislation. They are the ones who must live with the law, translate it into administrative procedures, and see that the legal intent is carried out. As a consequence, opposition from the department of social services tends to decrease a bill's chances of passage. The opposite is also true. When a bill is supported by the relevant state agency or, better yet, requested by it, chances of passage are high.

How well does agency-sponsored legislation do? The findings in the Washington State studies indicate that such bills do well. In each study, agency-requested legislation had a significantly better chance of being reported out of committee than bills without such requests. In the forty-fourth session, for example, 75 percent of all agency-requested bills were passed out of committee, compared to 55 percent of all bills. In the pilot study, 39 percent of all 227 bills were reported out of Social and Health Services Committees, in contrast to 54 percent of all department-requested bills.

Other data lend strong support to the contention that agency-requested legislation has a high probability of success and an excellent chance of becoming law. In the analysis of 465 successful bills from the forty-fifth biennium, 115, or a full 25 percent, were agency-requested legislation.

5. The advocate should seek influential legislators as sponsors of proposed legislation, provided that they are willing to exercise their influence in promoting the bill. Given the obstacles to the passage of legislation in state legislatures, it seems logical to select as sponsors individuals who enjoy power and influence with their colleagues. Influence is at best an elusive phenomenon, easier to observe in concrete instances than to measure systematically in a global way. Since most advocates do not have the opportunity to become intimately familiar with the distribution of influence in a legislative chamber, it often becomes necessary to use readily observed characteristics as a basis for inferences regarding the possession of influence. Three such characteristics are thought to be particularly important in this regard: party leadership, committee leadership, and committee membership.

The influence of party leaders, including the majority and minority leaders, whips, and caucus officers, derives in large part from their experience and skill in the legislative process and their central role in formulating policy strategy on critical issues and in seeing that this strategy is implemented on the floor. In addition, as Truman suggests, party leaders often exert influence on their colleagues by virtue of the credibility and trust that they have come to enjoy over years of service:

> Legislative skill, usually acquired only after considerable experience in a law-making body, creates its own following; less experienced or overly busy members will often be guided by a skilled veteran when a vote is called for, and in a fashion that cannot be explained simply in terms of party loyalty or the trading of votes.[12]

Committee chairpersons tend to be particularly powerful in regard to the fate of bills that fall under their committee's jurisdiction. The following comment, although overstating the power of chairpersons, suggests something of the central position that such legislators occupy:

> The chairman of a committee...was in a particularly powerful position. He was responsible for scheduling committee meetings and had considerable leeway in determining the extent to which the committee met....He had control over the agenda, and given a surplus of bills could easily exercise a strategy of delay. Majority party members were faced with many committee assignments... sufficient to distract them from the procedural preferences of committee chairmen....The fate of much legislation could be determined by...the chairmen.[13]

The power of chairpersons is not this unbridled in many states, but even when their discretion is circumscribed by rules, procedures, or party discipline, these individuals are influential in determining the outcome of bills that are within the purview of their committee.

Committee members are also likely to be influential with bills that come under the scrutiny of the committees on which they serve. Legislators, faced with an enormous range of issues in diverse fields, seek to handle this load by dividing the labor among committees. Members of these committees are expected to develop a special expertise in specific areas. Others, preoccupied with work in their own committees, come to rely on the judgment and advice of these specialist colleagues in a given area, although legislators known for hard work, loyalty, and playing by the rules also come to enjoy the respect and trust of colleagues.[14]

One study of influence patterns in Washington State tends to confirm these observations regarding the influence of certain legislators. When lawmakers were asked to indicate fellow legislators who were most influential in legislative matters, party leaders, committee chairpersons, and members of key committees were most often nominated. Party leaders were perceived as generally influential, and chairs and members of committees were thought to have a disproportionate influence in their areas of specialization.[15]

The data from the study of legislative outcomes in the forty-fourth session of the Washington State legislature again bear out these observations. Of the 183 bills referred to the senate and house Social and Health Services Committees, 101, or 55.2 percent, were reported out of committee. The rate of success experienced by the chairpersons and members of these two committees who were prime sponsors of bills was somewhat greater than that of nonmembers. Nonmembers succeeded in getting favorable committee action on slightly less than 45 percent of the bills for which they were prime sponsors. Chairpersons had 65 percent of their bills reported out, and members of the committees succeeded with 59 percent.

The authors' data do not support the contention that party leaders are particularly effective prime sponsors of social legislation. To begin with, party leaders sponsored relatively few such bills in the forty-fourth session. Moreover, their success in achieving favorable committee action was about the same as that of other legislators and decidedly less than that of chairpersons and committee members. One possible explanation of this finding is that party leaders must attend to a wide array of issues, some of which, such as taxation and appropriations, are likely to have higher legislative priority than health and welfare measures. Lack of time and a disinclination to expend political capital on bills that touch the interests of a narrow constituency may have contributed to the relative ineffectiveness of party leaders as sponsors of social legislation.

Although the chairpersons and members of human services committees who sponsored legislation had better success in moving their bills out of committee than other legislators, the differences were not as great as some observers of the legislative process have contended. In part, this may be attributable to the fact that members of these committees, including the chairpersons, sponsored a disproportionate share of the bills that came to their committees—almost 74 percent of the total. Some of these bills were no doubt sponsored merely as a courtesy to constituents or out of a desire to be associated with a cause that had some popu-

DEAR and PATTI

larity among voters but little chance of being enacted. In any case, this large workload may have forced them to focus energy, time, and influence on the bills that were considered most important or most likely to be acted on. This suggests that although committee leadership or membership confers power on legislators, it remains only potential power until they exercise it with respect to a particular bill.

Therefore, although it behooves the advocate to seek sponsors who have influence with their colleagues, it is equally important to determine, so far as possible, whether the lawmaker will exercise this influence in promoting the bill. This may be difficult to determine, but the policy priorities established by the legislators' party caucus and their voting records on related issues may provide some important clues. In addition, research suggests that on controversial issues, legislators with secure electoral margins are more likely to be responsive to proposals from interest groups and to work for unpopular causes; the evidence also suggests that when a bill touches on the vital interests of the legislator's constituency, active sponsorship is likely to follow.[16]

6. The advocate should press for open committee hearings on the bill and, when such hearings are held, attempt to arrange for testimony in behalf of the bill by expert witnesses. It is generally recognized that open hearings are not the most effective forum in which to inform and persuade legislators. Milbrath, in his study of legislators and lobbyists, found, for example, that hearings had less impact on legislators than either personal contacts or presentations of research results. This is not to say that hearings lack any value as a means of persuasion. For legislators who are wavering on issues or who are looking for additional information to buttress a decision that has already been made, hearings can have an impact.[17]

Perhaps the major value of hearings for the advocate, however, is the opportunity they afford to draw public attention to a bill. Truman argued that a primary function of hearings is to create a channel for propaganda.[18] Especially if a hearing draws the attention of the media, the interested public can be sharply expanded and thus can indirectly influence legislative decision making. Hearings often reveal sources of both support and opposition to a bill. Thus, although hearings may extend the constituency of a measure, they also involve the risk of providing a platform for legislators or groups opposed to a measure and giving them an opportunity to extend and consolidate their opposition.

Data from the authors' study suggest that hearings may facilitate the progress of social and health legislation. Of those bills heard in open meetings during the forty-fourth session of the Washington State legislature, 71 percent were reported favorably out of committees in the senate and house. Conversely, only 22 percent of the bills not heard in public hearings were reported out of committee. However, the data do not support a conclusion that hearings lead to favorable committee action. It is possible, indeed likely, that a decision to schedule a bill for hearing reflects a favorable disposition to the bill. Nevertheless, the strong association between positive committee action and hearings supports the notion that pressing for a hearing is, in general, a desirable tactic.

When such hearings are held, it is helpful to arrange for testimony by expert witnesses, especially staff members from relevant governmental agencies. There is some evidence that informed presentations based on systematic study or intimate familiarity with the subject can be persuasive to legislators. Rothman, for example, cites several studies that support the conclusion that advocates should seek the involvement of relevant governmental agencies in their lobbying efforts.[19] Smith's review of the literature on interest group influence suggests that legislators are receptive to groups that have factual knowledge about matters they are considering.[20] The authors' study supports this conclusion. When the Washington State Department of Social and Health Services testified in behalf of bills, over 81 percent of these measures were favorably reported out of committee. When personnel from that agency testified against a bill or adopted a neutral stance, only 50 percent of such bills received favorable committee action. Obviously, the fate of these bills was not influenced solely by the testimony of agency witnesses, but this does appear to have at least a marginal impact. This is not to suggest that only agency witnesses should be recruited to appear at hearings. Depending on the nature of the bill, other people, including former or potential clients, front-line workers, community leaders, representatives of special interest groups, and independent professionals, can also be effective witnesses.[21]

7. The advocate should use the amendatory process as a strategy for promoting a favorable outcome for a bill. The authors have observed elsewhere that advocates should expect to compromise on the substance of their proposals at every step in the legislative process.[22] Indeed, there is probably nothing more axiomatic in the legislative process than the notion that successful action requires an accommodation to diverse and sometimes conflicting interests.

The amendatory process in legislatures is one of the vehicles through which these accommodations are expressed. In standing committees, on the floor, in conference committees, and in negotiations with the governor, the language of the bill may be changed to neutralize opposition or gain support for the bill. To the extent that advocates are parties to these decisions, they have to decide whether the cumulative impact of the changes is a worthwhile price to pay for passage.

Data for the authors' study of social and health services bills in the forty-fourth session of the Washington State legislature strongly support the relationship between the amendatory process and favorable outcomes. Of the 183 bills under consideration in both houses during that session, 31 were amended and 152 were not. Nearly 97 percent of the amended bills were reported out of committee, and only 47 percent of those not amended were reported out. Even more significant was the finding that 64.5 percent of the amended bills were signed by the governor and became law; a mere 5 percent of the unamended bills achieved this status. (The authors' study of social and health services bills in the forty-third session yielded similar findings.) These figures must be interpreted with caution because the probability that a bill will be modified increases as it progresses through the legislative process. Thus, the extent to which amendments to a bill contribute to or result from the legislative process cannot be determined. In any case, the findings reported here, when joined with the widely recognized importance of compromise in the legislative process, argue for the tactical value of amendments as a means for promoting desired bills.

Dilemmas to Be Faced

Thus far this article has suggested tactics that appear to increase the probability of bill passage, all other factors being equal. Unfortunately, other things, most notably the substance of bills, are seldom equal. Bills vary considerably along a number of dimensions, including, for example, the extent of social change called for, the cost, and the target groups affected. Table 2 suggests the relationship between these substantive variables and legislative outcomes.

In a conservative political and economic climate, for example, proposals that seek to substantially extend benefits or services to some undervalued group, such as recipients of Aid to Families with Dependent Children, are unlikely to receive favorable legislative consideration, the tactical skill of the advocate notwithstanding. This poses a critical dilemma for professionals who are attempting to effect significant social change through the legislative process. In the face of anticipated resistance, the advocate has two alternatives. The first, described by Howe in her recent analysis of the strategy employed by the New York City Human Resources Administration, is to reduce the scope and costs of proposals to avoid likely rejection by the state legislature.[23] A second alternative is to proceed with the measures, even though the prospects for enactment are slim, hoping that through compromise some incremental policy improvements can be achieved. There is no happy way to resolve this issue. The first strategy, based on considerations of feasibility, may increase the likelihood of success, but it often requires the advocate to defer proposals that deal with significant and pressing social problems. The second course may focus attention on the magnitude and urgency of a social problem and the real costs of adequately addressing it, but it is a course likely to result in failure. How is the advocate to decide? Several considerations seem important:

- If the advocate has the skill and resources necessary to mobilize an active constituency around a measure, it may be feasible to pursue legislation that calls for far-reaching change at considerable cost.

- In some cases the advocate may wish to proceed with a more ambitious proposal to dramatize an issue or to introduce a policy principle into legislative consideration. In this instance, the purpose is not to achieve immediate success, but to establish a basis for future advocacy.

- When the advocate is pressing several proposals, it may be wise to defer introducing ambitious measures to conserve legislative cooperation and support for measures that stand some chance of passage.

DEAR and PATTI

- When the advocate is interested in building a reputation as a political realist, it may be necessary to focus on bills that have some prospect of succeeding. This can help establish the credibility that is often an important asset in advocating for major change.

Although these considerations provide little help in resolving the problems of a conservative political and economic climate, they may help the advocate assess the costs and benefits of alternative courses of action.

Table 2. Relationship between the Content of a Bill and Its Chance of Passage

Low Probability of Passage	High Probability of Passage
High fiscal impact: Implementation would require large appropriations of money.	*Low fiscal impact:* Implementation involves little or no cost.
Major social change: Implementation would affect many people, programs, and agencies.	*Minor or no social change:* Implementation may involve merely a regulatory or housekeeping matter.
Unpopular content: The bill deals with a subject or group unpopular with the public.	*Popular content:* The subject of the bill or the group it affects is well thought of by the public.

In summary, empirical research indicates seven tactics of legislative advocacy that are associated with favorable outcomes for human service legislation: (1) prefiling or introducing a bill early in the legislative session, (2) obtaining multiple sponsorship for the measure, (3) arranging for sponsors who are members of the majority party, preferably the Democratic party, and, if possible, obtaining bipartisan sponsorship, (4) seeking the support of the state agencies that would administer the proposed legislation, (5) seeking sponsorship by influential legislators, such as committee chairpersons, provided they are willing to exercise their power in promoting the bill, (6) pressing for open hearings on the bill, and (7) using the amendatory process to acquire support and neutralize opposition.

These tactics by no means account for all the variance in legislative outcomes. However, used singly or, preferably, in combination, these tactics appear to increase significantly the probability of favorable legislative action on social welfare legislation. Unfortunately, in a climate of political and fiscal conservatism, bills that propose extensive and costly social programs for disadvantaged and often undervalued groups are likely to be rejected by legislators regardless of the tactical skill of the advocate. This reality poses a critical dilemma for the professional seeking significant social change through the legislative process. Recognizing this dilemma and resolving it, however imperfect the solution, may be the advocate's most difficult challenge.

A number of tactics frequently proposed as a means of promoting desired legislation have not been considered in this article because there is insufficient research that links their use to legislative outcomes. The hope is that research can be extended to examine the effectiveness of other tactics, such as campaign support for legislators, the introduction of a bill in successive legislative sessions, the use of constituency pressure, and various forms of interpersonal influence. As research on tactics used in advocacy is extended, it will be important to know what combinations of tactics have the greatest impact. The investigation of these and related questions will help establish an empirically based model of legislative advocacy in social welfare.

Notes and References

1. Of the nearly 200,000 bills introduced into the fifty state legislatures during the 1975 and 1976 legislative sessions, only 42,445 were passed into law, a scant 21.4 percent of all bills filed. *See The Book of the States, 1978-79,* Vol. 22 (Lexington, Ky.: Council of State Governments, 1978-79), pp. 36-38.

2. *See,* for example, Maryann Mahaffey, "Lobbying and Social Work," *Social Work,* 17 (January 1972), pp. 3-11; and Peter Rossi, "Power and Politics: A Road to Social Reform," *Social Service Review,* 25 (December 1961), pp. 359-369. [For a revised version of Mahaffey's article, *see* p. 69 of this book.]

3. *See,* for example, Rino J. Patti and Ronald B. Dear, "Legislative Advocacy: One Path to Social Change," *Social Work,* 20 (March 1975), pp. 108-114.

4. Malcolm E. Jewel and Samuel C. Patterson, *The Legislative Process in the United States* (New York: Random House, 1966), p. 138.

5. *The Book of the States,* pp. 36-38.

6. Personal communication from James Gunther, past executive secretary of the Legislative Council of the Washington State legislature.

7. Wayne L. Francis, "Simulation of Committee Decision-Making in a State Legislative Body," *Simulation and Games*, 1 (September 1970), p. 257.

8. *See*, for example, Richard Reeves, "Why Congress Is Weak," *Seattle Times*, October 11, 1979.

9. Thomas R. Dye, "State Legislative Politics," in Herbert Jacob and Kenneth N. Vines, eds., *Politics in the American States: A Comparative Analysis* (Boston: Little, Brown & Co., 1971), p. 165.

10. Arthur Wang and Dick Van Wagenen, "Human Service Votes in the 1979 Legislature." Unpublished manuscript, Olympia, Washington, 1979. (Mimeographed.)

11. Jack Rothman, *Planning and Organizing for Social Change: Action Principles for Social Service Research* (New York: Columbia University Press, 1974), p. 232.

12. David B. Truman, *The Governmental Process* (2d ed.; New York: Alfred A. Knopf, 1971), p. 345.

13. Francis, op. cit., pp. 243–244.

14. *See* Truman, op. cit., p. 345.

15. James Best, "Influence in the Washington House of Representatives" (mimeographed, undated), p. 17.

16. Rothman, op. cit., pp. 233–240.

17. Lester Milbrath, *Washington Lobbyists* (Chicago: Rand McNally & Co., 1963), pp. 213 and 230–231. *See also*, Truman, op. cit., pp. 376–377.

18. Truman, op. cit., pp. 272–273.

19. Rothman, op. cit., pp. 244–245. *See also* the previous discussion on the importance of state agency support in pressing for legislation.

20. Virginia W. Smith, "How Interest Groups Influence Legislation," *Social Work*, 24 (May 1979), p. 235.

21. *See*, for example, Truman, op. cit., p. 374, for a discussion of the point that people without technical knowledge are sometimes used to draw attention to the issue under consideration.

22. Patti and Dear, op. cit., p. 109.

23. Elizabeth Howe, "Legislative Outcomes in Human Services," *Social Service Review*, 54 (June 1978), pp. 173–188.

Monitoring the Bureaucracy: An Extension of Legislative Lobbying

WILLIAM G. BELL
BUDD L. BELL

8

CLIENT advocacy is a traditional role for social workers, one that is increasingly articulated through legislative lobbying. The thesis of this presentation is that this advocacy role can and should be expanded to include monitoring the human service bureaucracy charged with implementing the social legislation produced by the lobbying effort. Lobbying and monitoring can be complementary tasks, and both are integral to the legislative activities of social workers.

Although monitoring represents a new role for social workers, the rationale for social workers to enter the domain of program oversight is implicit in the characteristics of legislators, legislation, and watchdog agencies. One cannot always expect legislators to oversee the manner in which legislative programs are operationalized. They are interested in the passage of legislation rather than its implementation. Politicians prefer to espouse causes that can muster broad support. They develop legislation in a form conducive to its passage, work to obtain public support and legislative approval, and ultimately seek the appropriations necessary for program purposes. They often spend considerable energy to obtain passage of a favorite measure, but once this is accomplished, they look ahead to the next political challenge, not back at previous achievements. Aside from seeking credit at election time, legislators usually regard their task as complete when the work of the implementing agency begins.

The process of getting legislation passed is usually consensual and often requires reducing the measure to its lowest acceptable level.[1] Thus, by the time the program reaches the bureaucracy for implementation, its goals are often watered down from the original legislation, and its intended programmatic form is open to subtle or flagrant administrative deviations. Legislation is drafted in broad, often vague terms for the practical reason that any attempt to incorporate inclusive administrative directions and constraints would require a document of immense size. However, this vagueness suits the bureaucrat's interests: keeping program goals broad and general not only ensures administrative flexibility but eases the agency's drive for political survival.

Nor do government-designated watchdog agencies exert much influence on how bureaucracies interpret or carry out legislative mandates. Such agencies usually confine themselves to measuring financial and general administrative compliance with legislation; they are neither empowered nor staffed to ensure that human service systems provide the services the legislation intended.

In the absence, therefore, of effective scrutiny of social programs by either legislators or watchdog agencies, the client advocacy role, which social workers increasingly carry out through legislative lobbying, should be expanded in concept and practice to include monitoring the implementation of social legislation. Monitoring the bureaucracy, the agency of legislative implementation, is a concomitant responsibility to legislative lobbying; it adds a measure of assurance that change sought by legislation will take place.[2]

This position on the complementarity of monitoring and lobbying activities derives largely from some ten years of experience by coauthor Budd Bell. Since 1971 she has pursued these dual responsibilities as a full-time volunteer for the Florida Chapter of the National Association of Social Workers (NASW), which sanctioned her activities. Out of this reservoir of experience in lobbying the legislature and scrutinizing the state's human service bureaucracy, the Florida Department of Health and Rehabilitative Services (HRS), there emerges a model for monitoring a bureaucracy.

In this article, the author who undertook the monitoring activities just described is referred to as the advocate–social worker. She had formal social work training, had administrative and consultative experience in social work, and was knowledgeable about the workings of the human service network in Florida. Because she was not employed by the human service bureaucracy, she was in a position to deal comfortably and effectively with the upper echelons of HRS without the usual constraints imposed on social workers employed by the agency.

Monitoring Defined

The approach to monitoring used by the advocate–social worker is distinctly different from either legislative oversight or internal monitoring by in-house agency staff. Legislative oversight, as described by Bragg,

> conveys a notion of constitutional responsibility of a legislature to monitor governmental operations and policies that are established and implemented by the executive branch and interpreted by the judicial branch....Vehicles of legislative oversight include auditing, budget review, program evaluation, sunset laws, zero-based budgeting, administrative rule review, legislative hearing and public reporting.[3]

In-house monitoring, which is frequently a vehicle for quality control, reviews specific services or administrative procedures in a given agency.

Monitoring as described in the case studies to follow consists of scrutinizing the actions and performances of both public and private social agencies as they implement social legislation. This scrutiny includes such activities as reviewing and attempting to influence the direction and content of bureaucratic rules, administrative or legal decisions, program guidelines, and similar matters related to the implementation of social legislation. The aim of this form of monitoring is to protect the interests of clients targeted by the legislation and to ensure that the benefits intended by the legislation are obtained by the target population.

At least four reasons can be cited in support of this form of monitoring:

- All agencies, including human service agencies, have vested interests to protect.

- Social agencies, despite the lofty language in their charters and in social legislation, are not necessarily benign with respect to protecting clients' rights.

- There can be legitimate differences in interpreting legislative intent in legislation. Bureaucratic interpretations often emerge in the form of administrative regulations and it may be necessary to enter an early challenge to these regulations before they harden into policy with the same effect as law.

- State and federal budgetary oversight agencies have the power of veto over the administrative decisions state agencies make in the course of implementing social legislation. This power is sometimes exercised to the detriment of groups of clients intended to benefit from the legislation. In such cases, budgetary agencies need to be challenged on their interpretation of legislative intent.

Social workers, therefore, should look closely at program implementation and ask whether the mandate incorporated in recently enacted legislation has been translated into appropriate service provisions. Are the newly appropriated funds being spent to achieve the program intended for clients? Are federal resources directed to the state for programs meeting the legislative intent? Equally important, are clients' rights and entitlements being respected in program implementation?

Climate for Advocacy in Florida

Client advocacy is an adversary process, but in Florida, since 1975, legislative approval for outside advocates to operate within HRS has tempered the hostility agencies usually show toward advocates. Client advocacy was incorporated as a formal part of HRS through legislative changes in the HRS Reorganization Act of 1975. Testimony before legislative committee hearings on HRS's reorganization claimed that the location of the administrative headquarters of the state's human service agency in the extreme northern portion of the state made the agency inaccessible and thereby unresponsive to clients' needs. "Bring client services closer to the people" became a slogan attractive to state legislators pressing for reorganization. Subsequently, HRS was decentralized into eleven administrative and service delivery districts distributed geographically throughout the state. Each district was placed under the control of a district administrator with considerable discretionary power over the district's budget, program, and staff.

In keeping with this emphasis on increasing the linkage with people served by HRS, the authors, among others, asserted that establishing client advocacy committees within HRS would give further assurance that the legislature's desire for client linkage would be achieved. Legislators found merit in these arguments, and the HRS Reorganization Act of 1975 included a feature whereby district administrators were required to appoint human rights advocacy committees (HRACs) for their districts and encouraged to appoint HRACs for all major HRS facilities in their districts, such as state mental hospitals and institutions for the developmentally disabled.[4] The legislation excluded HRS staff from membership in HRACs and stipulated that members of the committees be drawn from a broad range of citizens and professionals.

These developments thus suggested that the monitoring role the advocate–social worker had been exercising since 1971 was compatible with the client advocacy provisions incorporated in the 1975 HRS reorganization. Further legitimation of this role occurred when the secretary of HRS, the agency's key administrator, recommended that the advocate–social worker head the HRAC for the largest state hospital in the HRS system.

In the period since 1975, the concept of outside advocacy for HRS clients has taken root in Florida. All district administrators have appointed HRACs for their respective districts, and HRACs were appointed for all six state institutions serving the developmentally disabled. In 1979, the secretary of HRS stated "his commitment to client advocacy and to human rights advocacy committees in helping maintain the quality of services to HRS clients and for future improvement of HRS services."[5] Subsequent HRS secretaries have implicitly or explicitly affirmed this position, although in 1981 only three of the four state hospitals for the mentally ill were served by an HRAC.

It should also be noted that the reception accorded the monitoring activities of the advocate–social worker underwent a change after the 1975 HRS reorganization. Resistance to her monitoring activities diminished as it became apparent that she reflected client needs with some accuracy. Her expertise was particularly valuable in the resolution of problems encountered during the early stages of the reorganization, when executive staff were sensitive to the legislature's directives with respect to client advocacy and sought advice and counsel on the subject from several outside sources.

Acceptance of the contribution of the advocate–social worker did not, however, result primarily from the legislature's directives but from the following tangible indications of her competence to serve HRS in the role of client advocate:

- A capacity to avoid simplistic proposals for complex problems related to the delivery of human services.
- An ability to negotiate solutions rather than to threaten reprisals.
- The provision of help for the HRS administrators in anticipating and identifying potential crises so that they could avoid a reactive posture on policy issues.
- The suggestion of useful criteria whereby program standards and client equity could be measured.
- The introduction of research findings to support proposed solutions.
- The presentation of alternatives in the formulation of administrative regulations and program implementation.

The relationship between the advocate–social worker and HRS administrators could be described as one of mutual respect at a distance, a form of professional interaction that is not uncommon but that remains untreated in the literature. The advocate–social worker was not privy to intimate decisions made within the organization, but she was invited to contribute to major policy questions in regard to which her background, role, and experience appeared useful to HRS. On occasion she more aggressively stepped forward to involve herself in the review of HRS policy issues when she deemed these areas relevant to her monitoring and advocacy function.

Actions taken by the advocate–social worker were situation specific: she supported HRS on some issues and opposed the agency on others. For example, on occasions when the annual HRS budget was under consideration by the legislative appropriations committee, she testified in support of specific funds. In such cases, she and HRS mutually determined that her support was necessary and useful. At other times she openly opposed efforts by HRS, appearing before state legislative hearings or the appropriations committee to question or suggest modification of legislative actions desired by HRS.

Case Illustrations

The monitoring efforts by the advocate–social worker did not constitute an independent undertaking but were integrated with her lobbying efforts in behalf of the Florida Chapter of NASW. Monitoring complemented the lobbying effort, and because it continued in the period between the annual legislative sessions, it created a year-round program of client advocacy. The lobbying served as the base for the monitoring, and the results of the monitoring helped shape the direction of subsequent lobbying.

Monitoring activities dating back to 1971 generated a host of experiences that would be useful in describing the monitoring role. Four abbreviated case studies are offered here to illustrate how monitoring relates to various activities by governmental bodies—to legislative and administrative behaviors likely to be encountered in equivalent bureaucracies elsewhere. The cases to be described involved the following activities:

- Challenging an inappropriate emphasis in the state budget for services to children.
- Challenging the state's interpretation of federal administrative regulations concerning day care funding.
- Exposing a state agency's resistance to expanding community-based services for the impaired elderly.
- Monitoring the amendatory activities of the state's bureaucracy and legislature with respect to voluntary commitments to state hospitals.

CHALLENGING A BUDGETARY EMPHASIS

What began as a challenge to the direction and emphasis in the state budget concerning services to children and youths led eventually to the establishment of a new, freestanding child advocacy agency, the Florida Center for Children and Youth. Two developments precipitated action by the advocate–social worker. First, a trend in legislative cutbacks in children's services was brought into sharp focus in 1974 by the lack of state funding for the School Health Act. Second, despite an HRS policy of decriminalizing status offenders, the legislature continued to support increased institutionalization or incarceration of youthful offenders rather than alternatives in community-based services.

The strategy initially selected by the advocate–social worker was to request a friendly state legislator to sponsor a bill establishing a commission on children and youths in the executive branch of the state government, specifically the Department of Administration, which handled statewide planning. The bill did not achieve passage, but this came to be regarded as a positive outcome. After the bill had been filed, it became clear that the proposed commission would have been placed in a situation involving a conflict of interest—one element of the executive branch would have been monitoring the program activities of another part of the executive branch.

The revised strategy was to establish a freestanding advocacy agency able to speak in behalf of children and youths, but without formal association with the state apparatus. A proposal prepared by the advocate–social worker sought funds to establish an independent Center for Children and Youth under provisions of the Law Enforcement Assistance Act (LEAA). Because the $67,000 requested from LEAA called for a 10-percent local match, this required a statewide appeal to selected groups and thus provided a natural opportunity to discuss widely the limitations in the state's budget for children. Funds were sought and obtained from three state organizations: the Junior League, an organization committed nationally to a program of child advocacy; the state's chapter of the National Council of Jewish Women, because the national counterpart had recently completed a study on juvenile justice; and the Florida Association of Youth Services, an organization of professionals and citizens concerned with improving services for young people. The outreach to these state organizations laid the groundwork for their subsequent affiliation with the new center.

Obtaining the LEAA grant made possible the employment of two full-time professionals and a secretary, who worked under a state board of forty citizens.[6] The center's board was made up of representatives of state and local organizations, professionals not in HRS, state legislators, volunteers associated with child agencies, and youths.

An immediate goal of the board was to help redirect the state's budget for child and youth programs, primarily those programs under the aegis of HRS. Because the state's budgeting process for social services is complex and often arcane, this goal required extensive training of center volunteers and staff. The training attempted to facilitate an understanding of the budgetary process and to identify the most promising points of influence accessible to volunteers.

It is not possible here to do more than summarize the training undertaken by the lay and professional leadership associated with the Florida center. They were taught to trace the flow of the budget process, starting with basic discussions at district HRS levels, continuing with analysis by the state's HRS budget staff, and culminating with further analysis and review by the Department of Administration, which advises the governor and his budget staff prior to submission of the governor's budget to the state legislature. In the legislature, the budget is considered in substantive and procedural committees in both chambers, in negotiations and hearings, and, eventually, in floor debate in both houses. Volunteers were told where to obtain the budget document and taught how to interpret its various subsections. Essentially, they were taught that they are entitled to ask questions of bureaucrats and legislators and probe for the human service priorities in each version of the budget. They also learned how to form coalitions for legislative impact, how to testify before committees, how to marshal facts, and how to lobby legislators. Citizens thus acquired knowledge of where and how to intervene in the budgetary process to influence its final form.

This extensive training of volunteers had long-range as well as short-range benefits. For example, in 1978 the Florida legislature appropriated $9 million for the state's Department of Education to develop educational alternatives for disruptive youths in the school system. The center-initiated bill, drafted with the help of two friendly legislators, one in the senate and the other in the house, was instrumental in helping to keep disruptive youths in the schools rather then expelling them and having them slide into the juvenile justice system. This aspect of client advocacy illustrates Edelman's suggestion that "to develop a children's lobby we have to interlock with all those constituencies who are concerned first about the survival needs of children, and then their rights."[7]

INTERPRETING FEDERAL REGULATIONS

The 1974 amendments to Title XX of the Social Security Act established funding for public child day care services, using a formula that matched national, state, and local funds. The intent of the federal child care provisions was to reduce the dependence of low-income families by enabling parents, especially single parents, to enter or reenter the labor force. Each state was permitted to devise its own plan and funding approach to implement the day care program. Florida did not produce a state plan but adopted the policy of leaving it to local providers to petition the state for participation in the program for children funded by Title XX.

The year 1974 also saw the culmination of a four-year effort by the Legislative Office of the Florida Chapter of NASW to secure the passage of the Day Care Licensing Act. The measure was achieved with the assistance of a coalition of social service agencies, related organizations, and parent groups concerned with the quality of child care services in Florida.

Responsibility for setting the fees to be paid by parents using day care services funded under Title XX was assumed by the director of the Budget Division of Florida's Department of Administration. He persuaded the governor to mandate a weekly fee of thirty dollars per child, a fee the Florida Chapter of NASW considered excessive in light of the existing fee of twelve dollars a week per child. Not only was the thirty-dollar fee beyond the reach of most low-income parents, it was counter to the federal intent to provide a service that would help reduce financial dependence on the part of low-income families. The Florida Chapter of NASW marshaled data in support of the weekly fee of twelve dollars but was unable to persuade the governor to alter his decision even though the HRS secretary endorsed NASW'S position.

A broad coalition of parents, service providers, NASW members, and representatives from such groups as Church Women United, the National Organization for Women, Catholic Charities, and the Junior League was assembled by the advocate–social worker to articulate opposition to the proposed thirty-dollar fee. Responsibility for organizing the local response at each of the hearing sites was assigned to five social work students from Florida State University who had been placed with the NASW legislative lobby for field experience. Using the Wide Area Telephone Service (WATS) line in NASW's Legislative Office, students helped organize statewide networks of opposition to the fee policy. They developed position papers for use by members of the coalition, staffed organizational meetings, and used role-playing techniques to train individuals to testify.

The intense public response and the quality of the testimony offered at the thirteen state hearings had their effect. When the hearing tapes urging a return to the twelve-dollar weekly fee were played for the governor by the HRS secretary, the response was dramatic. The governor rejected the advice of his budget director and yielded to the secretary's recommendation to adopt the lower and more reasonable fee.

Out of this positive achievement emerged a quasi-permanent organization of service providers to monitor state plans on day care. In 1979, the coalition mapped a preventive strategy to influence changes in day care regulations. After holding meetings of their own, coalition representatives met with the governor, with local legislative delegations, and with the appropriate legislative committee heads. From this experience came the realization by Title XX service providers that it is vital to influence proposed state regulations before they are cast and hardened into administrative stone.

EXPOSING BUREAUCRATIC RESISTANCE

Florida's painfully slow progress toward developing alternatives in long-term care for elderly people who are functionally impaired may partly be attributed to early resistance to innovative change on the part of a key social worker in HRS. Although Florida's lack of progress in this area was not atypical, given the federal bias toward the institutional solution and the absence of comparable comprehensive community-based programs for elderly people requiring long-term care, there was one essential difference in Florida. In 1973, the Florida legislature passed the Community Care for the Elderly Development Act but failed to attach an appropriation to it. The act was based on the recommendations of a 1971 policy study commissioned by the planning arm of HRS.[8] The legislation proposed a time-limited demonstration to test the impact of a community-based service in diminishing inappropriate or premature institutionalization of elderly Medicaid patients.

Implementation of the act was the responsibility of the director of HRS's Division on Aging, a social worker with many years of service in the bureaucracy. She argued that in failing to attach an appropriation, the legislature absolved the division from responsibility to implement the act. The advocate–social worker argued that outside funds could be sought, and she pressed publicly for efforts toward seeking federal funds to undertake the demonstration. In keeping the issue alive, the NASW advocate–social worker thus created considerable discomfort for the director of the Division on Aging, an NASW colleague in HRS who viewed the persistent NASW pressure as a personal attack. The advocate–social worker held that the source of resistance to change within the human service agency had to be identified regardless of the colleague's membership in NASW, a position supported by the chapter's leadership.

Lobbying to obtain a legislative appropriation in 1974 and 1975 was without success despite strong interest by several house and senate members. In 1976, a senator from Dade County assumed the leadership of the senate's Committee on Health and Rehabilitative Services and held hearings around the state on problems of the aging. The NASW Legislative Office alerted members around the state to testify and have others testify in favor of community care for older Floridians. NASW submitted a position paper to the legislative committee. In light of the growing support for community care, the committee redrafted an expanded version of the 1973 act, retitling it the Community Care for the Elderly Development Act of 1976. The new act called for demonstration programs to test four variations of community care. An appropriation of $1.3 million was approved, and seven demonstrations were mounted in 1977.

In the face of evidence that the concept of community-based care for the aging could become a workable and productive service, the new director of the program on aging in HRS recommended a $7.3 million appropriation for community care for 1978. A fiscally conservative governor cut the $7.3 million out of the state budget despite the measure's wide support. Instead, the 1978 budget contained an appropriation of $1.3 million, a repeat of the 1977 level. By 1979 it was clear that the extensive work by legislators, NASW, and other advocates for the aging had taken hold. The new governor—the former Dade County senator who had sponsored the 1976 hearings on the problems of the aging and who, in his successful campaign of 1978, had been endorsed by Florida NASW's Political Action for Candidate Election (PACE) organization—approved a biennial budget that contained funds to initiate a statewide program of community care for the aging.

The NASW lobby thus contributed to the ultimate acceptance of community care for Florida's elderly by virtue of its persistence in helping to keep the issue alive. The lobby made community care for the elderly a high priority despite opposition by a top-ranking social worker in HRS, and it allied itself with citizen and legislative forces in support of legislation that promised to improve the welfare of Florida's elderly citizens.

MONITORING AMENDATORY ACTIVITIES

The monitoring of HRS's amendatory activities is illustrated by the efforts of the advocate–social worker to neutralize HRS's attempts to undo the legislative and policy changes achieved in the state's Baker Act of 1971. The importance of monitoring the amendatory processes can best be understood in the light of a brief historical background on the law at stake, the Baker Act.

Named after its prime sponsor, Representative Maxine Baker of Miami, the 1971 act originated from a long-standing concern about a consistently high rate of involuntary admissions to the four state mental hospitals administered by HRS and about the disproportionate ratio of geriatric patients in these Florida state hospitals. In 1970 involuntary commitments to the state hospitals amounted to 90 percent of all admissions. For years Representative Baker and others had been aware of this flagrant abuse of civil rights, but earlier efforts to reform Florida's mental health legislation had been unsuccessful. Resistance to changing the pre-1971 regulations on hospital admissions was led by an HRS-organized coalition composed largely of HRS administrators, professionals in the mental health network, and circuit court judges, who had legal power to order voluntary commitments.

When invited by Representative Baker to assist in modernizing the commitment procedures specified by earlier legislation, the advocate–social worker suggested the formation of a countercoalition of individuals and organizations sharing a disenchantment with the procedures then in force. The coalition assembled by NASW included professors at law schools in the state, the Florida affiliate of the American Civil Liberties Union, mental health professionals, and like-minded others. The Baker Act was approved in 1971 over the objections of HRS administrators who argued that they were apprehensive about the emphasis on patients' rights and counseled against "haste" in changing civil commitment procedures.

The passage of the Baker Act did not end HRS's efforts to water down the act's original provisions, and by 1975 HRS had mobilized a consortium seeking to amend the 1971 act. This 1975 effort was successfully blocked in part because of a landmark ruling that year by the United States Supreme Court in the case of *Donaldson* v. *O'Connor*, which provided additional momentum for the reform movement.[9] Donaldson had been a patient at Florida State Hospital since 1956, and the Supreme Court ruled that he had been denied his rights. In the wake of this ruling, reform forces pressed for and obtained additional safeguards for the mentally ill in state hospitals, including assurance of due process and a policy mandating the choice of the least restrictive treatment alternative for mentally ill individuals.

Despite these additional reforms, efforts to amend and thereby water down the Baker Act were continued by forces not always located in HRS, including legislators and mental health practitioners, some of them social workers. Although the number of involuntary commitments to state hospitals dropped dramatically shortly after initial passage of the act, a gradual and sometimes subtle erosion of the act's enforcement since the enactment of 1971 has resulted in a gradual but steady climb in the number of involuntary commitments.

The case of the Baker Act brought Florida NASW to the recognition that some issues never attain legislative closure. The task of monitoring the agency administering the commitment procedures for Florida's mental hospitals remains a perennial issue; it reappears at each legislative session and hence remains a constant focus of the NASW lobby, HRACs, and other advocacy groups in Florida. NASW, in particular, has consistently called for adoption of the statute on civil commitment proposed by the Mental Health Law Project.[10]

Monitoring as Advocacy

The ten years of monitoring the human service bureaucracy in Florida thus suggest a modest set of guidelines for improving the effectiveness of this form of client advocacy:

Know the process by which policy is implemented in state government. Be conversant with both the covert and overt actors in the legislative and implementation processes. Identify and work with those whose decisions and actions are central to the process of policy implementation. It is also important to understand the administrative and budgetary procedures and to know how the executive branch and the legislature relate to one another in policy-making, decision making, and policy implementation.

Develop credibility with legislators and legislative staff. Client advocates from the ranks of the profession cannot be viewed by legislators and their staffs solely as adversaries; at some point in the relationship, advocates have to be seen as allies. Social workers can offer their particular expertise to illuminate nuances of a bill that may not be easily discernible to legislators. As others have indicated, legislators have assumed an awesome task in attempting to be knowledgeable on a broad range of major social issues. The professional's offer of help is often welcome; it may eventually be solicited by legislative staff, providing the professional establishes a claim to competence and is able to deliver on that claim.

Neutralize the potential resistance and hostility of bureaucrats. Although monitoring involves actions likely to generate controversy, not all controversy is antithetical to positive change. Controversy is not incompatible with effectiveness. Until actions prove otherwise, client advocates should assume that bureaucrats share their goal of effective program implementation. In Florida, not all state human service staff were threatened by the advocate-social worker. Many HRS staff, especially the client support staff, some of whom had done fieldwork under the advocate–social worker, reached out to work creatively with her. The path to diminishing potential resistance and hostility on the part of state officials and workers is through demonstrated competence and through candor in relationships.

Organize and develop linkages with citizen groups. Client advocacy is not the exclusive province of professionals. In addition to filling the traditional role of service volunteer, citizens can become lay advocates and agents of social change.[11] They can be trained to understand and work with complex issues in service provision, in state legislation, and in policy implementation. As Sparer, Thorkelson, and Weiss suggest, there is more work for lay advocates than can be done by social workers, staff attorneys, and other professionals concerned with the performance of service agencies: "There is not only a valid role but a definite need for a new type of local citizens' organization, a center for lay advocacy."[12] In Florida, once the process of state budgeting had been demystified, citizens were effective in achieving a redistribution of state resources in human services. Both as clients of HRS and as advocates for clients of HRS, they gave testimony to legislators, they lobbied, and they participated in monitoring and measuring program objectives. It was apparent that citizen groups had greater influence on decision makers than some professionals could achieve.

Coalitions and Class Advocacy

A persistent theme in this article has been the use of coalitions as an effective strategy in client advocacy. The formation of a coalition is a technique for marshaling fragments of power to achieve political success beyond the reach of groups acting independently. Because coalitions are temporary alliances organized around common, interim goals, they are not meant to be long lasting. As the case studies indicate, the Florida NASW volunteer lobbyist made extensive use of coalitions to achieve political objectives. Coalitions brought together groups representing HRS clients, advocates for HRS clients from lay and professional ranks, legislators, lobbyists associated with other organizations, and service providers. The specific mix of a coalition depended on several factors, such as the nature of the issue, the stake each member of the coalition had in the issue, the readiness of the group to compromise individual goals to achieve the central objective, and the skill of the leadership in bringing the coalition together and holding it together.

Participation in coalitions and the other forms of political behavior required by advocacy creates certain dilemmas for social work professionals, as Brager attests.[13] Although social work has a strong tradition of providing articulate representatives for the dependent, the disadvantaged, and the deprived, the profession also espouses norms of objectivity and neutrality. Moreover, for some social workers, the difficulty in assuming the client advocacy role suggested by this article arises from their professional training, which tends to emphasize case advocacy in behalf of clients seeking help with psychological and emotional difficulties. Social workers are less comfortable with class advocacy, which requires them to serve as intermediaries for clients who may not seek them out directly but who nevertheless need assistance to cope with adverse social conditions shared by a broad category of people. Perhaps the discomfort experienced by social workers in acting as class advocates is attributable to the requirement that they function, in Brager's phrase, as "political tacticians," with all the demands and consequences that the phrase implies.[14]

The field training currently provided for students in some schools of social work helps them to become reasonably sophisticated in dealing with the political aspects of social welfare. This trend and the heightened interest of the profession in such organizations as PACE give some promise that social workers will, in time, become more attuned to functioning as class advocates. As governments intervene to improve the social conditions of people, they often generate imperfect bureaucracies to carry out the mandates of social legislation. Do social workers have any alternative but to assume some responsibility for monitoring the behavior of bureaucracies of which social work is a part?

Notes and References

1. For a detailed analysis of political limitations on policy intervention, policy adoption, and policy implementation, *see* Robert Binstock and Martin Levin, "The Political Dilemmas of Intervention Policies," in Binstock and Ethel Shanas, eds., *Handbook of the Aging and the Social Sciences* (New York: Van Nostrand Reinhold Co., 1976), pp. 511–526.

2. *See* Budd Bell and William G. Bell, "Lobbying as Advocacy," in Bernard Ross and S. K. Khinduka, eds., *Social Work in Practice* (Washington, D.C.: National Association of Social Workers, 1976), pp. 154–167.

3. Kenneth N. Bragg, paper presented at the National Conference of the American Society for Public Administration, Phoenix, Arizona, April 1978. (Title unavailable.)

4. The powers of the HRACs include "serving as third party mechanisms for protecting the constitutional and human rights of any client in a program or facility operated, funded, or regulated by the department" [Florida Statutes, 20.19 (7) (g) (1), 1979, p. 110]. HRACs have considerable freedom to act independently. In 1981, for example, the HRAC at Florida State Hospital sued HRS, albeit unsuccessfully, to reverse the agency's plan to construct a $17 million forensic center for mental health patients convicted of crimes.

5. Statewide Human Rights Advocacy Committee, Florida Department of Health and Rehabilitative Services, "Summary of Proceedings," Tallahassee, Fla., January 11, 1979.

6. Five years after its inception, the center had grown to employ a staff of twenty, operating on an annual budget of some $600,000 from multiple project grants.

7. Marian Wright Edelman, *Developing a National Agenda for Children* (Washington, D.C.: Children's Defense Fund, 1979).

8. William G. Bell, "Community Care for the Elderly: An Alternative to Institutionalization," *Gerontologist*, 13 (Autumn 1973), pp. 349-354.

9. For an excellent review of Donaldson v. O'Connor by a mental health professional active in the pro-Baker Act coalition, *see* Kent Miller, *Managing Madness: The Case Against Civil Commitment* (New York: Free Press, 1976), pp. 19-22.

10. Mental Health Law Project, "Suggested Statute on Civil Commitment," *Mental Disability Law Reporter,* 2 (July–August 1977), pp. 77-159.

11. *See* Benjamin B. McIntyre, *Skills for Impact: Voluntary Action in Criminal Justice* (Athens, Ga.: Institute of Government, University of Georgia, 1977).

12. Edward V. Sparer, Howard Thorkelson, and Jonathan Weiss, "The Lay Advocate," *University of Detroit Law Journal,* 43 (1966), pp. 493-515.

13. *See* George A. Brager, "Advocacy and Political Behavior," *Social Work,* 13 (April 1968), pp. 5-15.

14. Ibid., p. 6.

Organizing Social Action Coalitions: WIC Comes to Wyoming

WILLIAM H. WHITAKER

9

ONE blustery winter day early in 1980, the governor of Wyoming signed a bill authorizing the establishment of the Supplemental Food Program for Women, Infants, and Children (WIC). Bringing WIC to the one state in the nation without it required twenty-two months of work by members of the Wyoming Coalition for WIC in collaboration with an outside organization, the Children's Foundation of Washington, D.C.

The Wyoming WIC campaign offers a model of successful coalition building with implications for achieving social welfare objectives in the face of concerted conservative opposition. This article first describes the political context and the sequence of events in the Wyoming campaign. Next, using a multidimensional model for analyzing change efforts, it examines the structure and strategies of the Wyoming coalition, identifying principles of coalition building and management that have general application elsewhere. Because Wyoming is predominantly a rural state, this account is of special interest to social workers in rural settings. Wyoming's character, however, is by no means uniquely rural, and most of the lessons of the WIC campaign are generalizable to urban situations as well.[1]

Wyoming is sparsely populated but, like many of the rural Sunbelt states, is rapidly growing. With an area of 97,914 square miles and an estimated 1979 population of only 468,678, it has a population density of only 4.8 people per square mile. From 1970 to 1979, however, the state's population increased by 49.6 percent.

Wyoming is a wealthy state. Median family income in 1978 was nearly twenty thousand dollars a year. Nevertheless, many Wyoming citizens lacked the means to pay for nutritionally adequate diets, and the state's nutrition-related neonatal death rate was eleventh worst of all the states in the nation.

Wyoming is a conservative state. Republicans outnumber Democrats nearly two to one in the Wyoming legislature, and Wyoming Democrats frequently are likened to moderate Republicans elsewhere.

In common with other sparsely populated states, Wyoming has a proudly nonprofessional "citizen legislature." Legislative sessions are constitutionally limited to a twenty-day budget session one year and a forty-day general session the next.

Most Wyoming Republicans and many Democrats view federal money with considerable distrust. Federal funding for social service programs for the poor is especially suspect. Legislators frequently worry that federal funds will dry up, leaving the state to pick up the tab. When it comes to social welfare spending, the Democratic governor and the Republican-dominated legislature often seem to agree that while "small is beautiful," none is even better.

Between 1971 and 1975, nearly 9 percent (2,805) of all live births in the state were low–birth weight babies. With low birth weight linked to an increased likelihood of brain damage, mental retardation, respiratory disorders and other diseases, stunted growth, and infant death, Wyoming faced a tragic and expensive public health problem. Premature babies must be kept in costly intensive hospital care until they gain enough weight to be taken home—at a cost figured at approximately six thousand dollars for every pound of weight gained. The cost of later remedial medical and social services is additional.

WIC, a federally funded food and nutrition education program begun in 1972, provides supplemental foods rich in iron and protein to infants, children under 5 years old, and pregnant and nursing mothers in low-income families. No state funds are required for its operation.

Research evaluating WIC programs in other states shows that participation in the WIC program reduces the incidence of premature births and iron deficiency anemia. One study indicates that every dollar spent for WIC saves four dollars in medical costs.[2] Yet Wyoming chose not to make WIC available to the eight thousand women and children in the state estimated eligible for the program.

Coalition Formation

In the summer of 1978, the Children's Foundation, a nutrition advocacy organization based in Washington, D.C., targeted Wyoming for action because it was the only state without WIC. From their extensive network of contacts with national organizations and individuals concerned about hunger-related issues (including, for example, an aide to a former Democratic senator from Wyoming), the Children's Foundation staff compiled a list of potentially sympathetic contacts in Wyoming. Letters were sent and follow-up phone calls made to religious, health, community action, university, nutrition, and social welfare organizations to search out people who might work to bring WIC to Wyoming. Both public and private organizations were approached. In most instances, these contacts were not blind but were made through links in existing networks. As good connections were established, the Wyomingites were asked, in a kind of pyramid operation, to suggest other potential supporters.

Quite early, connection was made with the executive secretary of the Wyoming Church Coalition, a retired minister who previously was the hunger action coordinator for the Board of World Ministries of the United Church of Christ. He drafted a resolution urging the establishment of a Wyoming WIC program as soon as possible. The resolution was passed by the Wyoming Hunger Task Force and Church Women United, two organizations related to the church coalition, and copies were sent to Governor Ed Herschler and Chief Medical Officer Laurence Cohen.

Shortly thereafter, two Children's Foundation staff members flew to Wyoming to visit their contacts, expand the network of interested individuals, and urge as many people as possible to attend a workshop planned to be held, with the help of the church coalition, during the annual conference of the Wyoming Human

Services Confederation in Laramie. The confederation includes many of the social and human service workers of the state. Its annual meeting is an opportunity for professional continuing education, networking, support, and informal socializing among human service people throughout Wyoming. The confederation once included an active social action committee, but that committee was moribund in 1978.

Children's Foundation staff made personal contact with more than thirty-six people during their initial groundwork. Twenty people, including several drop-ins, attended the confederation workshop on WIC coalition building.

After a slide show describing the WIC program, a discussion of the need for WIC in Wyoming, and consideration of what a coalition might do to foster WIC, several of those present decided to organize as the Wyoming Coalition for WIC. They decided to seek endorsements from as wide a range of Wyoming organizations as possible, to focus on the governor and his chief medical officer as the principal critical and facilitating actors, to find out how other states in the region were implementing WIC, and to reconvene in the state capital several weeks later.[3]

Half the people present at the workshop agreed to participate actively in the campaign. Three of them—a Catholic nun social worker, an unemployed member of the Laramie School Board, and a University of Wyoming professor of social work (the author of this article)—and the executive secretary of the Wyoming Church Coalition were to play major roles in the campaign. Several others who had expressed initial interest dropped out in the early stages of the effort. However, at least half the people initially contacted by the Children's Foundation became involved to varying degrees. One key Republican contact who did not become a WIC advocate refrained, apparently as a result of the Children's Foundation contacts, from joining the opposition that was to emerge.

Before the confederation conference adjourned, WIC coalition members won endorsement of their resolution by the Wyoming Chapter of the National Association of Social Workers (NASW) and the membership of the Wyoming Human Services Confederation. A few days later the NASW president secured WIC endorsement from the Wyoming Commission for Women, of which she was a member. Throughout the campaign, the network of endorsing groups was expanded as WIC advocates sought official approval from additional organizations to which they belonged or in which they knew leaders who could be convinced to lend their support.

As new groups endorsed the coalition's objective, they became informal members of the coalition and were invited to send representatives to planning and strategy sessions. A few became active strategists. Others encouraged their members to sign petitions, write letters, and contact legislators when requested to do so by coalition partisans. Still other endorsing groups did little more than permit the use of their names.

In preparation for the first postworkshop WIC strategy session, the nun social worker, the social work professor, and the church coalition executive met and decided to propose themselves to the group as a steering committee for the coalition. If the nascent group agreed, formal responsibility would be divided with the nun as treasurer, the church executive as secretary, and the professor as chair. Although they desired to minimize formal structure, they believed that at least this much organization was necessary to carry out the work of the coalition. Because they were prepared for the planning meeting with a reasonable and tangible proposal and because no one else had prepared an alternative plan, their recommendations were adopted and their positions in the coalition formalized.

In its next meeting, the coalition also adopted an initial strategy for action. With the legislature out of session, the governor had the authority to establish new federally funded programs subject only to ratification by the next legislature. All that was necessary, coalition members believed somewhat naively, was to get the governor to approve. They knew that he would turn for advice to the state's chief medical officer, a pediatrician with long involvement in Wyoming medicine. Dr. Cohen was known as a fiscal conservative and was reputed to reject the use of federal dollars for what he saw as welfare programs. However, his reputation as a pediatrician was excellent. Armed with the knowledge that WIC had been endorsed by the National Academy of Pediatrics, the steering committee made an appointment with Dr. Cohen, hoping to gain his support as well as access to the governor.

To their dismay, they soon learned that Dr. Cohen believed that WIC was primarily a way to enrich grocers and the dairy and cereal industry. His professional opinion was that malnutrition was not a problem in Wyoming and that milk products should be avoided in the diet after the age of 6 months because they were, in his view, major contributors to heart disease in adults. The doctor stated that although he believed coalition members could probably garner enough support to force WIC on Wyoming, he hoped they would desist. His department, he said, was already overworked. If WIC were added, what program would the coalition propose dropping?

Having failed to win the backing of a key facilitating actor, yet unwilling to concede that the governor could not be won over to their point of view, the coalition's leaders continued a strategy of rationality seasoned with increasing citizen pressure. The steering committee prepared a report to the governor documenting the efficacy of WIC, proposing how the program might operate, and, using statistics from Dr. Cohen's own division, supporting the need for the program in Wyoming.

By six weeks after the coalition's founding workshop, the governor had received pro-WIC resolutions from seven major church, social welfare, and women's organizations. He did not respond. Hoping to use the demonstrated interest in WIC as a trump in the bitterly contested gubernatorial election then nearing completion, two steering committee members, aided by a longtime activist Democratic precinct captain, buttonholed the governor at a campaign picnic and questioned him about WIC. He acknowledged receiving the resolutions, claimed familiarity with the program, but refused to state his position. He promised, however, to meet with a coalition delegation, if he were contacted after the election.

Coalition members also lobbied the Republican candidate, who claimed to support WIC but chose not to make it an election issue. Had he openly supported WIC, he might have alienated conservative backers essential to his campaign. The incumbent Democrat narrowly won reelection.

After considerable delay, an audience was granted the coalition by the governor. The coalition delegation consisted of the three-person steering committee, a Democratic state senator who was a member of the Commission on Women, and a nutritionist whose expertise the committee hoped would help counter the medical halo of Dr. Cohen.

The governor, supporting his medical officer, refused to authorize WIC while the legislature was not in session. The coalition would have to negotiate standard legislative channels of approval. If it succeeded, which seemed unlikely, given the Republican domination of the legislature, neither the governor nor Dr. Cohen would oppose the program.

The director of the state's Department of Health and Human Services, Dr. Cohen's *de jure* superior, was also at the meeting and agreed to meet with coalition representatives to draft a state plan, the state's application for WIC to the U.S. Department of Agriculture. The plan was to be the matter for which legislative approval was sought and would be included in the 1980 budget request for the department. (Acceptance of federal funds required legislative approval.)

Without state collaboration on the plan, the political task of the coalition would have been far more difficult. Perhaps recognizing this, the administration later tried repeatedly to dissociate itself from its plan, claiming that it was the property and responsibility solely of the coalition. Nevertheless, the coalition was able to claim at least a degree of state support, a factor which proved crucial in rallying Democrats in the eventual political showdown over WIC.

It has never been entirely clear why the director volunteered departmental participation. Perhaps he perceived the coalition as so unlikely to succeed that a totally united front by the administration against WIC was regarded as unnecessary. Perhaps an internal departmental power struggle reportedly occurring between this official and Dr. Cohen had something to do with it. Or perhaps there was a genuine difference of opinion within the administration, with the director believing in WIC. Whatever the genesis of this opportunity, coalition strategists recognized it and exploited it. Had they been less well informed about departmental politics, they might have missed their chance. When, despite the director's promise, the coalition was not invited to send representatives to participate in the departmental task force set up to study WIC, it became clear that a new degree of organization would be necessary.

Grass-Roots Work

With the governor displaced as critical actor by the Republican and Democratic legislative leadership—eventually the coalition had to target the entire membership of the legislature—it was essential to strengthen commitment to WIC among constituents in legislative districts. Grass-roots support was vital.

At their monthly planning meeting, coalition members agreed not to try further to pressure the governor to accept WIC while the legislature was out of session. Instead, they decided to follow the normal budget route, to work as closely as possible with the administration in developing an official state plan, and to expand their local efforts to get more organizational endorsements. A petition drive was launched with a goal of one thousand or more signatures of Wyoming voters, a large number in a state whose total population was under half a million.

The steering committee kept in touch with the Children's Foundation. Through foundation efforts, a grant of fifteen hundred dollars (later increased to two thousand) was provided by the Community Nutrition Institute, another link in the nutrition advocacy network in Washington, D.C. The grant funded a series of regional educational workshops to promote public awareness of WIC and build support for the forthcoming legislative campaign.

In September 1979, more than a year after the Children's Foundation made its first contacts in Wyoming, workshops were held in Cheyenne, Casper, Worland, and Green River, population centers located in the eleven counties ranked most in need of WIC. Cheyenne and Casper are the state's two largest cities, each with a population of about sixty-five thousand residents in 1979. Local legislators and their constituents were invited to each of the workshops to learn about WIC. Although few legislators attended, WIC had been publicly called to their attention, groundwork important in preparing a place for the program on the legislative agenda.

The workshops were run by Wyoming volunteers and a Children's Foundation staff member who flew into Wyoming for a week to assist. Until this time, all coalition work had been carried out by volunteers or quasi-volunteers, such as the three steering committee members who had, with the approval of their employers, worked long hours on the campaign. After a year of work and little tangible evidence of success, key volunteers were tiring and other demands were being placed on their time. No one was prepared to undertake the volume of work that the workshops would entail. The Community Nutrition Institute grant made it possible not only to pay for printing, postage, telephone, and other workshop expenses but, more important, to hire a part-time staff person to coordinate workshop logistics. Once again the campaign might have foundered without outside support.

Approximately one hundred and fifty people participated in the workshops. Many, convinced of the need for WIC, went home to circulate petitions in their neighborhoods, churches, and clubs. More than a hundred postcards were sent to Governor Herschler urging him to keep WIC in the budget. Volunteers agreed to serve as WIC contact people for specific legislators in their districts. Considerable news coverage was generated.

It was evident, however, that the major task of coordinating the legislative lobbying effort could not be carried out solely by existing volunteers. No single volunteer or group of volunteers had the necessary expertise, commitment, and time. Once again the Children's Foundation came through, this time with fifteen hundred dollars from the Ms. Foundation for Women, which made it possible to hire a part-time campaign coordinator for the five months through the end of the legislative session.

Knowing that the governor was readying his recommendations on specific budget items, the coalition attempted to meet with him to present its petitions. Members hoped to make the presentation a media event that would increase pro-WIC pressure. When the governor refused to attend a meeting, copies of the 1,029 signatures were sent to him, and the originals retained for future use. A widely carried news release reported that the petitions and a list of thirty-four organizations supporting WIC had been forwarded to the governor. Although supporters now included every major social welfare, nutrition, and nursing organization in the state, the governor recommended rejection of WIC.

The coalition's attention turned to the Joint Appropriations Committee of the Wyoming legislature. From across the state and from the Washington offices of the Children's Foundation, dozens of contacts were made in search of every possible source of support. A telegram from U.S. Secretary of Agriculture Bob Bergland to the Wyoming Appropriations Committee and a letter of support from Senator Warren Magnuson, chairman of the U.S. Senate Committee on Appropriations, promised that federal funding for WIC was secure and that Wyoming would not have to supplement or take over the program with state funds once it had begun.

State Senator June Boyle, a Democratic member of the Joint Appropriations Committee and a member of the WIC coalition from its inception, moved in committee to restore authorization for WIC. The coalition's chairman was permitted to speak for two minutes before the committee and presented the original petitions to its conservative Republican chairman, who pointedly ignored them. Later the governor appeared and expressed the anti-WIC views he shared with Dr. Cohen. By supplying milk and milk products to beneficiaries, Herschler asserted, WIC would only cause "heart problems for fat babies." Opposed strongly by both the governor and Dr. Cohen and supported only feebly by the director of Health and Human Services, the motion to reinstate WIC failed.

In his vocal opposition, however, the governor provided essential ammunition to the coalition. The media picked up his "fat babies" remark, and angry nutritionists, who had been for the most part only passive supporters until then, became activists. Stimulated by a professor of agriculture who had close ties to the coalition, cattlemen of this major beef-producing state, concerned lest beef become the governor's next anticholesterol target, joined the fray. Calls registering protest flooded the offices of legislators and the governor. Wyoming's major statewide newspaper, already anti-Herschler, ran a half-page editorial headlined "Have a Heart, Governor." Almost overnight, WIC became one of the hottest issues of the legislative session. On street corners, in supermarkets, and in beauty shops, people talked of WIC. Many also contacted their representatives.

With time in the forty-day legislative session running out, petitions and endorsements continued to come in from new WIC advocates. As a last major effort, the coalition organized valentine parties from which hundreds of cards flooded the legislature urging lawmakers to "give WIC to Wyoming for Valentine's Day." A valentine booth operated by social work students in the university's student union sent several hundred cards, each signed by a constituent, to legislators throughout the state. Students used radio talk shows to urge further support. At home and in the capital, buttonholing and lobbying continued.

The budget bill from which WIC had been deleted was referred to the house, where a freshman Republican representative, a grocer, introduced a WIC amendment. As representatives rose to vote from desks piled with valentines, WIC carried the vote by forty to twenty-one.

In the senate the battle was hotter. Once again the Finance Committee voted WIC down. On the floor, a Republican senator, carefully recruited by coalition members, reintroduced the WIC amendment. The amendment failed by one vote.

In Wyoming each bill is read three times before final action is taken. Gearing up for the third reading, WIC advocates in Wyoming put in two full days of hard lobbying, and Children's Foundation staff explored every possible Washington contact who potentially could influence a Wyoming vote. When WIC was introduced for the third time, it passed by a vote of sixteen to fourteen. Ten Democrats and six Republicans voted for the measure; one Democrat and thirteen Republicans voted against it.

Now the wait began. Would the governor use his line item veto power to crush WIC? The coalition could do nothing more; political insiders warned that further pressure on the governor would probably result in an angry veto. Days dragged by. Finally, on March 18, some twenty-two months after the Children's Foundation made its initial Wyoming contacts, Governor Herschler signed the bill.

Care and Feeding of Coalitions

A coalition is a "temporary alliance of two or more groups or individuals for the purpose of limited cooperative activity."[4] Over the last decade or so, an enormous amount of research has been published on coalitions. Most of it, however, relates to the social psychology of coalitional games or to governmental coalitions of political parties. Far less has been written about the commonly occurring social action coalitions, of which the Wyoming Coalition for WIC is an example. In recent social welfare literature, Cox and his associates, Grosser, Humphreys, Wachtel, and Warren have made observations about social action coalitions.[5]

Although coalitions are relatively impermanent, they persist for varying periods of time. Political coalitions may—but often do not—endure for several years. The life of coalitions in sociopsychological game theory is often measured in hours or even minutes. Social action coalitions fall between these poles. It is possible to imagine a permanent coalition, but few social action coalitions last longer than a year or two without transformation into organizations with a life of their own; they then cease to operate as genuine coalitions of independent organizations. The relatively brief duration of social action coalitions reflects their typical creation for single-issue campaigns that are won or lost in limited periods of time. Coalitions focusing on more than one issue are more difficult to organize than single-issue efforts but, when successfully organized, are likely to endure longer.

Coalitions arise when organizations or individuals are unable to achieve their objectives through independent action. Especially at their inception, coalitions have an ad hoc quality that may permit rapid mobilization for social action. They provide a degree of distancing that may permit participating organizations to use more militant strategies than they could under their own auspices. In a study of local branches of the National Urban Coalition, a business-dominated, antipoverty effort of the 1960s, Grosser unexpectedly found that the locals tended to be "more change-oriented, risk-taking and radical than other welfare-influencing bodies."[6] This may have been because the locals did not themselves operate social welfare programs. Similarly, Grosser observed that in a struggle over New York State welfare budgets, certain groups were willing to attack the state administrator or engage in mass demonstrations under the auspices of an ad hoc committee, whereas they were unable or unwilling to do so directly.

Social action coalitions may have certain dysfunctions also. For example, Warren has noted that the development of ad hoc, single-issue coalitions of social agencies and organizations may threaten the ability of planning councils to coordinate health and welfare activities.[7] Humphreys expresses similar concern about the effect of coalitional interest groups.[8]

Warren provides a six-dimensional framework for examining purposive change efforts.[9] His dimensions—change objective, target system, change-inducing system, strategies, resistance, and stabilization—provide a theoretical backdrop for the comments that follow on the Wyoming Coalition for WIC and on social action coalitions in general. The analysis begins with a discussion of the campaign's change objective and target system and then examines questions of coalition structure, use of existing networks, and motivation of participants. After considering several problems related to maintaining coalitions, the analysis concludes with a look at issues of strategy, resistance, and stabilization.

CHANGE OBJECTIVE

In any attempted purposive change, the change agent must first define the change objective and decide whether the desired change is one of behavior, relationships, ideas, or a combination of these. The primary objective of the WIC coalition was behavioral change by the governor and legislature to permit the establishment of WIC in Wyoming.

TARGET SYSTEM

The second key consideration in any change effort is the identification of the target system, those critical actors who have the authority to consent to the change proposal and the facilitating actors able to influence decisions by critical actors. At first the WIC advocates perceived the Wyoming governor as the principal critical actor and a relatively small number of his political allies and friends—notably Dr. Cohen—as key facilitators. Failing to win the governor's acquiescence, it was necessary to set a new target system: the legislature and all those who might be able to influence its members.

ORGANIZATIONAL STRUCTURES

Any change agent intending to work via coalition must consider a series of problems related to organizational structure and the internal functioning of coalitions in general. A primary task of the organizer of coalitions is to develop enough structure to achieve the desired objective but to avoid goal displacement—the deflection of the coalition from action by overemphasis on maintaining and nurturing the organization itself. Although frequently joined by unattached individuals, social action coalitions are made up of already existing groups that come together to try to achieve mutually desired objectives. Such coalitions function best when limited to one or a small number of related objectives. The maintenance of a coalition frequently requires the organization's tacit neutrality on issues that divide the members.[10] It would have been entirely inappropriate for the WIC coalition to have addressed an issue such as abortion, about which there was no possibility of organizational consensus.

In common with other forms of collective behavior, such as social movements, coalitions go through a life cycle beginning with a relatively loose structure and ending in bureaucratization or dissolution. If an effort to bring about change must persist for more than a short time, a fine line must be negotiated between goal orientation and organizational maintenance. To succeed, coa-

WHITAKER

litions must be more than will-o'-the-wisps and must have at least the appearance of strength and even permanence—must be something more than ad hoc. At the same time, their organizers must strive to avoid or at least retard the natural progression toward bureaucratization, with its focus on organizational maintenance.

The structure of the WIC steering committee reflected the need to keep records, handle funds, communicate with members, and limit the number of people officially speaking for the coalition. Other trappings of formal organization—constitution, bylaws, incorporation, and the like—were consciously avoided.

Decision making may become a point of contention in an organization lacking bylaws. In change campaigns, decisions must frequently be made rapidly and often cannot wait for monthly planning sessions. Yet if rank-and-file members feel excluded from the decision-making process, their zeal may diminish, and their willingness to act may fade. To counter this possibility, organizers must keep open the channels of participation whenever possible.

Throughout the first year of the campaign in Wyoming, much of the coalition's strategy was developed in the steering committee and ratified by the larger monthly meetings. The willingness of the steering committee to accept the responsibility to think through and propose programs filled a void and was essential to the success of the campaign. The work of the committee provided the glue that held the campaign together. Whenever possible, however, major decisions on strategy were discussed, modified if necessary, and ratified by the monthly meetings before action was initiated.

EXISTING NETWORKS

The temporary, time-limited nature of most social action coalitions makes them especially dependent on existing social networks. Engagement with existing networks is particularly important in rural areas where populations are small, the number of social welfare activists is limited, and many activists already know one another. In rural areas, links already exist even over considerable physical distance. This, of course, requires the change agent to pay careful attention to local mores and values. Offending a few key contacts can preclude cooperation by whole networks of potential allies. The same principle holds true in more populated areas, although greater numbers may provide increased latitude for error.

Existing networks are often based on relationships that have been developed in other arenas. In the WIC campaign, for example, the wife of the social work professor had voluntarily prepared media materials for the election campaign of a state representative who later played an active role in the WIC coalition. The church executive and the nun social worker had collaborated on many earlier projects. A key state senator joined the coalition because of her long-time friendship and association in the State Commission for Women with the president of the NASW chapter. The social work professor worked with both of them early in the WIC campaign in an unrelated action to prevent legislative rescission of endorsement of the Equal Rights Amendment. The importance of the change agent's putting down roots in the community and building relationships with others cannot be overstated.

In some rural areas, a change agent's being "from away" may be a significant handicap. This did not prove to be insurmountable in Wyoming. The social work professor who served as chair had been in the state only two months when the WIC coalition was formed. Both he and the staff of the Children's Foundation had to overcome the suspicions of some long-time Wyomingites, but after an initial period of testing, they were for the most part accepted. The Children's Foundation staff consciously kept as low a profile as possible but did not hesitate to act and speak as necessary.

MOTIVATION

As the attempt to forge a coalition is undertaken, the question of motivation—of "what's in it" for the participants—must be reckoned with. Humphreys has described a coalition organized around interest by social agencies in securing revenue-sharing funds to replace money lost through categorical grant-in-aid reductions. Key leadership here came from an NASW chapter, even though the chapter could not apply for this kind of funding.[11] Frequently, participants in coalitional social action seem to take part for a variety of reasons that range from genuine altruism to simple self-interest. Many are in all likelihood affected by multiple motivations. In the WIC effort, concern about the nutrition and health of Wyoming children and their mothers and interest in saving the state money, in laying the groundwork for future hunger-related campaigns, in acquiring experience about which to write and teach, in strengthening the church coalition, in embarrassing the governor, in enhancing the status of nurses and dieticians in the state health system, in selling milk products, in preserving the market for beef, in gaining the good will of university professors, in winning reelection, and—as the freshman legislator who introduced the WIC amendment in the house put it—in "doing what's right" were only some of the sources of motivation.

COMMUNICATIONS

Effective and consistent communications enable a coalition to maintain group solidarity, gain new supporters, and influence facilitating actors. In Wyoming, considerable effort was spent preparing and writing proposals for action. This both permitted sharing by mail and created a record and action guide. Careful minutes were kept of planning meetings and of sessions with the governor and his administrators. Statements of understanding were sent to officials after meeting with them to create a record reducing the likelihood of future misunderstanding about who said what and what commitments were made by the administration and the coalition. This helped avoid the danger pointed out by Grosser of ad hoc groups being open to outside manipulation because they are virtually without memories.[12] The record also made possible the writing of this analysis and perhaps will enable others to benefit from the WIC experience.

All minutes were circulated to the coalition's "key list" of everyone who had attended one or more planning meetings and to some people who were being cultivated as potential facilitating actors. Whenever possible, the coalition used the newsletters of its constituent groups to communicate with supporters and to expand the action network. At a key point in the legislative process, a special mailing was made to several hundred contacts. Monthly meetings were rotated among three key towns, and the workshops were similarly dispersed to support the efforts of local mini coalitions.

FUNDING

The resources of volunteer time and energy, organizing ability, and money that are required by all social action coalitions are to some extent interchangeable. As campaigns become prolonged, there is usually a finite limit on how much can be undertaken by unpaid volunteers. In her report on the revenue-sharing coalition, Humphreys noted that the successes achieved "were costly, particularly to the leadership group, which had to spend increasing amounts of time and energy orchestrating the coalition's activities."[13] The WIC coalition was able to offset this problem by the use of part-time, underpaid staff to coordinate its workshops and the final lobbying effort. The woman selected for the coordinating task was also a part-time lobbyist and coordinator for the Wyoming Chapter of NASW. When the Wyoming Church Coalition made WIC its top legislative priority, she was hired part time by the church coalition as well. By wearing three hats, she was able to spend over half her time on WIC, and at crucial points worked more than full time on the project.

Although some may argue that ad hoc organizations can operate with few tangible assets, money was necessary to the WIC effort in Wyoming.[14] As Grosser has aptly put it, "Fundraising on a makeshift basis is exhausting and inefficient and may produce resentment that does little to enhance spontaneity or esprit de corps."[15]

The WIC coalition received its initial funds for postage, printing, telephone, and even some transportation through the University of Wyoming Department of Social Work. By the time these funds were no longer available, the campaign was well under way. About three hundred dollars were raised from direct organizational and personal contributions, and a total of thirty-five hundred dollars came in two grants via the Children's Foundation. The Children's Foundation paid for the travel and expenses of its staff on three trips to Wyoming and must have incurred an enormous telephone bill in behalf of the WIC program.

STRATEGY SELECTION

Determination of the strategy appropriate to the coalition's change effort is another important task of the change agent. Warren's classification of situations is useful in this regard. He classifies each situation in terms of issue consensus, difference, and dissensus, and he identifies the strategies corresponding to these situations as collaboration, campaign, and contest.[16]

The strategy used should maximize the forces working for

change and minimize the effect of those arrayed against the change objective. Brager and Holloway offer many useful insights on how this may be accomplished through the application of force field analysis.[17] Participants in the revenue-sharing coalition described by Humphreys had to forgo using the argument that their private organizations were more cost-effective than public agencies. In part they wished to avoid undercutting public programs, and in part they needed to avoid mobilizing the public agencies and public agency unions as new sources of opposition.[18] Because the Wyoming governor had not learned this basic lesson well enough, he made statements that energized the nutritionists and brought the cattlemen into the conflict in aid of WIC.

One goal of any change agent is to infuse the attempt at change with a modicum of rational planning. Such is, after all, the nature of purposive change. Planning efforts, however, must make allowances for the unexpected and the irrational. In Wyoming, in planning strategy for the introduction of the WIC amendment in the house, coalition leaders carefully considered which legislators might best advance their cause. A Republican member of the house leadership agreed to undertake the task and was thoroughly informed about the WIC program and the coalition's efforts. On the night before the crucial vote, a freshman Republican, completely unaware of the plans that had been made, volunteered himself for the job and refused to consider any alternative. The legislator previously selected so carefully agreed to second the motion and yield the limelight. The newcomer performed well and the vote was favorable. But, as Peter's grandfather always said, "What if Peter had *not* caught the wolf?" What then?

COUNTERMOVES TO RESISTANCE

In the process of devising a coalition's strategy for action, the change agent must anticipate the types of resistance to be overcome. Warren, in his treatise on social change, distinguishes among habit, disruption, vested interest, ideology, psychopathology, and rational conviction.[19] The varieties of resistance may exist singly or in combination. The development of intelligence regarding the characteristics—including both strengths and weaknesses—of adversaries permits the change agent to verbalize sources of potential opposition and to advance the change effort by using opponents against themselves. Unaware of the strength of

Dr. Cohen's aversion to milk products, the WIC organizers misjudged the likelihood of his cooperation. However, even had they been certain that Dr. Cohen would oppose their efforts, it might have been necessary to make the contact with him so that they could not be charged with failing to use normative channels. Having exhausted all avenues open to them before resorting to norm-violating behavior, they were protected from the criticisms of opponents and could argue successfully in the coalition that contest strategies were required.

Intelligence may also enable a change agent to use the opposition against itself. Throughout the WIC campaign, the coalition made effective use of both public documents prepared by the state and internal memorandums leaked by state employees who, although supporters of WIC, believed their open opposition to Dr. Cohen might jeopardize their jobs. The information from these sources strengthened the needs assessment prepared by the coalition for the governor and made it possible to keep abreast of internal developments in the Department of Health and Human Services that might have harmed the coalition's effort.

In a similar manner, the two legislators active in the coalition provided essential information about the functioning and internal dynamics of the Joint Appropriations Committee and the legislature in general and contributed significantly to the formulation of the coalition's strategy. Doing one's homework thoroughly is a necessary ingredient of successful campaigns.

As campaigns heat up, "the empire strikes back." Cooptation is a common response. In the WIC campaign, the nutritionist who attended the meeting with the governor and who played a prominent role in the early stages of the change attempt was offered and accepted a job in another program directed by Dr. Cohen. Prevented from attending coalition planning sessions, she kept in touch with the steering committee and continued to provide inside information. When, during the final legislative push, she was asked by the media to respond as a nutritionist to the governor's "fat babies" remark, her superior grudgingly permitted her to reply. She spoke forthrightly in favor of WIC and stated that she felt the governor was misinformed. Shortly thereafter she was warned that her further involvement could jeopardize her husband's promotion from acting to permanent head of a major state bureau.

A less direct attempt was made to influence the WIC chair-

WHITAKER

man when the governor's office contacted the university administration to inquire whether a professor had followed appropriate university channels in forwarding the WIC petitions to the governor. The message was transmitted from president to dean to department head to professor. Although no attempt was made by the university to hinder the professor's participation in the coalition, the message had a chilling effect. Later, a state administrator alleged to the head of the Department of Social Work that a legislative supplemental appropriation in excess of one hundred thousand dollars had been denied the department because of conservative dissatisfaction with the professor's activities. Friends in the legislature, however, denied the allegation.

STABILIZATION OF GAINS

After the change objective has been attained, it is still necessary to stabilize and preserve the gain. Enactment of a law is insufficient. Enforcement and implementation are required. In Wyoming, after WIC was authorized by the legislature and the governor, Dr. Cohen, as a good administrator would, hired a competent WIC state staff and vowed that Wyoming's program would be the nation's best. In several counties, the program began smoothly, but in Natrona County, home of the most adamant Republican opponents, the medical association continued to fight against WIC. After mobilization of eligible mothers and children and a dramatic facing down of the county commissioners, the program was approved. The once-available federal funds had been allocated elsewhere, however, and as of this writing, the WIC program is still not serving Wyoming's most populous county.

With the coming of block grants and President Reagan's 25-percent reduction in funding for social programs, WIC will be cut back in Wyoming as in every state. Ironically, the election of a reactionary president and Congress has partly brought about the loss of federal funds for WIC that was feared by Wyoming conservatives, although without the requirement that the state pick up the tab.

Change and Political Conservatism

In the struggle for progressive social change, it is necessary to prepare for the long haul of years rather than weeks and months.

Many of the people initially involved in the WIC campaign were concerned about the broad question of hunger in this nation and abroad. WIC was chosen as a short-term, limited, and readily attainable objective. Nevertheless, it was brought to Wyoming only after nearly two years of struggle. The achievement of even such modest goals as WIC requires the expenditure of substantial energy, money, and time.

In Wyoming, distance was a problem. Participation centered in Laramie, Cheyenne, and Casper in spite of efforts to expand the geographic base. Telephone and written communications could not substitute for face-to-face interaction. The geographic rotation of monthly meetings was necessary but costly in time and resources. It is a three-hour drive between Laramie and Casper and over an hour between Laramie and Cheyenne when the weather is good. During at least six months of the year in Wyoming, ground blizzards and ice often more than double driving times, when roads are open at all. Travel frequently is possible only at great risk.

Although the population of Wyoming is sparse, much of it is concentrated in a relatively few population centers. There is no single dominant city; neither are there hundreds of small towns and villages. A statewide legislative campaign potentially reaching a large majority of the state's residents—and their elected representatives—needed to cover only about a dozen locations. The success or failure of efforts of the coalition to establish local groups in Laramie, Cheyenne, and Casper depended on the ability of the local leadership and the time it could commit. When convinced of the value of a program and of the possible success of efforts for change, many concerned people are willing to learn how to work for change.

In retrospect, Wyoming's rural characteristics—communication hampered by distance and weather, sparse population, sensitivity to outsiders, and conservative legislators—do not appear to have demanded coalition strategy and action qualitatively different from those required in an urban setting. The tasks faced by the change agent in both rural and urban areas are more similar than different. Overall, however, the limited population probably increases access to the political process and lightens the work required for social change.

The WIC experience in Wyoming offers hope that progressive change is possible even in the face of heavy conservative opposition. The conjunction of positive programs, political sophistication, community roots, personal commitment, and resources can result in social action coalitions with a reasonable likelihood of success. Not all battles will be won, but they must be engaged. Social workers must not yield the arena to those of the self-righteous minority without a fight.

Notes and References

1. Portions of this article appeared earlier as "Making Waves in a Sea of Peanut Butter: Implications for Social Work Practice in Sparsely Populated, Conservative Areas," in Joseph Davenport et al., eds., *Social Work in Rural Areas: Issues and Opportunities*, proceedings of the Fourth National Institute on Social Work in Rural Areas (Laramie, Wyoming: University of Wyoming Department of Social Work, 1980), pp. 194-204, and as "WIC Becomes a Household Word in Wyoming," *Children's Rights News*, 6 (Summer 1980), pp. 9-11.

2. Joseph C. Edozien et al., "Medical Evaluation of the Special Supplemental Food Program for Women, Infants and Children," *American Journal of Clinical Nutrition*, 32 (March 1979), pp. 677-692; Barbara Bode, *The Scientific Basis for WIC* (Washington, D.C.: Children's Foundation, undated); and James E. Austin and Eileen Kennedy, "Cost Effectiveness of WIC Prenatal Supplementation," Memo 6 (Cambridge, Mass.: Harvard University, November 1978) (photocopied).

3. For an elaboration of the concept of the *facilitating* actor as a person who has significant influence on a *critical* actor who has the authority to make a desired decision, *see* George Brager and Stephen Holloway, *Changing Human Service Organizations: Politics and Practice* (New York: Free Press, 1978), pp. 115-116.

4. George A. Theodorson and Achilles G. Theodorson, *A Modern Dictionary of Sociology* (New York: Thomas Y. Crowell Co., 1969), p. 54.

5. Fred M. Cox et al., eds., *Strategies of Community Organization* (3d ed.; Itasca, Ill.: F. E. Peacock Publishers, 1979); Charles F. Grosser, *New Directions in Community Organization: From Enabling to Advocacy* (New York: Praeger Publishers, 1976); Nancy A. Humphreys, "Competing for Revenue-Sharing Funds: A Coalition Approach," *Social Work*, 24 (January 1979), pp. 14-18; Dawn Day Wachtel, "Structures of Community and Strategies for Organization," *Social Work*, 13 (January 1968), pp. 85-91; and Roland L. Warren, *Social Change and Human Purpose: Toward Understanding and Action* (Chicago: Rand McNally & Co., 1977).

6. Grosser, op. cit., p. 146.

7. Roland L. Warren, "The Impact of New Designs of Community Organization," *Child Welfare*, 44 (November 1965), pp. 494-500.

8. Humphreys, op. cit., pp. 16-17.

9. Warren, *Social Change and Human Purpose*, pp. 56-57.

10. William A. Gamson, "Coalition Formation," in David Sills, ed., *International Encyclopedia of the Social Sciences*, Vol. 2 *(New York: Free Press, 1968), p. 533.*

11. Humphreys, op. cit., p. 16.

12. Grosser, op. cit., p. 133.

13. Humphreys, op. cit., p. 16.

14. Grosser, op. cit.

15. Ibid.

16. Warren, *Social Change and Human Purpose*, pp. 119–157.

17. Brager and Holloway, op. cit.

18. Humphreys, op. cit., p. 17.

19. Warren, *Social Change and Human Purpose*, pp. 49–52.

PART **III**
ELECTIVE PROCESS AND
OFFICEHOLDING

Ragtag Social Workers Take on the Good Old Boys and Elect a State Senator

WILLIAM H. WHITAKER
JAN FLORY-BAKER

10

OLDER MAN: It's about time, you know.

HOUSEWIFE: It's time we had a state senator who *cares*.

MAN: It's time we had a state senator who *listens*.

BLACK MAN: It's time we had a state senator *nobody owns*.

HOUSEWIFE: Michael Schwarzwalder is that kind of a man. He's a Democrat. And he's a *good* man.

OLDER MAN: He's running for the Ohio senate because he wants to work for lower utility bills.

BLACK MAN: He says the gas company and the electric company have been so busy trying to outsell each other that the average customer has been forgotten. And we're the ones who pay the highest rates!

HOUSEWIFE: The state senate is the place to do something about that.

MIKE: And I'm sure going to try. I'm Mike Schwarzwalder. I need your vote. I'll work hard for you.

ANNOUNCER: Paid for by the Schwarzwalder for Senate Committee, who believe in Mike Schwarzwalder. Jon Marshall and Helen Evans, Chairpeople.[1]

THIS sixty-second radio script helped kick off a media campaign that played a key role in a successful election drive to defeat an incumbent state senator and replace him with a candidate more sympathetic to social welfare issues. According to the experts, the incumbent, Donald Woodland, had everything going for him. A former wrestling coach in sports-conscious Columbus, Ohio, he was a six-year veteran of the Columbus City Council, had made many political friends during his four years in the state senate, and was an entrenched member of the "good old boys" who made many of the decisions of central Ohio politics.

As an executive with Columbia Gas of Ohio, Woodland could also count on the money and influence of the business community. In addition, his work in the senate for labor-written legislation on workmen's compensation, collective bargaining, and minimum wages had won him the staunch support of organized labor. Woodland seemed to have carved for himself the best of all possible worlds.

The challenger, Mike Schwarzwalder, appeared to have few of Woodland's advantages. A young lawyer, he had served in the Peace Corps and had chosen to work for the Legal Aid and Defender Society rather than pursue corporate law. Although his father some years earlier had been an extraordinarily popular municipal judge, Mike lacked access to extensive support in the business community.

Schwarzwalder's initial backers consisted of a small group of social welfare activists and radical attorneys, plus others who simply disliked Woodland for a variety of reasons. Their assets were dedication, creativity, a capacity for hard work, a common set of values, and a willingness to enjoy the process of a campaign.

From the beginning of the campaign until late into the evening on primary day, virtually all the smart money was on Woodland. Nevertheless, the coalition supporting Schwarzwalder—labeled "ragtag social workers" by a local magazine—carried the primary by a narrow margin and went on to win the general election in the face of vicious Republican opposition.

We, the authors of this article, are professional social workers who were members of Schwarzwalder's policymaking core group, the eighteen people who made the major decisions and ran the campaign. Jan Flory-Baker served as campaign scheduler. Bill Whitaker helped develop campaign issues.

Both of us shared with the other core group members sore feet from walking precincts, bleary eyes from twice weekly late-night strategy sessions, and newsprint-stained hands from separating and folding thousands of campaign "tabloids," the basic item of literature in the campaign, which we could not afford to have folded commercially. We also experienced the severe psychological stress that characterizes campaign conflicts. All the tension and fatigue, however, was more than compensated for by campaign camaraderie and the eventual accomplishment of the goal.

During the campaign, Whitaker was the associate director of the South Side Settlement, a seventy-seven-year-old, neighborhood-based, interracial social agency; Flory-Baker was vice-president of its board. On several previous occasions, the settlement had antagonized United Way by organizing political protests by welfare mothers and students. More than once, funding had been in jeopardy. We made every effort, therefore, to identify our participation in the Schwarzwalder campaign as that of private individuals who in no way represented the agency. Nevertheless, our involvement generated threats to the programs of the settlement.

The hope behind the writing of this article is that it will encourage our social work colleagues throughout the country to try out the electoral process and help replace opponents of social welfare with elected officials sympathetic to social work values and concerns. The article tells the story of the Schwarzwalder campaign, analyzing it as a social movement, but it may be helpful, first, to consider briefly the process by which a campaign organization emerges and develops.

According to Mauss, the structure of a social movement may be visualized as a series of three concentric circles.[2] The outermost ring consists of a sympathetic public made up of people with some degree of concern about a given problem. Although these people are not activists, they may provide support in the form of finances or votes if their sympathies are in the right direction.

The second ring consists of a much smaller number of active participants in the movement. The movement has an important but not an exclusive billing on the agenda of these individuals and organizations. From this ring are drawn the volunteers so necessary to carrying out the hard, nitty-gritty daily tasks required for success.

The movement's innermost ring is its core. The core consists of the most zealous and committed members of the movement, including ideologues prepared to sacrifice other interests to advance the movement's cause.

The success of a social movement depends on both the quality and the number of members in each of the three rings. The size of the sympathetic public is important, but it is no substitute for dedication and skill in the inner circles, especially in the core.

Warren's five-stage action system provides a useful model for analyzing the Schwarzwalder campaign as a social movement. Warren suggests that any campaign may be analyzed in terms of (1) its initial systemic environment, (2) the inception of the action system, (3) the expansion of the action system, (4) the operation of the expanded action system, and (5) the transformation of the expanded action system.[3]

Initial Systemic Environment

The initial systemic environment of a political campaign is the focus of two major questions:

- What conditions exist in the community that create a seedbed favorable for the germination and growth of a particular action campaign? Problems, felt needs, strains in the social structure, and perceived opportunities for achieving positive gain all need to be taken into account.
- What activities and relationships exist in the community that the proposed campaign can build on? Associations among people sharing common ends, values, or experiences are potential building blocks for new or renewed organization and action.[4]

A significant part of the initial systemic environment for the Schwarzwalder campaign was the inadequacy of public assistance grants, which had been a serious issue in Ohio for many years. A variety of reform campaigns addressing these needs were mounted by social welfare proponents between 1959 and 1970.[5] In 1975, a statewide lobbying effort was mounted. Four future Schwarzwalder core group members were active in this campaign. Modest reform was achieved as grants under Aid to Families with Dependent Children (AFDC) were raised by $11.25 a month per recipient. Although this was the largest single increase in the history of AFDC in Ohio, families still received only about 60 percent of the state's minimum standard of need.

During the AFDC campaign, delegations from the Franklin County Hunger Task Force Legislative Committee, which was cochaired by the present authors, met with each of the Franklin County legislators to enlist their support. One Democrat, Senator Woodland, proved especially uncooperative. After several invitations, the senator agreed to meet with a delegation of his constituents that he knew would include several mothers with small children. He set the meeting time for 5:00 P.M., a time when mothers would normally be preparing supper.

Nevertheless, a delegation of fifteen or sixteen people, all voters from his district, arrived at the appointed time. For nearly an hour the group waited. There was no word from the senator. Finally, he arrived as half the group, angered by the apparent runaround, was leaving the statehouse. One of the organizers muttered something about the need for real representation, and the seed of a future political campaign was sown. During the next year, Senator Woodland would come to know the fury of a group of women and men scorned.

During this period, another kind of structural strain was generated that contributed to the success of the Schwarzwalder campaign. Beginning late in 1972, an effort was launched to reform the Franklin County Democratic party. Substantial numbers of young, liberal Democrats who were dedicated to the grassroots politics of participatory democracy joined forces around the county party convention scheduled for April 1973. They assumed leadership in preconvention committees on party rules, platform, and structure. Many supported a shift in party structure from ward to precinct representation, arguing that increased participation in party affairs could rejuvenate the party and shift it in a liberal direction. At least five people who later became members of the Schwarzwalder core group, including Mike Schwarzwalder, were active in the convention.

At the convention, the proposed shift from ward to precinct representation was opposed by the party regulars and was narrowly defeated. A party platform containing strong liberal planks on social welfare, civilian police review, and freedom of sexual preference was passed in spite of opposition by party regulars. However, during the next few months the revised platform was never printed or distributed. The only copy was reportedly lost. The hours of meetings, statement drafting, and conventional political activity by the reformers seemed for naught. Frustration and disillusionment resulted.

Nevertheless, some minor change did come about. Several of

the dissidents were elected as ward committee members and representatives to the party's central committee in the 1974 primary election. Most of these ran against party opposition. Serving on the central committee, on the screening committee for candidate endorsement, and in other party positions, the reformers gave their best efforts, but they were further frustrated by the grip of the good old boys on the party's affairs. Two of the dissident committee members later became members of the Schwarzwalder core group, and at least one other was an active participant in the campaign.

Two other factors deserve mention in relation to the initial systemic environment out of which the Schwarzwalder campaign emerged. In 1973 Mike Schwarzwalder served as chairman of the campaign that elected the first Democratic judge in Columbus in many years. Like Schwarzwalder, the participants in this campaign were told they had no chance. But they won, learning in the process. Having upset the solidly entrenched incumbent and having tasted victory, some people were anxious to try again.

A final factor in the initial environment was public concern about the rising cost of utilities. The Arab oil embargo had accelerated the increase in utility rates. Consumers were already feeling the impact of increased prices for gasoline, heating, and lighting. An organization called Ohioans for Utility Reform was established and quickly began building strength for a petition campaign in support of several issues. Among them was a populist "lifeline" proposal setting price ceilings for a family's minimum gas and electricity requirements. The proposals received considerable attention in the media.

During the summer of 1975, as public utilities continued to press for the price increases claimed to be necessary to preserve their profit margins, they became the enemy in the eyes of more and more of the inflation-pinched public. Although most of the utility reformers were leery of the Schwarzwalder campaign and stayed out of it, they did a great deal to help create the issue that would carry Schwarzwalder to victory.

An error in political judgment by Senator Woodland and the Democratic party regulars contributed as well. Like most Ohio legislators, Woodland held a full-time job in addition to his employment as state senator. He was an area development director for Columbia Gas Company of Ohio. He also served on the senate committee that was about to rule on a reform bill on utility regulation that was strongly opposed by Columbia Gas.

Challenged in the press to disqualify himself from voting because of a potential conflict of interest, Woodland instead requested a ruling from the senate's Ethics Committee. Before the ruling came through, however, the Democratic leadership discovered that Woodland's vote was needed immediately so the committee could move this popular election-year issue to the floor of the legislature. Seemingly caught between employer and party, Woodland resigned from the committee. But the damage was done; by this time he was already identified in the public eye as a tool of the gas company.

Inception of the Action System

In the inception stage, the principal task of the change agents is to set goals and decide what parts of the community must be involved to accomplish them. Relationships between change agents and necessary allies must be contemplated and strategy developed to forge relationships where they do not yet exist.[6]

Although general concern about the issues of hunger among the poor and rising utility costs continued through 1975, the desire to oust Woodland did not become a formal goal until early 1976. Shortly before the deadline for filing candidacy, a small group of friends who had shared experiences in the AFDC campaign and the Democratic party reform activities began to discuss running a candidate to oppose Woodland.

They approached an incumbent Democratic state representative with the idea. Although he could count on strong support from the university community, he felt the primary was unwinnable from an incumbent Democrat and was unwilling to risk his house seat and incur the wrath of the party.

The group next considered running a political unknown, Jan Flory-Baker, in an intensive grass-roots campaign against Woodland. There was much interest in having a female candidate and also in running a winnable campaign. Learning that Jan's home was one block outside the senate district, the group contacted and was turned down by a number of other unknowns, including Karen Schwarzwalder, a popular organizer in the university community.

The insurgence might have ended there had not the editor of

publications of the American Federation of Labor–Congress of Industrial Organizations (AFL-CIO) in Ohio, a dedicated Woodland antagonist, been a member of the group. At his urging, the group decided to spend one more week in search of other potential candidates.

Mike Schwarzwalder, the young attorney married to Karen Schwarzwalder, was interested. His involvement with poor people through the Legal Aid and Defender Society, his participation on the boards of several social welfare agencies and in campus community groups, and his possession of a family name long-respected in Columbus politics looked good to the fledgling core group. After a long discussion about the mutual expectations of candidate and campaign group, the decision was made to enter the campaign with Mike as the candidate.

For most of the core group, the decision entailed a commitment of time and energy and a willingness to butt heads with the Democratic power structure at little personal risk. For Mike, however, the decision was more momentous. If he won the general election, all would be forgiven; the party would overlook his having challenged an incumbent. If, however, either he or Woodland lost the general election, and a Democratic seat went Republican, Schwarzwalder would be sentenced to political limbo.

The stakes were made clear when, shortly after the candidacy was rumored, Mike was visited by a team of political "heavies." Representatives of the Central Labor Body AFL-CIO, the United Auto Workers, the Columbus Education Association, and the laborers' local came to inform him bluntly that if he persisted, he would be ruined and could never run for any office. If, however, he were "reasonable" and withdrew from the senate race, they would support him for any number of races, including judge, a position that paid fifteen thousand dollars more a year. Throughout the primary campaign the Democratic and labor power structure did everything it could to bully and co-opt the candidate and members of the campaign core group.

Having selected a candidate and survived the first onslaught of the good old boys, the campaign group turned to the questions of campaign organization and strategy. How should we structure ourselves? What kind of campaign should we run? What allies should we seek? What offers of support, if any, should we reject?

A key fact distinguishing the Schwarzwalder campaign from many others was that a group of noninfluential, fairly ordinary citizens joined forces concerning several issues and searched for a candidate to carry their banners. It is more usual for a party to handpick a candidate based on a presumed ability to win, with little or no concern for issues, or for a candidate to select himself or herself and then seek support for whatever race seems winnable. The central role of values advocated by the social workers and other core group members made this campaign unusual.

It was decided early that the campaign would be a collective one. The candidate and core group members would be mutual participants in the policymaking process, rather than the candidate or his manager calling the shots while "go-fers" jumped to carry out their assignments.

With people as the campaign's primary resource, it was essential to deal sensitively and carefully with process as well as to keep an eye on the task. As much as possible, policy was decided in the core group on the basis of consensus; few formal votes were taken during the course of the campaign. Although this practice added considerably to the length of the group's twice weekly meetings, the strengthened group identification that resulted more than offset the cost in time.

A certain amount of paranoia accompanies any campaign and characterizes the core of most social movements.[7] The Schwarzwalder campaign was no exception. The core group's practice of consensus seemed to leave the door open to infiltration and sabotage by the Woodland forces. Although the group wanted, wherever possible, to make inroads into the Democratic party and organized labor, it needed to feel confident that it was not being manipulated or co-opted by these other groups. As new individuals came into the core group, trust developed through the common commitment to hard work and through the thrashing out of issues and strategy in group meetings. No one was likely to stay involved in the face of the heavy daily demands on the group unless he or she was committed to the common goal.

Policymaking through consensus, however, did not mean that the program decisions needed on a daily basis were the equal province of every core group member. Each member of the core group was asked to take responsibility for some major task. In addition, three core group members were available to make daily decisions and provide coordination and direction.

One person was the scheduler, with the responsibility of seeing that the candidate's twenty-four hours each day were used fully and with maximum exposure. Another was the coordinator of volunteers. Still another was chief fund raiser. Others coordinated neighborhood teas, voter registration drives, the placement of yard signs, advertising, press relations, and issue monitoring and development. About one-third of the core group members devoted all their time to campaign responsibilities; the others had employment and responsibilities for children as well. Everyone helped with the mundane, tiring, necessary work of the campaign's details.

The selection of campaign issues was another key task during the campaign's inception. Committed to values, the core group was determined to run an issue-oriented campaign. Win or lose, the campaign would at least contribute to the public debate of important matters.

Each member of the core group had personal priorities among the issues. For a few, improved AFDC benefits were foremost. For others, the question was one of utility rates and corporate irresponsibility. Still others were advocates of participatory grass-roots democracy.

Each concern had its strengths and also its limitations. For example, improved welfare benefits might win supporters from the social work community but lose heavily elsewhere in the candidate's predominantly blue-collar district. In many precincts, even the mention of public assistance might be enough to scuttle the campaign.

Ultimately, the group chose to emphasize Schwarzwalder's strengths and Woodland's weaknesses. The candidate did not lie or evade questions on unpopular topics, but the stress was on general values rather than on specific issues. And so it goes with virtually all political endeavors. The core group agreed that a state senator should care about poor and working-class constituents, groups too often neglected by the good old boys; that an elected representative should be accessible, willing to listen to constituents' concerns, and ready to knock on doors and meet people on their own turf, not just when it was convenient; and that a senator should not be in the pocket of any set of special interests, including the campaign's managers and biggest backers, but should be free to vote according to his or her own best judgment after being counseled by close advisers and any other interested parties.

Although the heart of the campaign was the volunteer effort, the attempt to communicate the ideas of the Schwarzwalder campaign to the electorate was critical. The campaign was fortunate to recruit to the core group several highly creative professionals. One was the group's token business executive, who had an excellent background in advertising. The materials that were developed for distribution in the precincts and for newspaper and radio ads (and, during the general election campaign, for television ads) were essential to the success of the campaign. The theme "It's about time we had a senator who cares, who listens, and nobody owns" was used throughout the campaign.

In keeping with the idea that nobody owned Schwarzwalder, the core group decided to accept no campaign contributions from registered lobbyists or from organizations whose values seemed in conflict with its own. For support, the group decided to look especially to the university community, to working-class neighborhoods, to social welfare activists, and to the network of political dissidents of which several of the group were members.

Expanding and Operating the System

Expansion of the action system, according to Warren, involves building the relationships necessary to achieve the campaign's goals.[8] Clarity about goals and strategies is essential in making choices about whom to try to involve in the campaign. The choices depend on what is needed from individuals and groups either during the operation of the action system or later. Recruits may be sought for their specific expertise, to carry out essential tasks, to provide linkages to other groups whose support will be needed sooner or later, or to build a sense of ownership in the long-term effectiveness of the campaign.

The operation of the expanded action system is the carrying out of campaign strategies.[9] During this stage, maximum numbers of people participate in campaign activities, obstacles are confronted, and the most visible activities of the campaign occur. The operation stage culminates in the apparent success or failure of the campaign.

In the Warren model, the expansion and operation of the action system are two distinct analytic stages. They call attention to two important processes that may take place concurrently in the hurly-burly of a campaign. The processes are especially likely to coincide in an election campaign, which is characterized by fixed deadlines and a short span of time.

From a modest beginning with a few friends sitting around a living room floor, the action system of the Schwarzwalder campaign grew to include substantial numbers of social activists, social welfare liberals, Woodland haters, street people, students, personal friends of the candidate and the core group, neighborhood residents, lawyers, ministers, dissident Democrats, and just plain folks who agreed with the issues and caught the enthusiasm of the campaign. Although there was some growth in the core group as the campaign progressed, most expansion took place in the middle ring of active participants and the outer ring of the sympathetic public.

Personal contact was the key to the campaign's successful recruitment of volunteers. All of us in the core group pestered our friends. Believing in what we were doing, we soon overcame our reluctance to ask others to help. Every friend and colleague who might be willing was contacted; volunteer cards listing name, address, phone, what the volunteer was willing to do, and other pertinent information were prepared. Many of us even became able to ask for money for the cause.

Every meeting, every conversation became an opportunity to enlist additional support. There was a volunteer task for everyone. If a person could not walk to precincts to pass out literature, he or she could give money. If money was a problem for someone, he or she could help with a rummage sale or by baby-sitting or by writing postcards to friends. The few ward committee members working with the group contacted their booth workers, getting commitments to help deliver literature, to hold neighborhood meetings for the candidate, and to allow the placement of signs in their yards. Name by name the list of volunteers grew until by the day of the primary, more than five hundred people had played an active role in the campaign.

A major strength of the core group was its ability to enjoy itself. Too often, those of us with a vision of how life should be tend to become inflexible, unsmiling adversaries of the system we wish to change. Obsessed with product, we neglect process. Taking ourselves too seriously, we pay little attention to organizational maintenance and our groups deteriorate. The Schwarzwalder campaign tried to avoid that danger through humor and festivity akin to that advocated by Cox:

WHITAKER and FLORY-BAKER

The celebrators of life today and the seekers of justice tomorrow need each other in the world. Celebration without politics becomes effete and empty. Politics without celebration becomes mean and small. The festive spirit knows how to toast the future, drink the wine and break the cup. They all belong together.[10]

Festivity and celebration were evident in the unorthodox and newsworthy launching of the Schwarzwalder campaign. Following a 6:00 A.M. pancake breakfast at the Schwarzwalder home, fifty volunteers descended on downtown Columbus to leaflet the crowds on their way to work. The form of the leaflet was an excellent facsimile of a bill from Columbia Gas, Senator Woodland's employer. Few of the eight thousand "gas bills" distributed were crumpled and tossed into the street, a frequent fate of such hand-outs. Most were folded and tucked away into pockets. We thus launched the campaign in a way that touched a public nerve and that was genuine fun for everyone involved. The press conference called to explain the campaign generated considerable coverage in the news media.

A few days later the campaign fired round two and again received good media coverage. Campaign headquarters opened in a storefront on the main bus line through the Bottoms, a working-class neighborhood in the senate district. Each day, hundreds of potential voters drove or rode by the headquarters and read the Schwarzwalder name. The headquarters opened with a humorous guerrilla street theater skit in which Senator Woodland and the president of Columbia Gas, in the form of huge papier maché heads, were portrayed conspiring to do further damage to utility consumers. This, too, was fun as well as serious work.

PRECINCT TARGETING

In a political campaign, all efforts point toward election day, toward the final count of votes. Precincts are targeted, attempts made to make the candidate's name a household word, personal appearances by the candidate scheduled, money raised, and election day activities planned—all toward that single end.

Targeting is an exacting and absolutely essential component of a well-run political campaign. It is a method of determining in which precincts to concentrate efforts. Good targeting identifies areas where personal contact by the candidate and other election-eering strategies are likely to have the greatest payoff in votes and sets priorities for carrying out these strategies.

Having the candidate's name widely recognized among the voters by election day is essential to electoral success. Mike was fortunate in having a distinctive surname that had been popularized with older voters during his father's service as a judge from 1954 to 1971. The Schwarzwalder name had last appeared on a ballot in 1966. That alone, however, would have been insufficient.

The campaign developed several pieces of campaign literature that were delivered by hand door to door by the volunteer corps in targeted precincts. In addition to the gas bill, the printed items included a four-page tabloid newspaper consisting of photographs and brief quotations from the candidate, and a "door hanger" with a sample ballot that could be taken into the voting booth by a voter. One hundred and twenty thousand tabloids and thirty-five thousand door hangers were distributed by volunteers during the primary campaign.

Yard signs displaying the Schwarzwalder name were silkscreened, and four hundred of them were placed in front yards in urban areas and on telephone poles and fence posts in rural parts of the district. A unique two-piece campaign button—creating name recognition by emphasizing that "Schwarzwalder" was too long for one button—was designed. Several hundred sets were produced with a one-at-a-time button-making device. The buttons were worn by volunteers as they campaigned and added to the esprit de corps.

Several radio spots keyed to the theme of "a senator who cares, who listens, and nobody owns" were written, produced, and scheduled for broadcasts on the stations most likely to be listened to by district voters. This required another kind of targeting.

During the primary campaign we had no money for television time. Small, relatively inexpensive ads were therefore placed on the much-read entertainment pages of the two metropolitan daily newspapers and in several smaller weeklies, including the city's black newspaper. A series of press releases on campaign issues generated additional publicity and name recognition at no cost beyond that for photography.

The use of the candidate himself also demanded attention. The group secured "walking lists" of registered Democrats in the targeted precincts, and during the primary, Mike personally knocked on an estimated eight thousand doors. Other door knocking was done by Karen Schwarzwalder and the core group members.

As the campaign proceeded, more and more candidate's nights and neighborhood coffees crowded into the schedule. Mike attended at least seventy-eight community meetings throughout the district, shook hands in bowling alleys and at shift changes at factory gates, and spent sixteen hours riding the city bus lines introducing himself to potential voters.

The campaign had a lucky break about a month before the election. Mike was the first politician to show concern for the plight of striking workers at an appliance factory in the district. The union local reciprocated with some volunteers for the campaign, and some rank-and-file support developed in spite of the opposition of the AFL-CIO hierarchy.

Funding is a crucial element even in a volunteer-based campaign. The rental and utilities for the storefront headquarters, the printing of literature, and the purchasing of media time were the major expenditures and made up $13,000 of the total primary expenditure of $14,800. The campaign accepted and sought funds from all sources except from registered lobbyists and from organizations whose anticonsumer philosophy seemed in conflict with the campaign's principles. Core group members "put the arm on" friends and colleagues, asked for contributions at neighborhood coffees, held special fund-raising events for which admission was charged (wine and cheese parties, a beer blast, a rock concert), and held rummage sales.

THREATS TO SUCCESS

Many threats to the success of a campaign are likely to emerge before election day. Campaigns founder as a consequence of external attack or seem to dissolve as internal problems destroy team spirit and the will to continue. The Schwarzwalder campaign had to surmount threats of both types.

Not long after the campaign began, a third candidate emerged with a platform that also attacked the utility issue. With no volunteer organization and no big money to conduct a traditional political campaign, he had no chance to win. But if he remained in the contest, he was likely to draw off enough of Schwarzwalder's support to throw the race to Woodland.

After much internal debate, we confronted the newcomer

and offered to withdraw and leave the race to him if he could show that he had a better organization and resources than we did. He refused to withdraw. He was subsequently declared ineligible by the board of elections because he had failed to establish residency for the required period of time. This was uncovered by a neat piece of detective work by the core group.

The visit to Schwarzwalder by Democratic labor "heavies" has already been described. A similar attempt was made to bully core group member Whitaker. The business manager of the laborers' local visited him and threatened to defeat him as a Democratic committee member. Getting nowhere with that tack, the union official then threatened the South Side Settlement where Whitaker was associate director. Unless Whitaker got out of the Schwarzwalder campaign, the union representative would guarantee that the million-dollar capital building campaign the settlement was conducting would fail. In a special meeting the settlement board decided to risk calling the union's bluff. The building campaign continued unaffected.

Such threats, and the general discrediting of the campaign by Democratic party regulars and so-called political experts, only strengthened the resolve of the core group. Schwarzwalder's status as an underdog seemed to have the effect of eliciting ever-increasing volunteer efforts. Righteous indignation proved to be a powerful organizing force.

Internal conflict, however, arose to create a severe threat. Ideological differences between the candidate and some core group members reached a boiling point under the pressure of the campaign.

For Mike, exposing himself to the core group and its process of consensus decision making was a new experience. Building trust among core group members and working through many kinds of conflict—ideological, strategic, and personal—was a process that both Mike and several members of the core group sometimes resented when immediate, task-oriented decisions needed to be made.

Six members of the core group were personal friends and professional colleagues of the candidate and knew him fairly well. Others, particularly those working with him on a daily basis, were only acquaintances. To trust another person to plan your day every day for eight months is not easy.

Another unusual characteristic of the campaign was that

most of the key positions were held by women. Many had experience with the political process through issue campaigns, but the electoral process was new to them. As "ragtags" and women who were sensitive to the fact that many in the community had written them off, they were anxious to prove their capabilities both within and outside the core group. Conflict was a frequent result, and this, too, had to be resolved through process.

Finally, election eve arrived. We shivered until the 3:00 A.M. shift change at factory gates, holding posters urging workers to "Vote Schwarzwalder." A bed sheet was painted with the slogan "Good Morning, Vote Schwarzwalder" and set aside to be suspended from a freeway overpass during election morning rush hour. The office was organized for the next day's activities. Almost reluctantly, we went home to get a little sleep.

On election day, activity continued until the polls closed. Volunteers were dispatched to key precincts with sample ballots to distribute from outside the legal limit of one hundred feet from the polls. With the last remaining funds, the campaign rented a city bus for use as a billboard. Transportation was readied to take supporters to the polling places.

Volunteers hit the pavements one final time to ring doorbells and get out the vote in targeted precincts. People wearing billboards were stationed at key locations throughout the district. Coffee and doughnuts were delivered to volunteers. By late afternoon, as activity dwindled, we were too tired to chew our fingernails.

Everyone straggled home for hot showers, naps, supper, and then the planned victory celebration in the local Croatian hall. Finally, late that night came the word. A total of 13,580 voters had lined up for Schwarzwalder, a 962 vote margin. We had won.

General Election Campaign

It was June, but there was no time to relax. The November general election would arrive all too soon.

For the general election, the basic strategy was to carry on with more of the same. The ranks of the volunteers continued to grow although some fell away, incorrectly believing that the big battle had been won.

Some volunteers began to emerge from the ranks of the regular Democrats and the Ohio Education Association, which during the primary had been aligned against Schwarzwalder. We debated as a core group and decided to accept an endorsement and money from the Ohio AFL-CIO.

People who previously would not give the Schwarzwalder campaign the time of day suddenly proclaimed themselves allies and began to offer advice. The core group accepted their volunteers and their money, considered what they had to say, and consciously continued to pursue its basic grass-roots strategy.

In midsummer, the Schwarzwalder campaign expanded the utility issue with a "lucky" Friday the thirteenth door-hanger leaflet against the telephone company. The candidate continued to knock on neighborhood doors. A new round of fund-raising events, neighborhood meetings, and candidate's nights got under way. A new tabloid was produced and one hundred and fifty thousand copies distributed. Just before the election a new sample ballot was placed on thirty-five thousand doorknobs. The radio spots from the primary were revised, and with more money available, the campaign was able to buy time for television ads.

The Republican party, anticipating a possible Schwarzwalder victory, forced its duly nominated candidate to withdraw, replaced him with a stronger person, and mounted a smear campaign against Schwarzwalder, accusing him of being a campus radical who counseled draft dodgers and who was arrested for rioting during a demonstration against the military. The smear campaign was countered with a major newspaper ad setting the story straight. Ironically, the Republican smear tactics helped pump new energy into the Schwarzwalder volunteer effort and brought to the ranks some civil libertarians who might otherwise have stayed at home.

In any case, the smear attempt was unsuccessful. On election day Schwarzwalder defeated his Republican opponent by 19,400 votes, receiving 60.8 percent of the total ballots cast.

Transformation of the System

The final stage in Warren's model is the transformation of the action system.[11] During this stage the campaign organization, having achieved or failed to achieve its goals, may attempt to stay in business to monitor the results of its labor or may disappear, perhaps leaving behind a residue of relationships and shared experiences that may contribute to the formation of a future action system.

The core group of the Schwarzwalder campaign continued to meet periodically, certainly not with campaign fervor, but as a sounding board and support group for the newly elected senator. Mike, in turn, provided community leadership, using his senate seat as political leverage even on issues that could not be resolved in the statehouse. When, for example, a powerful corporate landlord attempted the mass displacement of poor people in a portion of his district, Mike used his influence publicly and privately to enable tenants and other residents to have some control over their neighborhood.

None of the core group believed that the Ohio senate would change significantly with the election of one senator. It did not, but the seeds of future progress were sown. The campaign demonstrated to the regular Democratic party that grass-roots participants were a force to contend with. No longer could the party assume that incumbents were immune to democratic challenge— or that issues and value-oriented campaigns were impractical and idealistic.

A senator was elected who supported a wide range of social welfare issues. He provided significant leadership in trying to protect Ohio communities from runaway industry and became a serious enough voice to be criticized editorially by the *Wall Street Journal*.[12]

Mike Schwarzwalder believes that the campaign and his relationships with social workers helped sensitize him to the social and economic needs of all kinds of people. He also learned much from his social worker supporters about values, the process of decision making, and the need to involve people in the choices that affect their lives. The knowledge gained in these areas remains an influence in his life both inside and beyond the Ohio senate.

In addition to this, eighteen people learned through experience how to apply their values in developing the strategies, tactics, and skills necessary to conduct grass-roots electoral campaigns. Several hundred volunteers shared positive experiences in the democratic political process. Core group members and volunteers alike cut their political teeth and continue to be involved in progressive social action. For example, one core group member went on to direct the Columbus Metropolitan Women's Center, another to direct Ohio State Legal Services. Others provided leadership to a women's action collective and a citizens' crime watch program. One woman finished law school; another core group member worked for the legal aid society in a southern Ohio town.

Today, when the forces of reaction are organizing to dismantle the social welfare gains of the last several decades, the Schwarzwalder campaign offers hope to social workers and others committed to progressive social policies. It demonstrates that grass-roots efforts can succeed against what appear to be overwhelming odds. It challenges us to make the struggle our own.

Notes and References

1. Virginia Wallace-Whitaker, untitled script, Schwarzwalder for Senate Committee, Columbus, Ohio, 1976.

2. Armand L. Mauss, *Social Problems as Social Movements* (Philadelphia: J.B. Lippincott Co., 1975), pp. 47–48.

3. Roland Warren, *The Community in America* (2d ed.; Chicago: Rand McNally & Co., 1972), pp. 315–320.

4. Ibid.

5. For a detailed discussion of public assistance and the history of public assistance reform in Ohio, *see* William H. Whitaker, "The Determinants of Social Movement Success: A Study of the National Welfare Rights Organization," pp. 144–155. Unpublished Ph.D. thesis, Florence Heller Graduate School for Advanced Studies in Social Welfare, Brandeis University, 1970.

6. Warren, op. cit., p. 317.

7. Mauss, op. cit., p. 48.

8. Warren, op. cit., pp. 317–318.

9. Ibid.

10. Harvey Cox, *The Feast of Fools: A Theological Essay on Festivity and Fantasy* (Cambridge, Mass.: Harvard University Press, 1969), p. 120.

11. Warren, op. cit., pp. 319–320.

12. "An American Exit Tax," *Wall Street Journal,* December 7, 1978, p. 20.

Running for Office: A Social Worker's Experience

CECILIA KLEINKAUF

11

SEEKING elective office requires proven campaign methods, political awareness, organizational skill, and just plain hard work. This article is not intended as a guide to campaign management, however; many excellent sources are available for that purpose.[1] Instead, the intent is to relate some of the significant experiences and events in my campaign for the Alaska legislature, to discuss the assets and liabilities a social worker brings to candidacy for public office, and to comment on professional values and political participation. Because a major focus of the article is the effect a background in social work has on a person's involvement in politics, it will be useful to outline the details of my professional training and experience before discussing the details of my political candidacy.

Entering social work after teaching junior high school for five years, I naturally gravitated toward child welfare. Prior to and after taking my master's degree in social work at the University of Denver, I practiced as a county child welfare worker, supervisor, and administrator in Colorado; I also worked as the director of social services in a group home for teenage girls. After moving to Alaska in 1969, I conducted institutional licensing reviews and practiced as a private consultant until I joined the faculty of the University of Alaska in 1974 as an instructor and trainer in child welfare.

My professional and political activities have generally paralleled one another. I participated in voter registration drives and precinct activities in Colorado, and the nature of my social work employment there involved me in the legislative processes that set funding levels for human services. The scarcity of professional social workers in Alaska drew me into the political process again. When major legislative battles emerged over purchase of services, Aid to Families with Dependent Children, and day care, I became a lobbyist for the Alaska Chapter of the National Association of Social Workers. I was fortunate to become involved with a few legislative leaders who cared about social welfare services and who knew how to use social work knowledge; they were willing to teach me the ins and outs of the political process. As I gained experience in lobbying and began to develop and conduct workshops in lobbying, work in legislators' campaigns, and participate in party politics, more and more people began to urge me to run for office. I decided to do so—someday.

Start of a Campaign

The year 1978 was a congressional and gubernatorial election year in Alaska, as well as a year of the regular biennial legislative election, so dozens of campaigns were in high gear well before the June 1 filing deadline. My campaign was not one of them. Despite my long-standing intention to run for a seat in the Alaska House of Representatives, I had concluded that 1978 was not the year. Although one of the two Republican incumbents in my legislative district had decided not to seek reelection—an opportunity for a newcomer—the campaign managers, volunteers, and financial contributions were already committed to other candidates. Without those three vital ingredients, it appeared foolhardy to try to mount a meaningful campaign.

The day before the filing deadline, as I was about to begin working in another campaign, I learned that only one Democratic candidate had filed to run in the primary election for the two seats that represent my district in the statehouse. Because there are two seats, if only two Democrats run, both automatically survive the primary. The opportunity for developing name recognition with minimal effort seemed too good to pass up, and many friends, supporters, and active Democrats urged me to file. My district is predominantly middle class and upper-middle class and has traditionally voted Republican, but because only one incumbent was running and because a large number of voters were registered as Independents, a Democrat was at less of a disadvantage than in most years. Further, because significant changes in representation for that area of Anchorage were to occur following reapportionment in 1980, 1978 was a good time to run in preparation for future elections.

My hope that I would be one of only two Democrats filing for the primary was not fulfilled; three other candidates also filed before 5:00 P.M. on June 1. A total of eight candidates from both parties had filed in my district. Three weeks later the other woman Democrat withdrew in my favor after I agreed to assume her main issue of mobile home owners' rights. This left me as the only woman on the Democratic side and the only candidate who had never run before.

Alaska requires candidates to disclose comprehensive information about their personal finances, so a last-minute decision to run necessitated an all-out effort to gather detailed information and complete the required forms. On June 1, I found myself frantically assembling mortgage loan statements, bank account numbers, and property descriptions. I was thankful that the State Elections Office had assembled kits to guide prospective candidates in completing the forms. An hour and a half before the deadline, I submitted the necessary forms and became a candidate.

My hope that I would be one of only two Democrats filing for the primary was not fulfilled; three other candidates also filed before 5:00 P.M. on June 1. A total of eight candidates from both parties had filed in my district. Three weeks later the other woman Democrat withdrew in my favor after I agreed to assume her main issue of mobile home owners' rights. This left me as the only woman on the Democratic side and the only candidate who had never run before.

Once I had committed myself to run, my husband, a good friend, and two others who were willing to serve as advisers although they were working in other campaigns went to work with me to develop a plan for the campaign. All the books recommend against managing your own campaign, but I decided to proceed without a manager rather than settle for someone out of desperation. With my husband serving as finance chairman and with a small advisory committee, I performed many of the managerial tasks myself. I do not recommend this, however, unless absolutely necessary; being the candidate is exhausting enough. Moreover, an experienced manager has knowledge and skill that take time and exposure to the campaign process to acquire.

Because my budget was low and because voters tend to view women candidates as more responsive than men to constituents' needs, my advisory committee and I decided to run a people-oriented, direct-contact campaign that emphasized door knocking and neighborhood meetings.[2] To counteract possible negative reactions to my being female and a social worker, we also concluded that a sound approach lay in demonstrating to voters that I had significant knowledge and experience to bring to the legislative process and that my professional background prepared me especially well to listen to people's concerns and represent their interests. In the process of matching my political strengths and limitations to the character and interests of the district, we identified the five major issues that formed the cornerstone of the campaign: (1) responsiveness to constituents, (2) legislative reform, (3) increased development of the Anchorage campus of the University of Alaska, (4) coordinated and accountable human services, and (5) moving Alaska's capital.

My experience with legislative matters as a social service consultant, a budget adviser to the legislature's finance committees, a lobbyist, and a ballot initiative sponsor enabled me to speak knowledgeably about the legislative process and legislative reform. Because the Anchorage campus of the state university was in my district and because I was on the faculty there, I could also discuss university issues. The need to coordinate social service programs and to review their expenditures was an important issue in Anchorage, and it was one my experience as a professional social worker made me knowledgeable about. In 1974 Alaska voted to move its capital from Juneau to Willow; that the move had not yet begun in 1978 became a campaign issue all over the state.

A candidate must run on more than one issue, particularly a social worker. Not only are voters suspicious of single-issue candidates, but such candidates are also unable to appeal to a cross section of the electorate. The issues were presented to the voters through visits to voters' homes, through a campaign brochure that was hand delivered or mailed to voters, and through radio advertising, public appearances, neighborhood coffees, and some television advertising in the general election. Although I personally telephoned or visited at least 60 percent of the homes in my district, I also used volunteers for this work. My use of them had to be efficient because most were also working in other campaigns. Well-

KLEINKAUF

researched lists of Democratic and Independent voters, which a friendly statewide candidate shared with me, and low-cost voter identification lists enabled my campaign to make contact with a large number of potential supporters.

Campaign Highlights

Memorable positive moments in my campaign included emerging from the primary election as the top Democratic vote getter in my district and winning endorsements from influential women's groups, organized labor, public employees, teachers, and Anchorage's morning newspaper. The most negative moment, naturally, was losing. I spent election night in the headquarters of the Democratic gubernatorial candidate, and sharing his loss eased the pain of mine somewhat.

My loss was attributable primarily to my position as a newcomer and a Democrat in a Republican district. Most political observers believed that my being a woman and a social worker had little, if anything, to do with losing, particularly because I had significant legislative experience and a variety of issues on which to base a campaign. One of the winning candidates had his incumbency to thank for the victory; the other, a woman, had name recognition as the result of having previously run as a legislative candidate and school board candidate. A conservative, she had moved into the district to campaign in a compatible area, and the Republican party provided her with both financial support and campaign management expertise. Issues had little to do with the outcome because the four candidates espoused similar positions on several of the major issues in the campaign.

During the campaign, I became impressed by the positive sense of caring about government that voters exhibited. The experience of fund raising also made a lasting impression on me. Asking people to vote for you is easier than asking them to give you money. Because a vote involves a more pervasive commitment than a contribution and entrusts to the candidate the representation of the citizen in governmental affairs, it is odd that votes are often given more easily than money. Asking for money gets easier the more one does it, however, and candidates learn to have an established budget to identify what they are raising money for. Coaching from experienced campaigners, a diversified plan for raising funds, clear ideas about which contributions will not be accepted, and a good understanding of the legal requirements of the campaign disclosure statutes are also necessary.

My advisory committee and I decided that donations would not be solicited or accepted from groups whose positions on issues I could not agree with or that I would be unable to support if elected. These included antiabortion groups, the Alaska Teamsters Union, and right-wing groups, including some church groups. I did not seek endorsements or contributions from these groups, nor did I have to turn down their contributions, because they simply did not offer any after I stated my positions.

Making appointments to talk with union officials about a contribution was difficult, as was writing a fund-raising letter to mail to colleagues and friends. Fund-raising events were easier for me because three good friends, known for their great parties, each coordinated and hosted a fund-raising party, donating the food and beverages as in-kind contributions.

The large number of organizations and groups sending questionnaires to candidates or asking us to appear before their endorsement committees was something I was not prepared for, and I was surprised to find how much time it took. Endorsements were often followed by contributions and supportive advertising, so it was not only important to cooperate but to communicate one's position clearly. Pressure from special interest groups was notable in my campaign, a phenomenon that has become increasingly prevalent nationwide.[3] Ultraconservative groups, many of them church related, solicited and publicized candidates' opinions and positions on a wide range of moral issues, and the sophistication, organization, and advertising budgets of these groups were surprising.

Experience of Candidacy

Running for office is sobering, educational, exhilarating, rewarding, and exhausting. Working in a campaign gives some idea of what is involved for the candidate, but actually being the candidate is something almost impossible to describe. Even when you want to win more than you ever thought possible, part of you just wants to return to a quiet nonpublic life. Kirkpatrick, in her study of women legislators, notes that

> the psychological requirements for a successful campaign normally include a conviction that one is qualified, and a capacity for leader-

ship, rational calculation, gregariousness, social initiative, flexibility, and a capacity for supplication, and an ability to work hard and to engage in conflict.[4]

Having to be on display at all times, constantly smiling and moving from one campaign activity to the next, is a considerable drain on one's emotions. As election day comes closer, it becomes harder and harder to maintain a perspective on the world and life in general. I was warned that campaigning would pose serious threats to my self-esteem, ruin my marriage, and reduce me to an emotional wreck. The pressures of campaigning were unbelievable, but never before had I learned so much about my community, myself, my values, and my commitment to good government. Undoubtedly, my previous experience with the state legislature and the political process contributed significantly to my surviving the campaign with sanity and marriage intact. It also prepared me somewhat for the dishonesty and manipulation frequently seen in politics.

Women candidates are forced to prove themselves to a greater extent than are male candidates.[5] Many people believe that women do not belong in politics, and they do not expect women to be knowledgeable on budgets, policy analysis, or things outside such traditional women's domains as education and day care. It can be especially tough for a social worker to overcome these stereotypes.

One of the most difficult aspects of campaigning is the barrage of advice candidates receive. It is necessary to sift out what is useful and worth considering from what is simply the need of campaign voyeurs to involve themselves in other people's efforts. Absolutely everyone presumes to know exactly what the candidate should do about every aspect of the campaign. Usually such advisers do not want to work, just to advise. One called me up at 6:00 A.M. to recommend that I remove my nickname, "Pudge," from my yard signs so that people would take me seriously. Others tried to monopolize my time at a candidate's night to suggest different language for my radio ad. Television is a favorite focus of such advisers. They all seem able to quote statistics and experts about whether to film or videotape an ad, how much air time to buy, when to buy it, what to say, and so on. They had advice on my dress, my brochure, my volunteers, my husband, my door-knocking schedule, and my expenditures, but never did they commit themselves to do any work in the campaign.

The only valuable piece of advice I got was to trust my own instincts. Even when my campaign committee sat down with me for our regular strategy sessions, we generally would lay out suggestions, discuss pros and cons, and see if there was a consensus; if not, I would decide. For instance, toward the end of the campaign I decided, against advice, to save money by printing an inexpensive campaign brochure and to mount a major neighborhood walk with all my volunteers about two weeks before the election rather than at the very end when the blitzes of all other candidates would take place. These and other decisions may have been detrimental; it is hard to know. The mistakes I know I made were in waiting till the last minute to file and waiting too long to start aggressively raising money. I was also mistaken in expecting that other social workers would help me campaign; only a few actually did so. Some mistakes undoubtedly cost me money and votes, but at least I did not constantly feel at the mercy of every political expert who came along, and I was prepared to take the consequences of decisions knowing that I had been responsible for them.

One thing that surprised me was that I was not insulted or reviled during the campaign as frequently as I had expected. Nor was my social work background the subject of negative comment nearly to the extent I had anticipated. I believe that much hostility was averted by my willingness to discuss the concerns and issues that voters felt were important. I was guilty, though, of believing that just because people were gracious and friendly at their door, they would vote for me. Most people were friendly at the door, but I lost just the same. Losing is depressing, but it is manageable if you have maintained some perspective on the experience, not gone irrevocably into debt, been somewhat realistic about your chances, and have a job to go back to.

Social Work Assets and Liabilities

Both the knowledge base and the practice skills of social work are particularly useful in campaigning for office. As social workers, our understanding of social problems, social change, and human behavior renders us capable of speaking out about issues ranging from community problems to the difficulties of individual constituents. Furthermore, our ability to see the interrelationships between major social issues and individual lives prepares us to mount issue-oriented campaigns that relate to individual needs. Undertaking goal-directed activity is ingrained in the professional social worker and proves invaluable in all aspects of politics. The ability to analyze, think ahead, plan carefully, and work toward a goal are elements of problem solving that are used every day in campaigning, and nobody is more capable of such activity than social workers.

Innumerable skills carry over easily from social work practice to campaigning, and the most obvious are in the area of communication. Social workers are trained to meet people, listen to problems, and help people find solutions; we know how to manage hostility, reach out to shy and quiet people, and deal with groups as well as individuals.

Skills in both written and verbal communication are vital to good campaigning, especially the ability to speak clearly and with conviction. Campaigning demands frequent speaking engagements, interviews, and press releases, and the candidate must be prepared to speak extemporaneously, answer questions, and defend positions. Social workers are also trained in nonverbal communication, and this helps us avoid distracting mannerisms and observe and assess the feedback we receive from others.

Experience in the advocate role is also good preparation for political participation. Advocates seem to gravitate toward politics; their commitment to changing systems is a natural lead-in to policymaking in the public arena. Advocacy skills enable us to assist constituents to get information and solve problems, to deal with bureaucracies, and to mobilize others to confront and change systems.

Campaign liabilities for social workers include our long-standing focus on the individualized, micro approach to change rather than on societal or macro change. This emphasis still has far too many social workers avoiding politics; in consequence, policymaking in the political arena has usually proceeded without social work participation.[6] Time-worn misinterpretations of the Hatch Act and fear of agency reprisal for political involvement have also kept many social workers from political involvement. In addition, social workers, in my opinion, are afraid that politicians and the public will criticize the profession for the welfare cheaters, the unsuccessful alcoholism treatment programs, and similar unsolved problems. An inability to confront such criticism and to present the profession as a vital and necessary part of social change keeps most social workers safely and exclusively in direct practice.

Ignorance about political procedures is another major liability of social workers, most of whom do not understand politics or the legislative process and frequently do not even try to. Although they may bemoan a budget reduction for human services, for example, social workers fail to talk to their legislators about it, avoid learning about the budget process and how to influence it, and even neglect to gather and share data about the clients directly affected by the cuts.

Mahaffey identifies disdain and impatience as additional barriers to political participation (see "Lobbying and Social Work," p. 69). Lack of skills in competitiveness and assertiveness, avoidance of conflict, and discomfort with compromise also contribute to the social work professional's traditional avoidance of political involvement.

Professional Values and Candidacy

Whenever political participation by social workers is discussed, the issue of value conflicts arises. Such conflicts exist in all areas of social work practice, but in politics and campaigning for office, the concerns of professionals usually center on (1) conflicts between the values of candidates and constituents and (2) threats to social work values in the wheeling and dealing of politics.

Because the public tends to elect representatives whose values reflect dominant community attitudes, a successful candidate is usually one who convinces the electorate that his or her attitudes coincide with theirs and that he or she will be guided by these values as their representative.[7] Many politicians devote a great deal of time and money attempting to ascertain the interests and attitudes of their constituencies, and they use the results of polls and surveys to create their campaign positions. At times, such positions are clearly dishonest representations adopted merely to win votes. Many factors besides compatible values determine elections, but because voters deserve to know the candidate's principles and beliefs, a professional must be expected to state his or her positions honestly, recognizing that not everyone will agree with them. Candidates who are careful to keep in mind that positions taken today become commitments to fulfill tomorrow generally do not mislead either themselves or their voters.

The public holds certain negative attitudes toward the client groups social workers serve and toward the profession. Nevertheless, concern for humanitarianism, personal freedom, and quality are basic American values that closely parallel the primary values

KLEINKAUF

of social work. A social work candidate stating the belief that government exists to serve the needs of the people and to provide the necessary resources for individuals to exercise personal choice both reflects the basic value stance of the profession and finds common ground with many voters. Politicians also recognize the existence of strong public attitudes about government efficiency and accountability, and the social worker must come to grips with such issues as the careful and cost-effective management of government programs.

Candidates and constituents usually find much common ground, but the number of subjects on which positions must be taken and the frequency with which people disagree make it inevitable that conflicts will present themselves. What to do when the values of constituents and candidates conflict is no more simple than in any instance when worker-client values conflict. In direct practice, social workers are guided by the respect we hold for the client's right to self-determination, and we attempt to engage in problem solving that focuses on the difficulty, not on the values.[8] An appropriate warning for politicians, as for social workers, is to avoid adopting the client's values when under stress to be accepted. In situations of conflict, it is important to maintain flexibility while being guided by integrity and to distinguish clearly between knowledge and values. The development of self-awareness and a tolerance for ambiguity are also useful.

Most voters respect the candidate who does not equivocate about positions and often prefer to support someone whom they respect even though they disagree on some issues. They are also interested in a candidate who is willing to consider both sides of an issue. When value conflicts arise, it is helpful to remember that any elected official is expected to represent the interests of all the diverse elements of the constituency. A social worker can often be guided by the profession's commitment to the provision of opportunities so that people can exercise choices based on their own values. In the end, any elected official or candidate has to follow his or her conscience and be ready to answer to the electorate for a position or vote.

Political Behavior

Wheeling and dealing are generally thought to be necessary to achieve and exercise political power, and an aversion to wheeling and dealing is probably the most widely held reason for social workers' avoiding political activity. In many people's minds, wheeling and dealing is still conceived as arm twisting, bribery, vote trading, payoffs, and the like. Such tactics are obviously still in use, and they indicate either a lack of principles or a willingness to sacrifice principles for power. To generalize, however, that all politicians engage in unprincipled behavior to achieve power is inaccurate and unfair.

The nature of political power is complex, and the strategies to obtain and use it are many. Persuasion, bargaining, negotiation, compromise, confrontation, and rational argument are discussed in social work literature as elements of power to be developed and used in efforts to achieve social change through political action.[9] Khinduka and Coughlin also point out that

> there is no single source of power. On the contrary, power is achieved, consolidated and augmented on the basis of a variety of resources: money, votes, access to and control over information, knowledge, expertise, leadership, position, numbers, organization, status, loyalty of followers, prestige, political acumen, the communications media, strength of convictions and commitment, personal charm and charisma, interpersonal, organizational and interorganizational skills, support of other influentials, and so on.[10]

With so many points of leverage, it is unnecessary to rely on those that have resulted in the negative opinion many people have of politics. Although Kirkpatrick identified authority and force as the components of power, she also reported that "interpersonal skill, knowledge, drive and hard work have been reinforced by seniority and the product is power."[11] Power obviously can be achieved through constructive means, many of which social workers already know how to use.

Both candidates and elected officials interact constantly with party members, other candidates, other legislators, and governmental employees, and honesty must guide these interactions. As Kirkpatrick states,

> Personal integrity also has crucial legislative functions. To "do business" with each other, legislators must be able to count on the good faith and responsibility of their colleagues. Keeping one's word is important, but integrity, in its legislative context, involves more: declining to exploit one's colleagues, refusing to take unfair advantage or mislead, are part of integrity . . . . Deals

must be "square" deals in which both parties are fully and accurately informed and, once made, deals [must] be honored.[12]

The recognition that political behavior needs to be guided by integrity and square dealing is important for the professional whose conduct is guided by an ethical code. Although it is necessary to acknowledge that answers for every behavioral dilemma cannot be found in a code of ethics, many believe that such a code is a definite asset to political activity.[13]

A social worker's values and ethics are constantly being tested, and not just in the political arena. The manipulative aspects of human relationships, for example, must be dealt with in all areas of social work:

> Political behavior requires the same sensitivity to oneself and others as is required in all human interaction. It may even require more. Manipulation is neither self-defeating nor effective. The potential costs of political strategies must always be assessed against their potential gains, so that one's morality is supported by expedience. . . . Since people resent being treated as means to an end rather than as ends in themselves, those who appear to use them instrumentally are likely to be ineffective.[14]

The notion that politics is strictly a manipulative and secretive undertaking is more and more old-fashioned and belied by new sunshine laws requiring openness in politics and government. Legislation regulating conflicts of interest, campaign disclosures, lobbying, and other aspects of political behavior is being introduced and passed throughout the country. Election laws are also being scrutinized for their potential for voter fraud. The demand for such openness in government, coupled with aggressive new watchdog groups, is minimizing the dishonest aspects of political activity.

Conclusion

More and more, the social work professional recognizes the potential for policymaking through political activity, and slowly but surely social workers are becoming involved in electoral politics and legislative affairs. We are lobbying, managing and working in campaigns, and running for office. We are recognizing that it is possible for a social worker to be effective in politics without violating professional values and without losing sight of our commitment to the interests of those we serve as social workers.

Notes and References

1. *See* Chester G. Atkins et al., *Getting Elected: A Guide to Winning State and Local Office* (Boston: Houghton Mifflin Co., 1973); and Edward Schwartzman, *Campaign Craftsmanship* (New York: Universe Books, 1973) and *Campaign Workbook* (Washington, D.C.: National Women's Education Fund, 1978).

2. For a discussion of voters' views on the responsiveness of women candidates, *see* Irene Diamond, *Sex Roles in the State House* (New Haven, Conn.: Yale University Press, 1977), pp. 86–88.

3. "Single Issue Politics," *Newsweek,* November 6, 1978, pp. 48 and 60.

4. Jeane J. Kirkpatrick, *Political Woman* (New York: Basic Books, 1974), p. 91.

5. *See* ibid., pp. 3–23.

6. Alan D. Wade, "The Social Worker in the Political Process," in *Social Welfare Forum, 1966* (New York: Columbia University Press, 1966), pp. 52-67.

7. Kirkpatrick, op. cit., pp. 48–50.

8. *See* Allen Pincus and Anne Minahan, *Social Work Practice: Model and Method* (Itasca, Ill.: F. E. Peacock Publishers, 1973), pp. 37–52; Charles S. Levy, "The Value Base of Social Work," *Journal of Education for Social Work,* 9 (Winter 1973), pp. 34–42; and Charles S. Prigmore and Charles R. Atherton, *Social Welfare Policy— Analysis and Formulation* (Lexington, Mass.: D. C. Heath & Co., 1979), pp. 23–36.

9. *See* Rino J. Patti and Ronald B. Dear, "Legislative Advocacy: One Path to Social Change," *Social Work,* 20 (March 1975), pp. 108–114; and Pincus and Minahan, op. cit., pp. 76–78.

10. S. K. Khinduka and Bernard J. Coughlin, "A Conceptualization of Social Action," *Social Service Review,* 49 (March 1975), p. 9.

11. Kirkpatrick, op. cit., p. 131.

12. Ibid., p. 119.

13. *See* Daniel Thursz, "Social Action as a Professional Responsibility and Political Participation," in J. Roland Pennock and John W. Chapman, eds., *Participation in Politics* (New York: Leiber-Atherton, 1975), pp. 213–232; and Charles Levy, *Social Work Ethics* (New York: Human Sciences Press, 1976).

14. George A. Brager, "Advocacy and Political Behavior," *Social Work,* 13 (April 1968), p. 14.

A Social Worker-Politician Creates a New Service

MARYANN MAHAFFEY

12

ACCORDING to the 1975 Uniform Crime Report of the Federal Bureau of Investigation (FBI), police across the country received more calls for family conflict than for murder, aggravated assault, and all other serious crimes. Incidents of wife beating outnumbered those of rape by three to one. Responding to calls related to wife abuse accounted for 13 percent of all homicides of police officers and 40 percent of all injuries sustained by police officers.[1]

Families caught in patterns of recurring violence often turn to the police. The police are easily available through a phone call, and they come quickly. They handle the violence because they have the authority—the uniform and the badge. They are the twenty-four hour service of last resort. The director of the Police Foundation has publicly stated that such social problems occupy a major portion of police officers' time and that although officers are not trained for such work, they should be.[2]

Police officers across the nation know families that experience repeated instances of domestic violence. Such families are familiar to the local precinct and to the officer on the beat. These families are often not known to those who provide counseling services, however, nor are the families familiar with the services that provide the counseling they need. Far too often the death or handicapping of a family member is the "solution" to the conflict.

A variety of responses to the problem of domestic violence have developed. Social workers in the army in Europe worked with commanding officers and military police to defuse such situations and to begin the counseling process.[3] In the United States, social workers in some communities have been assigned full time to police stations. In other communities, psychologists have trained police officers in defusion techniques. In other cases, psychologists have trained police to refer cases of domestic violence to social agencies.

Despite the existence and success of such programs, social agencies in many communities have insisted that the family in trouble visit the agency only during regular office hours, and they have questioned the value of social workers going with police on "family trouble runs." The validity of this approach is questionable. The knowledge, ethics, and skills of social work are needed wherever individuals and families interface and problems are created. This implies that the problems and needs of families trapped in domestic violence can only be addressed if social workers develop strategies of change in close cooperation with the governmental agency most directly involved—the police department. Moreover, because any change process requires identifying and mobilizing support both inside and outside the systems targeted for change, attempts to influence the police department or any other department of government require attention to political considerations—to balancing the needs and interests of the elected officials who make policy with the interests of their constituencies and other sources of political power.

Events throughout the country in recent years have increased social workers' awareness not only of the importance of public policy in solving such social problems as family violence, but also of the need to take an active part in the political processes that shape governmental policies. As a result, increasing numbers of social workers have become involved in politics, some as campaign workers or lobbyists, others as elected or appointed officials.

In 1973, such considerations drew me to become a candidate for the Detroit City Council and to make family violence one of several human service problems I chose as campaign issues. At the time, there was some public recognition of family violence as a problem, and demands were mounting that the Detroit Police Department find a solution. By focusing attention on the public safety aspect of domestic violence, by proposing a rational effort to deal with the problem, and by drawing a large vote as a candidate for the city council, I hoped to show that a solution involving the provision of additional police and counseling services to families in crisis had broad public support.

This article describes my efforts, as a social worker, to create such services through direct involvement in the political process. Intended to provide a model for incremental change through political action, the article highlights the importance of understanding power in bringing about change—expert power, referent power, charismatic power, and the power of numbers. It also demonstrates the need for resourcefulness and flexibility in defining objectives and revising strategies and tactics.

Emergence of a Political Issue

In 1973, Detroit was caught in a political cross fire. The black mayoral candidate—with my support and that of the black community and progressive whites—had fought for and won changes in the city charter to create a civilian police commission, the Detroit Board of Police Commissioners, charged with making policy for and controlling the police department. The other candidate for mayor was the white police chief. Hysteria was rising in the community as the media focused on crime, muggings, and property damage. One headline screamed "Detroit Is Murder City." The media portrayed the problem as one of strangers killing strangers, creating fear among city residents. In the suburbs, hostility was rising toward the city as Detroit's black population crept toward a 51 percent majority. Some people were calling for more police and for "untying their hands." Others were campaigning against the police and for black control of the city. The black community viewed the police as a white occupying force, and verbal attacks by blacks had many police paranoid. In this climate, a political strategy of open confrontation would have been inflammatory and counterproductive.

As a candidate for city council, I defined as public safety issues the need to free police officers for crime fighting by filling more jobs with civilians and the need to reduce the injuries and deaths among police and citizens by training police to deal with domestic violence and social conflicts. I knew the deaths were mostly results of arguments among acquaintances. My objective was to pair social workers and police, namely, Family Service of Detroit and Wayne County and the Detroit Police Department, to defuse incidents of domestic violence and to provide social services to the disputants. The project I proposed would (1) train the police in crisis intervention to defuse domestic violence, (2) involve social workers in providing this training for the police, (3) have social workers on call in precinct stations, and (4) have the police make referrals to social workers. The success of the project depended on its acceptance by the decision makers in city government who had responsibility for training police and managing the police department and by the leadership in the family services agency and in the private social service system.

My position was strengthened by the large vote I received in November 1973. From a field of eighteen candidates, I was elected to the nine-member city council with the fifth highest vote. Soon after the new city council was sworn in, we marched, with the new black mayor, in a funeral for a police officer killed in the line of duty during a social conflict situation. The emotional impact on the council members was forceful—the dirge, the lines of silent officers, the crowds along the parade route, the rifle salute, and the solidarity of officers and families as they rallied around the widow, who was herself in police training. In June 1974, the council adopted my resolution establishing a task force to investigate the issue of social conflict among families, friends, and acquaintances, particularly the question of domestic violence, and find ways to reduce police and civilian injuries.

The resolution instructed the Social Conflict Task Force to report to the city council and the mayor within three months with recommendations for referral mechanisms to handle situations involving social conflict and with proposals for training Detroit police officers to deal with such situations. The task force, by resolution, was to be composed of representatives from a number of organizations and agencies, including Family Service, the National Association of Social Workers (NASW), the Association of Black Social Workers, community counseling and mental health coordinating agencies, the Detroit Police Department, and the department's corps of chaplains. The task force was also to include three people named by the mayor and the Detroit Board of

Police Commissioners. By asking the mayor and the board of commissioners to name three people, I hoped to avoid turf problems, lend credibility to the task force, ensure that the new mayor would feel involved, and avoid giving the community the impression that the council and the mayor were at odds.

The idea of a task force was new for the Detroit City Council. Although the council met every day of the year in committee of the whole, subcommittees were prohibited by the charter from 1918 to 1974. Some members of the council were reluctant to establish committees or task forces, for they felt it would then be impossible to know everything that was going on. Others thought establishing such bodies would reduce the power of the city council president, a position many members wanted. It seemed wise, therefore, to make this a task force with a time limit and, because it was a first, to have someone other than a council member chair it. A priest who was a trained community social worker was asked to head the task force in the hope that this would reduce turf-related problems. He would also do better, I believed, with the police department because his gender and priestly identification would help in dealings with the police chief.

It was also essential to involve a diverse group of human service professionals to avoid leaving the project to police department traditionalists or to professionals advocating one particular method, such as peer group counseling, which is based on the idea that one does not need professional training to deal with problems involving human relationships, but needs only to be a peer with a loving, caring heart. (In Detroit in 1973, untrained women were running rape counseling services without professional consultation; by 1975, such services throughout the country were applying for money to hire professionals because the problems to be dealt with called for more skills and training than the volunteers had.)

A central objective of my resolution was to address the lack of understanding between the social work professional and the police. I was convinced that if social work professionals were involved in the project from the beginning, some of the artificial barriers between the two professions would be eliminated, and the services developed would be better for it. However, some social workers had serious doubts about the project. They questioned whether a change from traditional social agency practices would improve the situation and whether social workers would lose their identity and begin to emulate police officers. They also wondered what the physical dangers would be. Many social workers see their role as one of offering therapy in traditional office settings. Neither psychiatrists nor social workers have traditionally worked with the police, although, as will be discussed later, some psychologists have begun to develop crisis intervention programs designed for police work.

Police traditionally view their work as the pursuit of criminals and the performance of patrol duties. Intervening in social conflicts is often seen as social work and as a less desirable assignment for the police officer. However, many police, like the public, are intrigued by the police activities portrayed in such television shows as "Baretta" and "Starsky and Hutch," although police admit that a show like "Barney Miller" is closer to reality. Police officers usually want to get the family trouble runs off their backs, but the programs to accomplish this are often ignored and the victims told that the problem is a civil matter: "Sorry, lady, there's nothing we can do."

As the task force began its work, it became known that a command officer in the Detroit Police Department had researched domestic violence in preparing a doctoral dissertation on the police emergency phone system. His findings highlighted the lack of crisis intervention training for the police operators and the low priority police gave to domestic violence. Although this officer was regarded by police officers, both black and white, as fair, tough, and a true police professional, the chief refused to appoint him to the Social Conflict Task Force. Instead, the chief intimated that the officer was being investigated by the FBI because of criminal contacts. This new, white chief was intent on proving his ability to rule the department. Therefore, the police officers appointed to the task force included one assigned to the Criminal Justice Institute (the local police academy) and an officer in headquarters command who was held in low esteem by the chief. The officers in charge of the institute were from outside the city and had little credibility in some levels of the police department. These appointments reflected the low priority the mayor assigned to the task force. The only hope was to use the task force to develop a base and a degree of understanding of family violence in the police department, social agencies, and the community and to develop a model for later program development.

Work of the Task Force

The task force studied crisis intervention programs conducted by police departments and other law enforcement agencies, examining them for their training techniques, their referral mechanisms, and their effectiveness. In 1974, most of the published work in this field had been done by psychologists, with the two major training packages having been developed by Bard from the Psychology Department of City College of New York and by Schwartz and Liebman, psychologists based in San Francisco. The Bard model emphasized teaching officers techniques for defusing conflict and for referring people to agencies.[4] This package was designed for special units in police departments, but, unfortunately, such units tend to be elitist and to arrive at the scene after other officers have already performed the difficult and sensitive parts of the assignment. Moreover, when problems with funding arise, special units are the most likely to be eliminated.

The Schwartz-Liebman model used in San Francisco's Bay Area also emphasized defusing conflict.[5] Although this approach involved the training of all police officers, the relationship between police and social service agencies was limited to the making of referrals and the developing of pocket-size referral books for officers. The police also tested whether the agency was receptive to police referrals and whether people were taken care of. Such referral mechanisms seemed to be afterthoughts. Both models had sexist overtones in how they viewed women victims of violence, and they built on the machismo emphasis of police training.

I joined a task force team that included representatives from the Detroit Police Department and the Criminal Justice Institute in conducting on-site research in California with police departments using the Schwartz model. The visit won support among some of the police officers for such a program and gave me additional information regarding links to community agencies and the experience of community agencies in social conflict interventions. For example, the experience of the program in Oakland, California, indicated that the peaks for conflict occurred on weekends and paydays and that once a situation was defused, 75 percent of the people being dealt with could wait until Monday morning for further intervention. Most families successfully referred needed from one to three interviews, and only 5 percent became long-term clients.[6] The task force also consulted extensively with the Police

Foundation in Washington, D.C., and one member of the task force attended an FBI seminar on social conflict in Virginia. Others attended a regional Law Enforcement Assistance Agency (LEAA) conference in Chicago.

The task force also examined the policies and practices of the Detroit Police Department in handling family violence. In 1974 the department gave a low priority to "domestic calls" on 911, the emergency line. People soon caught on that calls describing family problems brought a slow response, and callers began claiming there was "a man with a gun," which made the call a high priority and prompted a quick police response.

The General Orders of the Detroit Police Department in 1974 described social conflict situations as civil matters and not as a police responsibility. Several reasons were given for this point of view: (1) the large volume of other service demands for emergencies involving immediate physical danger and crimes in progress, (2) the lack of specific training for police mediating social conflicts, and (3) the service award system that emphasized arrests and convictions. Police recruits in Detroit received a total of seven hours of lecture-type training in topics related to social conflicts, a three-hour lecture on domestic complaints, and four hours of lecture on handling abnormal individuals, all of which constituted a tiny portion of the recruits' six-month training. Nevertheless, an estimated 25 to 30 percent of the calls to the 911 number in Detroit each week related to social conflicts.

Recommendations

In October of 1974, the Social Conflict Task Force reported to the Detroit City Council and the mayor, pointing out problems in many areas. The task force cited the lack of a legal way, in situations of marital conflict, to force a separation or to evict a violent person from the situation. It also criticized the failure of the police to treat with the same seriousness as crimes occurring between strangers domestic conflict or social conflict situations that involved people who knew each other; this problem was particularly noteworthy in instances of violence between husbands and wives. The lack of understanding and cooperation between social agencies and the police department was another problem discussed in the task force's report. Social agencies offered services during certain evening hours and ran some limited shelters for people who needed a place to spend the night. This was not enough, however, and what was available was often not made known to police officers. In Detroit, as in many communities, there are twenty-four-hour mental health clinics, but these are intended to deal with psychiatric emergencies, not problems in relationships, such as family conflicts. In addition, most of Detroit's social agencies did not set aside blocks of time during which clients caught in a conflict situation could walk in and receive services; with few exceptions, agencies had waiting lists for services. Two friends threatening to shoot each other do not need to be told to get at the end of the waiting list.

The task force also faulted the 911 priority list, which placed property crimes and crimes involving a weapon higher than family calls. An example of the 911 calls to which the operator could not send a car in 1974 was as follows: A 15-year-old girl called, screaming that her mother was hitting her and beating her up. She cried that she was frightened that her mother would kill her. The operator said that this was not a police matter and hung up. In turn, the police complained that when the calls came in at midnight on Friday or at 2:00 A.M. on Sunday from a family involved in physical violence, no social worker or social work agency was available.

The task force's report made five major recommendations: (1) that all officers be exposed to a forty-hour crisis intervention training program rather than just members of special units, (2) that a community resource referral system be established, (3) that social agencies set aside blocks of time and have extended hours to assist those calling the police department, (4) that changes be made in the police priority system and in the allocation of personnel, giving a higher priority to family calls and training 911 operators in basic interviewing and crisis intervention skills, and (5) that a service award system be established to recognize officers for their abilities to defuse volatile situations without injury to themselves or others.

When the report of the Social Conflict Task Force was completed in November 1974, I used my elected position to obtain media coverage for the report's findings. I also presented the report to the Detroit Board of Police Commissioners at a public meeting. Several members of the board believed in what we were trying to do; others thought it a minor matter. However, the police chief said that the recommendations of the task force could not be acted on until social work agencies were available twenty-four hours a day, seven days a week. He was unwilling to consider employing social workers in the police department unless they were uniformed officers; if they were uniformed officers, he was not willing to give them the assignment of working with domestic violence.

Other obstacles included the mayor's continuing to view the project as a low priority. It seemed obvious that the recommendations of the task force were not going to get far without better cooperation from the top of the police department. Therefore, the strategy became one of keeping the issue alive through meeting with the police chief and the mayor and through involving other community groups, including women's groups. For example, when representatives of the task force met with the Detroit Board of Police Commissioners, additional members of the Social Conflict Task Force and others were rounded up to be present as a show of support. The head of the task force organized an NASW committee on social conflict, and both of us continued to talk to the police, the police unions, and the corps of police chaplains. We also continued to work on the issue of 911 priorities, to talk with professionals and agencies about the necessity of closer work between social agencies and the police department, and to work with the National Organization for Women (NOW) and other community groups to keep the pressure on.

The Criminal Justice Institute had the officers most interested in the project. They even invited Schwartz and Liebman to conduct a week-long demonstration course on handling social conflicts. Not long afterwards, however, the institute was closed as a result of police department politics and Detroit's 1975–76 depression, during which every department of city government, including the police, took a 20-percent budget cut. The projection was that there would be no police to train for at least six months. It appeared the project was dead.

Breakthrough

Events quite apart from any efforts in behalf of the task force recommendations offered an opportunity for some progress. The police chief overreached himself in a departmental dispute and was fired. A new police chief was appointed. Also, the officer who had become the expert within the department on the issue of social conflict calls became deputy executive chief for several months.

In November 1976, in an effort to break through the stalemate, I held a meeting in my office to discuss social conflict calls. I invited the deputy executive chief of the police department, a representative of United Community Services, the priest who had headed the task force, the two area directors of Family Service of Detroit and Wayne County, and a representative of the Detroit unit of NASW's Michigan Chapter. Discussion at this meeting identified the two major areas of unmet need: emergency shelters to house and protect children in danger as a result of family trouble, and professional counseling. Family Service responded with a proposal for the Police Referral Project of Family Service of Detroit and Wayne County, which eventually became known as the Family Trouble Clinic. The agency's willingness to engage in this project was partly a result of community pressure and NASW involvement. A speech by the deputy executive police chief at a local NASW meeting on the issue of family violence and the police had interested many social workers in the problem.

The project was conceived as a three-month pilot effort. Family Service was to provide the finances for a social worker to be present in the precinct station and offer immediate service to clients during the peak periods for incidents of domestic violence, which were Friday and Saturday evenings from 8:00 P.M. until midnight. In addition, one or two visits by a social worker to the precinct during the week were planned to facilitate, coordinate, and direct referrals to Family Service. Objectives of the project were to demonstrate that referrals are expedited by precinct-based activities, make social services better known to more police officers, increase professional staff's appreciation of the problems police officers have in domestic relations calls, and give police officers a better understanding of the services offered. It was also hoped that the results of this police referral project would lend support to the task force recommendation of establishing night service for family counseling.

No movement took place regarding the proposal for several months. Finally, I discovered that the deputy executive chief had not seen the proposal, so I forwarded another copy to him. I then called him several times, and he finally agreed it was worth pursuing. At a brief meeting in March 1977, the acceptance of the project was confirmed and its location established for the Sixteenth Police Precinct, whose commander had volunteered to house the project. The precinct was the largest in the city, its population presented a racial and economic cross section, and the precinct station was close to an office of Family Service. As responsbility for the development and implementation of the project shifted from one step to the next, it was repeatedly necessary to confront obstacles, defuse emotions, and solve problems to keep the project moving toward the final goal. Social work skills and the modest power of my elected office were valuable assets during this stage.

Although an early problem arose when the precinct commander publicly supported a mayoral candidate in opposition to the incumbent mayor in the 1977 election, the officers working with the project were convinced of its value, and the two social workers assigned to the project by Family Service were pleased with their work. Everyone involved became supportive of the project, and both the police and the human service professionals said they had begun to appreciate each other. I lobbied the mayor and his staff in support of the project and, in my reelection campaign, described it as a success, thus building public acceptance and support. In the end, the project survived both the internal politics of the police department and electoral politics.

An ad hoc committee of Family Service studied the experiences of the police referral project and compiled useful information:

- Social workers and the police were received differently by families in crisis.
- All direct referrals resulted in clients' receiving crisis counseling services within three hours of the complaint.
- Follow-up counseling occurred in 89 percent of all situations in which families received crisis counseling from the social worker.
- In all situations of family conflict, at least one member of the family received some form of direct service from a social worker.
- The number of referrals the project generated in the test precinct would have doubled Family Service's total annual intake if the rate of referral were projected to all the city's police precincts.

- Ninety-nine percent of the people referred had not visited a human service agency before.
- Police officers were concerned about domestic violence, but most felt helpless and powerless in confronting the problem. Perceived as the authority in the community, police can force cessation of a violent situation, but they cannot keep people apart. In some situations, for a variety of reasons, the next day the wife would say that she wanted her abuser home. Social workers know and deal with the dynamics of relationships, the police officer with cessation of the immediate trouble. With the inception of the pilot project the police officer had something to say, to recommend, after stopping the hostile actions.
- Most disputants lacked communication skills and were not used to talking about feelings. There are also problems when only one of two marital partners is verbal.

Focus on Publicity

Once this information had been compiled, my office announced on a Friday that there would be a report to the Detroit Board of Police Commissioners. A newspaper reporter called me on Sunday afternoon, desperately looking for a story, and, as a result, the police referral project received a front-page headline Monday morning. Fortunately, the writer of the newspaper article spoke with a police sergeant who had worked with Family Service on the pilot project. The sergeant was pleased with the project and praised it, and the article had the effect of broadening public support. As planned, the report was presented to the board with two resolutions: (1) that the board approach the local United Foundation and its planning agency for the money to make the work of the pilot project permanent and to expand it to another precinct and (2) that the police department be instructed to work with Family Service to prepare a proposal to get funding for a similar program in all the precincts.

Time, place, and situation all influence process and strategy. As a result of Family Service's report and of the media coverage received by a national conference on domestic violence held in Detroit by NOW, the Detroit Board of Police Commissioners, on my recommendation, set up a task force on social conflict. A woman commissioner was to chair the task force, and I was to be vice-chair. We thus developed a publicly mandated support network as well as an entrée to the board of commissioners, the policymaking body for the police department.

Part of my function was to maintain community interest in the police referral project and to save the police from having to get into major battles with all kinds of groups in the community that might want to latch on to a hot topic. For example, after the task force was formed by the board of commissioners, two local feminists wrote a proposal for crisis intervention training for the police. One of them, a person with experience in sociological research, was to spend two months supervising a police sergeant in the development of a program to train police officers in defusion techniques. The researcher planned to develop a referral manual. The focus was on the victim without real consideration of the problems of the police officer. No mention was made of the training the police were already receiving or of any cooperation with other training programs. The sociological researcher and the other feminist, a planner in the city's planning department, did their political homework, and by maneuvering and taking advantage of internecine rivalry in the police department, they managed to obtain an LEAA grant despite the objections of several top officials in the police department and of the board of commissioner's task force. The grant was subsequently rewritten to incorporate the police officials' concerns.

Other groups also went to the board of commissioners to demand changes in police procedures. Some representatives of these groups were made members of the board's task force.

In 1977, I built my successful reelection campaign presentation on the theme "promises made and promises kept." One of the promises made in 1973 had been to do something about domestic violence. The promise had been kept: the police referral project had demonstrated that help could be given to families and to police officers and had resulted in some lessening of domestic violence. There was evidence that recidivism was lower among cases diverted to Family Service.

The pilot project demonstrated the need to spread the police referral program throughout the city. In November of 1977, the local United Foundation gave Family Service money to continue the program in the Sixteenth Police Precinct and to expand it to the Tenth Precinct. When the Criminal Justice Institute resumed training in 1977, it incorporated into its curriculum for all officers some of the material that was prepared as a result of the studies by the Social Conflict Task Force. As a whole, the project documented the overwhelming need for money to involve additional social workers in social conflict work.

Principles of Political Practice

It would have been impossible to establish the police referral system had there not been support inside the police department, as well as considerable support on the outside. Confrontation was avoided. The changing climate in relation to women contributed immensely to this. Despite the mayor's placing low priority on human services, his recognition of the general support the issue attracted, of my expertise in this area, and of my support for his administration kept the task force and the police referral project from being seen as too great a threat. In addition, success was ensured by using existing structures and by keeping small the amount of money initially requested. Sources of funding outside city government were relied on heavily until police acceptance of the idea for a different kind of training had been established. It was also important to the success of the program that the police department benefited through the positive publicity it received for its eagerness to find solutions to help people.

Given the dynamics involved in working with the Detroit Police Department, the mayor, and various elements of city government, a strategy that included picket lines and mass demonstrations would have been counterproductive. However, the strategy used did include a great deal of individual assessment, persuasion, expert information and documentation, lobbying, and the implied pressure of budget power, particularly the power to hold up contracts. It further required the ability to create publicity. The value of coordinating various forces was also demonstrated, because the Detroit Police Department has expert politicians in its ranks. In addition, police department officials were aware that, as a member of the city council, I had the power to call them to a public discussion or hearing. Like most bureaucrats, they dreaded the possibility of adverse publicity. Apparent throughout the long campaign for the referral system was the importance of timing and of keeping the issue alive during the many periods of waiting for favorable conditions and opportunities for progress.

A social worker entering politics cannot overlook the importance of conviction and assertiveness. In the Detroit City Council, where the members are elected simultaneously and at large, there is a natural competition for constituencies and for votes. There is also a tacit agreement that if a member successfully stakes out an issue of special concern and is firm and assertive on it, others will not seriously interfere with his or her leadership on that issue.

Social workers are trained to analyze complexity and see all sides. This, of course, is both a gift and a liability. Recognition of complexities can lead to indecisiveness, whereas police are trained to be decisive, to be in command, and to give short, quick answers. A consequence of these differences is that police and social workers are often intolerant of one another. What is needed is an integration of skills.

Social workers as a whole, and human service agencies as well, need to understand that if they have an idea for a solution to a problem and the professional expertise to carry it out, they must be prepared to fight to get the problem solved in a professional way. Social workers sometimes take the position that the best program will eventually win and so do not fight for proposals that would assure social work services. Too often, non-social workers become attracted by a social work idea and are allowed to take it over for personal gain as it becomes popular. It is important that social workers commit themselves to engage in action for the client's benefit and for equitable treatment to ensure the availability of social work services.

The solution to a problem on a limited scale creates new demands. As the police referral service demonstrated that it worked, the police in Detroit's Sixteenth Police Precinct made more referrals, and satisfied clients and others called the Family Trouble Clinic instead of the police. Those who returned seemed to want longer term counseling. Eventually, the clinic needed increases in workers and money. The workers became so overloaded they had trouble following up on calls and resorted to conducting most counseling via telephone. The solution to one problem thus created new ones, which had to be addressed in new ways. Flexibility is an essential complement to stability of purpose. The scientific method of problem solving—assessing anddefining the problem, analyzing the forces involved, establishing goals and objectives, planning and implementing intervention strategies, and constantly reevaluating process and substance to identify the need for any corrective action—provides a valid model for developing and delivering services to a needy population.

The steps outlined in this article can be translated for use by other social workers elected to office, by the many social workers who work with elected officials, and by community groups who have been successful in selling an issue to an elected official. The problem of domestic violence—its impact on the police as well as on families—was identified and then further defined through the use of a task force to gather information and bring various forces in the community together. At each step in the process, strategies were developed to continue the forward movement of the project. When some forces threatened to sidetrack the project, other routes were found and counterforces developed. Most important, throughout this long process, the goal was kept in focus and the pressure was continued. Perhaps the old maxim that change is slow should be extended to affirm that achieving the goal reached through long and persistent effort is even sweeter.

Notes and References

1. Federal Bureau of Investigation, *Uniform Crime Report* (Washington, D.C.: U.S. Government Printing Office, 1975).

2. Interview with Patrick V. Murphy, executive director, Police Foundation, Washington, D.C., June 1974.

3. Interviews with United States Army social workers, Fifth Army, Frankfurt, Germany, June 1975.

4. *See* Morton Bard and Joseph Zacker, *The Police and Interpersonal Conflict: Third-Party Intervention Approaches* (Washington, D.C.: Police Foundation, 1976).

5. *See* Jeffrey A. Schwartz and Donald A. Liebman, "Domestic Crisis Intervention" (Mountain View, Calif.: Law Enforcement Training and Research Association, Inc., 1971). (Photocopied.)

6. Interview with Betty Terrell, director of professional services, Family Service of the East Bay, Oakland, Calif., September 1974.

Empowerment: A Social Worker's Politics

RUTH W. MESSINGER

13

LIKE so many in our profession, I became a social worker out of a personal mandate toward service. Although trained in casework, I soon found myself in nontraditional settings, jobs that involved a mix of outreach, organizing, and administration. I worked, for example, as a community liaison and administrator in a parent-controlled elementary school and as a planner and field director of a professional training program committed to opening up human service employment for low-income urban adults. At the same time, I became politically active in my local community, working with the antiwar movement, in local day care struggles, against a highway construction project, and for low-income housing.

My decision to run for political office grew most directly out of this community involvement and also out of a desire to merge my social work vocation with my political concerns. I wanted to know whether, as a politician, I could make a difference in the decisions that were affecting my life and the lives of people in my community. I also wanted to know whether, as a social worker committed to the values and ethics of the profession, I could function politically in a way different from the way lawyers, business people, and others do.

I first ran for election to a seat on my local school board in 1975. I won and served two years as the board's secretary and legislative chair. My next campaign, in 1976, was a losing one—by seventy-three votes—for the Democratic nomination for the New York State Assembly. The following year I won a seat on the Council of the City of New York, defeating the Democratic incumbent in the primary by a three-to-two margin. At this writing, I am completing my first four-year term as the city council representative for the West Side of Manhattan. The district lies roughly between Columbus Circle and Columbia University. Its population of 240,000 is heterogeneous and politically liberal. About 25 percent of those living in the district are black and Hispanic; almost every income level, nationality, and religion is represented in the area. The people it has elected to Congress indicate the district's politics: for example, it was formerly represented by Bella Abzug.

The Council of the City of New York has forty-three members. It has the power to pass laws, vote on the mayor's budget proposals, and oversee the work of city agencies. It is not by charter a full-time legislature, and it has often been cited for its lack of independent action and its invisibility. That is changing. About half the council members now devote their full-time energies to the job, and members are learning to demand improved performance of city agencies and to focus public attention on governmental failures and inefficiencies. A group of us within the council constitute a progressive caucus. We often proclaim our disagreements with both our political leadership and the mayor, and we try to act as informed critics of a city administration that does not do enough in behalf of tenants, poor people, public education, or neighborhoods in need of services.

My social work training and experience condition my political activities and objectives in several specific and identifiable ways. First, I invest a good deal of my legislative time and energy in the increasingly less popular human service issues. I am considered by my colleagues to have expertise in these areas. This makes it more acceptable for me to pursue them and usually ensures that I will be listened to when I do. Second, I am sensitive to issues of process in a way different from my colleagues. My skills in listening and observing are sharply honed, and my training is also apparent in my ability to track what is happening in a debate and to intervene in ways that help clarify issues, determine possibilities, and build mutual understanding or agreement.

Third, and most important, there is a theme to the work of my office. The theme is empowerment—the transfer to others of the knowledge and skills they need to do more for themselves and on their own in future struggles. The goal of empowerment is founded on the conviction that the people most affected often know the most about what changes have to be made; that meaningful change will make many people more aware, self-reliant, and organized than they are now; that knowledge and skills social workers and other professionals have are not hard to share; and that we will all benefit if this sharing takes place. This theme is, of course, played out only imperfectly in my political activities. It is not always successful, but it is always visible in my electoral campaigns, in the organization of my office, and in my work with constituents and efforts toward broad social change. The remainder of this article explores this idea of empowerment in relation to my work with my staff and my constituents.

Campaigning and Office Administration

Empowerment, if it is to exist at all, must first exist for the people a politician works with and depends on each day—the aides, advisers, secretaries, receptionists, volunteers, and interns whose enthusiasm and commitment are crucial to most political efforts. Too often in political campaigns and offices the focus is only on winning elections and achieving specific legislative and political goals and not on the means by which such ends are achieved. Overlooked is the toll taken on people who are expected to subordinate themselves and their humanity to getting a task done; their competence and diligence in pursuit of the political objective are rarely acknowledged. It is not only demeaning to others to proceed in this way; it is counterproductive. The rate of burnout is high, and political staffs treated in this way often accumulate anger that leads to work done poorly or not done at all.

How much more rational and productive it is to take the time with staff and volunteers to see what their interests are, to explain to them in some detail the broader effort in which they are involved and how the tasks they have been asked to do fit into

MESSINGER

that effort, and to solicit from them on a regular basis their ideas on how to do those tasks better. Not everyone can or wants to grow or to expand personal involvement and responsibilities in the same way, but everyone must have such opportunities in order to remain happy and productive; empowerment means imparting the skills and structuring the environment that enable such growth to flourish. This is a philosophy that has a place in any office, whether political, social service, or business activities are undertaken.

Volunteers in political efforts who want to know what the work is all about deserve to find out. It is not hard to find ways to do more for interns and volunteers or for lower level employees. Many of the approaches used in my political office can be adopted elsewhere. There are monthly staff meetings, which are different in character from the weekly business meetings. They include everyone and allow time for the sharing of different work projects by each person; they usually feature one of the key staff people speaking on an issue of major importance. Questions are encouraged. Too often in the effort to manage or supervise efficiently, those of us in political office focus our exchanges with staff and interns on our questions about their work or on their questions about our assignments for them. Time needs to be provided, too, for their questions about their work and our work. Why are housing problems handled in another part of the office? What are we doing about the rash of problems with subway doors? Is there a better way to record constituents' concerns? As supervisory staff, we learn and adapt from reflecting on questions like these.

My office also produces a weekly schedule of the events to which I, my paid staff, or others are going and indicates when an interested intern might join us. Obviously, participation in government offers a wealth of such events, but so does social work. I know, because my staff goes to plenty of meetings on, for example, food stamp policy or foster care legislation. There are always human service professionals from social agencies in attendance, but rarely are the interns from their agencies included.

My office has taken gambles in assigning campaign projects, legislative research, performance monitoring, and conference-organizing responsibilities to novice workers. We supervise them closely and have the satisfaction of seeing our investment pay off for us and for them.

Some examples may be helpful here. Campaign volunteers conducted a telephone poll. An office intern organized a conference on how to save one of the city's parks, another did research on corporate ownership of single-room-occupancy hotels, and a third drafted new proposals for housing code enforcement. Interns are of particular help in doing on-site monitoring of city services. How many cars does a tow truck remove and from where? Does it obey traffic rules? Are litter baskets distributed evenly throughout a neighborhood, or are there fewer on those streets considered most dirty? What really happens to an individual who applies for food stamps or calls a police emergency number or enters a voluntary hospital without insurance coverage? Interns can follow, observe, interview, count, and check out the process.

My professional and political effectiveness increases tremendously when I can give such assignments to volunteers and interns, and those who have the work experiences benefit, too. They remain interested in doing similar work in the future; they are more likely to consider politics or government as a career than they would be if their assignments had been narrower and less meaningful. They can also pass on their skills to others.

Empowerment of Constituents

I try to apply the same principles of process and empowerment in my work with constituents. Many people, of course, telephone or visit any politician because they need something done. When it is efficient, practical, and reasonable to oblige such requests, I or my staff do so. We give them an address, make a phone call, track down a check, do whatever is necessary, but we try, always, to notify the people we assist about whom we are calling, what the most useful telephone number is, how they might do the same thing for themselves, and what to do if they do not get help.

Sometimes, too, it is necessary for my staff to intervene to rescue individuals from becoming victims of the system. We recognize that it takes a mass effort by many people to make systems work better, but we do not make this point on every occasion or turn every problem with the bureaucracy into a cause. Nevertheless, we look for patterns in this work with constituents and for areas in which it is of mutual advantage to organize a lobbying and advocacy force rather than just to give help.

It may be useful to look at two examples of our activities to involve interested constituents in doing more to help themselves, others similarly situated, and us. Tenants' problems can be handled in several different ways. My staff can take action on an individual tenant's problem with a landlord—a leaky roof, a possible rent overcharge, or harassment—and we can notify the tenant of how to register a complaint or file for an adjustment the next time. However, we can be even more helpful if we can find out to what extent the individual tenant's problems are endemic to the building. Often the tenant we speak to knows this or is willing to help us find out. The problem may have been a topic of discussion in the elevator or lobby for some months, or there may already be a tenants' association that the tenant we speak to can arrange to have us address. Perhaps the tenant is willing to work with us to set up both a meeting and an association. It is in our interest to talk the problems of the building over with a group of tenants and to structure for them not only what we can do to help, but what kind of help we need from them. We expect a tenants' association, for example, to circulate a questionnaire to every tenant to find out how many sinks do not work, who else has not received a lease, and what the most common building problems are. When the results are in, we meet with the tenants again. We apply pressure for them in crisis areas, but we also educate them about how they can work together effectively in their own interest. This may involve knowing whom to call or to write, or it may mean bringing in an attorney or engineer for technical assistance.

Sometimes in these discussions tenants express interest in the passage of legislation that would change the situation in which they find themselves. In such cases, we not only explain the content of the legislation but give people a reasonably accurate assessment of its chances for passage and tell them to whom to write to move the legislation along. My staff has been known to go to tenants' meetings with a ream of paper and lots of blank envelopes.

The Service Watch program operated out of my office is an example of how constituents can assume significant independent responsibility to work in behalf of their communities without either reporting regularly to my office or joining a local organization. At one point, this program was managed by a social work graduate student who was placed in my office for fieldwork.

A flier advertising Service Watch asks for people who want to help monitor city services. Individuals who respond to the flier are given a Service Watch packet and invited to come to an introductory meeting if they wish. The packet lists key phone numbers in the city bureaucracy for reporting anything from abandoned cars to broken water mains. The service monitors are also given specific instructions about what to say and how to keep a record of their conversations. They keep track of what works and what does not, and, depending on their resourcefulness and determination—that is, on the degree of their empowerment—they either follow up themselves or ask us to intervene.

My staff and I are still experimenting with this program and trying to determine how it can be expanded, what supervision it needs, whether occasional meetings are desirable, and what should be covered at those meetings. At some meetings, we have discussed major service delivery problems and developed ways to monitor them better; at others, we have shared information with Service Watchers about tenants' rights, city budget procedures, and other matters of general interest.

The benefits of this program are numerous. In buildings and on blocks that are watched by a constituent, my staff and I know more and find out about it more systematically than we would otherwise. This means that these segments of the community get more service. City agencies come to understand that there is follow-up on our calls from these areas and that it is to their advantage to do the work they promise. The magic list of telephone numbers, at least some of which work well, gets around, usually to other people who will use it responsibly.

Change Agents

Empowerment also makes an important contribution to the building of coalitions for legislative, policy, or more substantial social change. Many of the efforts of my office in this regard are quite traditional. In challenging a bill put forward by the city administration or arguing for a new amendment to the city code, legislators naturally want friends and do what they can to get them— talk to colleagues, arrange meetings for them with advocates of our point of view, and work with well-known lobbying groups (unions, staff of social service programs, the National Association of Social Workers, and so on), asking them to write and advising them about what needs to be said and when.

There are, however, significant differences in how a legislator concerned with empowerment proceeds in all this. My staff and I educate groups about why their item may proceed through the legislature in ways different from what they expect. We try to build coalitions around issues that previously attracted none. For example, we help strengthen forces opposed to the building of a highway by involving housing groups in their struggle, or we bring together several groups with an interest in opposing city tax exemption and abatement policies that limit the availability of city revenue.

I also believe that those who are the victims of current policies should be involved in the policy development process, and my staff and I work with them to make this possible. This means rejecting the standard model under which they are allowed to mass on the steps or wave banners at the right moment but are kept at bay by even the elected officials who support them most closely.

This scenario is worth examining in detail. The elected official whose recorded public statements are most sympathetic to, for example, the plight of tenants will in all likelihood be sought out by tenants. If the official feels that the demands of these tenants are worth holding firm for, there is no problem in terms of public statement and image. There may be a problem, however, convincing the rest of the legislative body, or there may not seem to be any chance of passage for the relevant legislation. In this kind of situation, the elected official, convinced that the best hope is a legislative compromise, might tell tenants, "I like what you are saying but don't know what I can do for you with the other members of the council. I'll try . . . ." The legislator then leaves the tenants and goes off to negotiate, maybe well or maybe badly; no one from the tenant group will ever know. The legislator simply comes back and says, "Here's the bill we will approve; it's the best I could do for you."

The tenants may be satisfied or unhappy. Certainly, though, they do not know how well they have been served or if all their arguments were made, and they do not understand any more about the legislative process or the thinking that motivates the people who do not support them. Further, they may be confused about why the legislator who expressed agreement with their position is now voting for something much less satisfactory. Even lobbying groups that have frequently experienced such disappointments are at a loss as to how to keep a check on how well their supposed legislative supporters are serving them.

My criticism of this process is that it keeps constituents in the dark, allows legislators to use a mechanism that makes them less than fully accountable, and lets them do much of their negotiating in behalf of the group behind closed doors. The constituents are not truly educated about the processes of government; they are not empowered to take more responsibility on their own shoulders in the future. Moreover, legislators who use this approach shield their colleagues from the full brunt of the pressure that might convince them to change their positions.

Empowerment requires a different process. Time needs to be spent educating strong lobbying groups about what their chances are and why and advising them how they might better their odds. Lobbies cannot, of course, be made to do anything they do not want to, but they can be given options to consider. Options might include organizing for additional public support in the district of key legislators or broadening the objective to draw the support of other groups that would be logical allies. They would almost certainly include direct lobbying of the group of wavering or unfriendly legislators. The exercise of such options often depends on information the legislator is in a better position to know than is the community or group concerned about a particular issue.

TASK FORCE ON WELFARE

Working out of a commitment to educate and empower constituents, my staff and I have helped a number of groups with special issues take their concerns further and become more fully involved in the process of government. Our best examples to date of this approach involve two task forces, each serving a different purpose and playing a different role. The first was the Task Force on Welfare Issues, which was set up out of my office, largely by me and the leading welfare rights organization in New York City. The task force helped my office with issues over which the city council has oversight authority, such as brutality by the representatives of institutions or agencies, poor administrative practices, and inappropriate rejections of claims in welfare centers. It also collected information for public hearings and used my minor clout as an elected official to get certain kinds of press coverage.

In addition, the task force's members produced a pamphlet

making the case for a welfare grant increase. By the time the pamphlet went into final production, all its authors had developed a sophisticated sense of the facts (which many of them began with) and a sophisticated sense of what would best convince their readers to be concerned. The pamphlet was used as a lobbying device with the state legislature, particularly during a demonstration of two thousand welfare recipients organized by the welfare rights groups involved in the task force. The pamphlet was also broadly distributed as an educational piece to citizens' groups, church and labor organizations, and others. It has been brought by me and my staff into health, housing, and environmental meetings, reaching a public that might not otherwise have even thought about the issue. Its sale in quantity through my office has helped raise funds for welfare organizing.

TASK FORCE ON PROPERTY

The Task Force on City Owned Property has had a full and rich life as a coalition that secured a special status in relation to the city administration. Formed at a time when a new administration was taking office in the city and a flood of buildings were being taken over by the city, the task force began as a small coalition of elected officials and housing and community organizations. It took advantage of the moment provided by the arrival of a fresh administration and drafted a policy paper with thirty pages of suggestions—both philosophic and specific—of what should be done. Because of the timing, because of the substantive content of the policy paper, and because the paper was presented to the administration with the support of several council members involved in housing issues, it was well received. The new commissioner responsible for housing recognized the value of working with this group. Not only were some of their suggestions adopted immediately, even with some credit given to the group in the press release of the commissioner's agency, but a schedule was worked out for regular meetings between the task force and the deputy commissioner to consult on program policy and legislation. The task force thus earned a role inside as well as outside the door.

This relationship has not, of course, proceeded smoothly. As a result of the existence of the task force and the pressure its members have mounted, more has gotten done and better policies adopted than would have otherwise been the case. Task force members understand this and take credit for it but do not stop their dogged pursuit of their goals, even those goals that are not consistent with the goals and policies of the administration. Because they understand government, they are vigilant and move quickly when they sense something is going on that they do not like. They can easily mobilize a demonstration. They have acquired a status and independence that permit them even to criticize the elected officials who helped them get started, without destroying the relationship they have and need with these officials. The Task Force on City Owned Property remains a major force for the city council and the administration to reckon with, even when they wish it would go away.

Although I had a central role in the formation of the task force, even its relationship with me has changed and evolved over time. The group has grown, weathered some internal policy differences, and taken on an independent existence. The task force has a nonprofit status and conducts business separately from my office. I still help to bring members in on key legislative discussions, including some with council members most philosophically opposed to the positions taken by the task force. Such council members listen longer and better to tenants who survive with the city as landlord and can support their arguments with facts than they would to me. The members of the task force know what legislative and governmental negotiation is all about. They understand that although they can often do more for their position by being uncompromising and by rejecting half-loaf solutions and even demonstrating against them, I can sometimes do more for the same position by bargaining with my colleagues or the administration. Well before any issue is voted on or decided, task force members know whether I think their position is correct, whether I am determined to stand with them even if we lose, and whether I feel that concessions are being offered that ought to be accepted. There have been bills on which we made too little progress for me to change my vote and bills on which I voted to secure some amendments, tried to make further changes, and then supported the legislation as worth the gamble.

The sophisticated ability of the task force's members to understand these processes and play these roles is impressive. They have become empowered in the legislative and governmental process. They represent the fullest development to date in my work of empowering others to play their own roles in government and in social change.

Politics and the Profession

Much of the profession and practice of social work is political in nature or occurs in a political context. What programs and services exist, who they are available to, and how they are funded are decided, at least in part, in the governmental arena, and anything decided in that sphere is affected by politics. Social workers and the populations they serve are influenced by matters as diverse as professional licensing, reimbursement statutes, levels of funding, the quality of the staffing in public agencies, regulations governing income maintenance and social service programs, and the relationships between public and voluntary service programs.

Because the context of social work is political in so many ways, it would benefit us and our practice if our behavior were political too. We are among the citizenry who ought to be in there slugging, professionally and personally, to influence regulation, law, policy, and budget as they affect us and our clients. We have an expertise that is needed in the halls of government on both sides of the desk: we should run for office, seek appointment to appropriate government positions, appear as lobbyists, urge our professional and agency associations to lobby, be active in our communities, and vote—drawing, in all these activities, on our knowledge, our skill, and our professional and personal ethics.

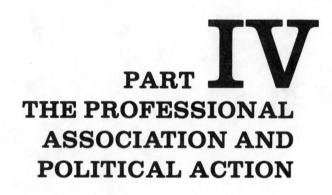

PART **IV**
THE PROFESSIONAL
ASSOCIATION AND
POLITICAL ACTION

Establishing ELAN
in a State
Chapter

DAVID J. DEMPSEY

14

THE National Association of Social Workers (NASW) began developing an Educational Legislation Action Network (ELAN) in late 1969 "to supplement and strengthen the activities of the Washington office of NASW."[1] The basic concept was to design a structure that, through establishing two-way communications between NASW's office in Washington, D.C., and the local chapters, would use the special knowledge of NASW members to influence members of Congress and advance human service policies and programs. ELAN would thus be a mechanism for constituent federal lobbying by NASW's national office. It was also conceived as a means for building coalitions through informing and mobilizing both social workers and their natural allies, such as lay persons on local social agency boards, community leaders, non–social work providers, and consumers of social services.

ELAN's tightly knit communication system came to be based on a spirit of cooperation that exists among the members, leaders, and coordinators in every state and that extends to the national legislative staff. The communication system is used to express to congressional and other legislative leaders the various needs and interests of the social work profession and its clients.[2] The pattern of communications outlined in ELAN's design is elaborate. A system of state coordinators and district leaders are the backbone of the organization. Members can develop an idea or legislative issue and process it up through the system, often through a state-level group organized as a social policy committee; or information, analyses, evaluations, and warning alerts can flow from the national ELAN office to the state ELANs. Communications from national ELAN to state ELANs are usually written, but events can necessitate the use of the telephone. States are encouraged to develop telephone trees for quick communication with constituent members. ELAN's members are expected to address members of Congress in various ways—through personal contacts, written communications, and phone calls.

The purpose of this article is to outline the organizational steps involved in establishing a state chapter of ELAN. Such an objective necessarily leads to a consideration of such other points as ELAN's functioning, its legislative and organizational relationships, and the problems likely to arise in organizing a network. Although the article presents this information in the context of the author's experience in developing ELAN in the state of Washington, readers should not assume that adherence to what is outlined here will ensure success. What was learned in organizing Washington State's ELAN has general applicability elsewhere, but in organizing there are always differences and exceptions. Nor should readers assume that all that is discussed or proposed in this article has been either totally accomplished or consistently successful in Washington State.

Because the experience in structuring ELAN in the state of Washington is so much a part of the ideas and recommendations set forth in this article, it will be useful to summarize the historical developments and political context in Washington State before attempting to extract any general principles from that experience. The Washington State Chapter of NASW was created in 1976 through the merger of five separate, geographically distinct local chapters. This consolidation, like that of other state chapters, was carried out in response to a mandate by NASW's 1975 Delegate Assembly that directed the reorganization into state chapters of what were then 172 local chapters. The Washington State Chapter's first two years involved establishing a central financial, budgeting, and programming process, hiring staff, and opening an office. Little attention was paid to ELAN until the early spring of

DEMPSEY

1978, when interest was stimulated by questions regarding ELAN's fiscal and organizational needs as budgetary recommendations were being prepared for the annual meeting of the state chapter's board in June. There was also interest in defining ELAN's scope, function, and capability because chapter members were exploring the possibility of establishing a state political action committee modeled after NASW's Political Action for Candidate Election (PACE), and they wanted to avoid duplicating efforts or functions undertaken by ELAN. Chapter members also wanted to know ELAN's actual condition so that they could realistically judge the chapter's capacity to mobilize for legislative lobbying.

It was a distinct shock to learn that the state's legislative action network was a paper tiger. On paper it existed in Seattle-King County and in a few other legislative districts scattered throughout the state. In actuality, a miniscule and primitive apparatus existed in only about half of Seattle-King County's eighteen legislative districts; not even a single contact person could be identified in the remaining legislative districts of the county. ELAN was thus barely alive in the chapter's most populous county and basically existed nowhere else in the state.

This was the beginning of the slow and arduous development of a legislative action network that is still in process; an effective network has not yet been fully established. In the attempt to achieve an effective network, chapter members, the author included, have made almost every mistake possible, uncovered more flaws, gaps, and deficiencies in the organization than could have been imagined, and frequently had the wrong people in important places and important people in the wrong places.

Conceptual Base

Despite this catalog of horrors, members of the Washington State Chapter learned many things about establishing a network that can be shared. A most important lesson was that an organization trying to develop an influential political mechanism must have clear conceptions of what is meant by such terms as "power," "politics," and "impact." The most appealing and sensible definitions of the first two terms were found in the work of the political scientist Dolbeare, who writes that "power denotes a capability in people, each of whom possesses certain resources (money, talent, reputation, institutional position and so forth) that may affect the thoughts and actions of others in various ways."[3] Because NASW is a membership organization, chapter members also kept in mind Alinsky's contention that power derives from two main sources— money and people.[4] Politics to Dolbeare "is a system of relationships in which power is employed consciously and unconsciously (in the sense that some anticipate the preferences of others whom they view as more powerful than they) to gain ends and to condition the behavior of others in ways deemed desirable."[5]

These definitions reveal the essence of politics as a system of relationships in which power is exerted. This simple but concrete definition contributes to the understanding that politics is the use of power to gain ends and is not a particular kind of political activity, such as campaigning or voting or running for office or lobbying. This valuable perspective offers a quick and accurate measure of the utility and effectiveness of political behavior. Money may be the mother's milk of politics, but people are the source of power in any state chapter's ELAN.

"Impact" is an important term because the network's purpose is to mobilize and deliver the impact of a state chapter's membership. Instead of defining the term, whose meaning is related to that of "power," it is more useful to borrow from another organization a succinct description of how an impact occurs. Schut, the highly respected lobbyist for Washington State's senior citizens' lobby, teaches that impact on the political decision-making process occurs when (1) it comes from organized activity, (2) it is done by a specific group, (3) it is done for a specific purpose, (4) it is aimed at a specific target, and (5) it is done at the appropriate time.[6] It is easier to recognize a desired impact than to achieve it. Nevertheless, knowing how an impact takes place is helpful in sorting out and organizing the steps that will create one.

Identifying and Organizing Resources

After several notable failures, the organization of Washington State's ELAN proceeded differently in a fundamental and significant way from the approach conceived by NASW's national office in Washington, D.C. Whereas ELAN is basically a creation of the national office—a classic attempt at organizing from the top down—the decision in Washington State in the spring of 1978 was to begin anew in developing ELAN from the ground up and to organize members by state legislative districts instead of by federal congressional districts. There were several reasons for this decision: (1) state legislative districts are closer and more familiar to chapter members and are consequently less threatening, (2) legislative districts are more congruent with communities and clusters of members, (3) the chapter's power would grow more naturally out of a statewide legislative network, and (4) because each congressional district in Washington State is composed of seven legislative districts, organizing the seven legislative districts would yield a fully organized congressional district.

What seems to be a deliberate contravention of NASW's national design was actually a state chapter's pragmatic decision to create an effective legislative network involving its members directly in, first, the state legislative process and then, less directly, in the federal lobbying network. Members are easier to organize around something familiar and are more susceptible to being influenced by it. The usefulness of this approach was the state chapter's most valuable insight.

Several resources are needed to organize the membership into an effective network. The most important are members, a central staff, training, accurate and current membership lists, intelligent direction and focus, a telephone tree, realistic budget allocations, a sense of the activities appropriate for a network, and time to organize these components into a coherent whole.

Of course, people are the most important resource. All sorts of people need to be involved. Basic network members are needed as well as district coordinators; committee, board, and staff members; and outside people, such as national consultants or other experts in particular areas who can provide training. People are thus the basic ingredient, the building block of a successful legislative network.

A central staff is also vital in establishing a successful network. Central staff can be paid or volunteers, or the role of a central staff can be performed by a committee or the board of directors. This role is a necessary one because it provides intelligent direction and focus and involves the making of the decisions a coordinated effort requires. Central staff functions in NASW's Washington State Chapter are handled by the chapter's hired professionals. Initially, hired staff may provide almost all the direction, focus, and decision making, but as the ELAN organization begins to develop, district coordinators and committees emerge that begin meeting and helping to influence both the direction and the decision making. Eventually, as the coordinators assume command of the ELAN apparatus through their committees, staff can retreat to perform the mechanical functions that assist the total network.

The most valuable mechanical functions that office staff can carry out for a legislative network are serving as a central point for planning, organizing, and communicating; providing accurate and current membership lists; maintaining up-to-date files for legislative districts; and performing reliable secretarial, clerical, and mailing services. The performance of these functions enhances the network's effectiveness. The importance of some functions is self-evident; others bear more explanation, such as the maintenance of membership lists and legislative district files.

Every month the national office furnishes each state chapter with an alphabetical list of the chapter's current members and an alphabetical list of all members in each of the chapter's different local branches. The lists reflect various membership changes, such as new members, resignations, people who have moved in and out of the state, deaths, terminations, and name and address changes. These changes are recorded on the membership lists as well as on four-by-six index cards. NASW annually provides each chapter with a set of index cards of the entire membership in the state as of a particular date. Such membership lists are essential to ELAN's functioning because they show the legislative districts in which a chapter's membership lives.

Legislative District Files

Membership lists can be used to create the single most valuable tool in building a statewide network: a legislative district file. The Washington State Chapter developed such a file by duplicating the index cards of the membership made available by the national office. One set of index cards was maintained alphabetically as a master file; the duplicate set was filed by state legislative district and then filed alphabetically. Because in Washington State seven legislative districts make up a congressional district, filing the members by state legislative districts also created a congressional district file. For example, the state's First Congressional District consists of the First, Thirty-second, Thirty-sixth, Forty-third, Forty-fourth, Forty-sixth, and Forty-eighth legislative districts. The master file is cross-referenced so that one can look up Mary Doe, see the notation "36," and know that her duplicate card can be found alphabetically within the cards belonging to the Thirty-sixth State Legislative District, which is also a part of the First Congressional District.

Developing a legislative district file is an immense but worthwhile task. Over a period of between six and eight months, a combination of volunteers and hired staff organized Washington State's list of over fourteen hundred members. The data in this kind of file are not only valuable for establishing ELAN but are also useful in other organizational and political efforts undertaken by a chapter because they provide accurate information about which districts have many or few members and which have none. ELAN can thus know exactly what strength in numbers might be available to the chapter in particular efforts. Information of this sort helps district leaders and coordinators recruit precisely and efficiently, which in turn gives members the feeling that the state chapter is mobilizing and organizing in a purposeful way.

Membership lists and legislative district files together provide the means by which a chapter can develop a telephone tree. Telephone trees are meant to facilitate quick communication through the network. They are designed so that one person makes a certain number of phone calls to others who do likewise until the whole network has received the message at hand. Usually, an ELAN telephone tree is used to urge chapter network members to communicate with their legislators on a particular issue. The members' communication with legislators may be by letter, postcard, telegram, or mailgram, by telephone, or, in Washington State, through a toll-free public opinion hot line that the state operates during the legislative session. A telephone tree's organization requires knowledge of local conditions, but some general tips include organizing the phone tree so as to avoid toll charges, letting friends talk to friends whenever possible, and having one caller responsible for no more than five other people.

The Washington State senior citizens' lobby notes four benefits of a telephone tree: (1) it encourages two-way communication between a legislator and his or her constituents, (2) it creates a feedback and monitoring mechanism, (3) it allows for selectively calling only those legislators targeted and can also be used to contact other public officials, and (4) it can be useful for functions other than political action, such as calling meetings and passing information.[7]

Direction of Activities

As noted earlier, two other important resources of an effective network are (1) intelligence in establishing a direction and focus and (2) a sense of appropriate network activities. The two are more related at certain points than at others, but some comments about direction and some discussion of appropriate activities will clarify the differences.

Intelligence in direction and focus means clear, purposeful activity by those working to establish a network. Direction and focus may initially come from various sources: it may shift back and forth between staff and coordinators, or between the chapter's board and staff, or among other constituents of the organization. This leadership and guidance must be provided, or else the grueling, tedious organizing activities of developing membership lists, legislative district files, and telephone trees will be seen as empty, meaningless, and, worse, unnecessary. As the network becomes established and its routines become secure, intelligent direction and focus should come from three different but coordinated sources: the ELAN committee's coordinators and staff and the state chapter's board of directors.

Enumerating a list of appropriate activities for a state ELAN is risky because readers will perceive tasks that were missed in Washington State. However, besides developing lists, files, and telephone trees, important activities included communicating with legislators and chapter members about issues, holding forums and workshops on certain issues, having training meetings for coordinators to standardize operations, recruiting new network members, deciding on network priorities, allocating money for ELAN's program, and finding ways to mesh these functions and components.

Time should be viewed as a resource because events occur in time. Because organized people are better able to influence events than unorganized people are, time spent organizing enhances the precious resource that people represent. "Time" can also mean timing or timeliness, which is a most important ingredient in using the telephone tree. Alinsky's point that "Timing is to tactics what it is to everything in life—the difference between success and failure" applies with special force to legislative lobbying by constituents.[8]

People are more accustomed to viewing money as a resource. ELAN needs money for phone trees, printing, mailings, coordinators' travel, training, workshops, and recruitment programs. There should also be some money allocated to buy the tickets that partisan legislative caucuses use to raise funds and maintain themselves.

One Way to Begin

When a chapter begins to organize ELAN, it may learn, as organizers did in the state of Washington, that there are certain advantages to beginning in the larger metropolitan areas and working from there. A chapter's membership units are usually better developed in these areas, although this is not always true.

Washington is a medium-sized state of 3.5 million people and seven congressional districts. Organizing for ELAN began in the state legislative districts in the major cities, starting with Seattle-King County and its eighteen districts, then moving into the Tacoma-Pierce County area with its seven districts. Next came metropolitan Spokane on the eastern side of the state, which included five districts. Finally, efforts were mounted in the medium-sized areas where small groups of chapter members met regularly—Everett, Bellingham, Vancouver, and Olympia.

Organizing in this fashion allowed ELAN to capitalize on strengths and get the bare bones of a network started. It also graphically revealed both organizational flaws in the chapter and political deficiencies in the chapter's ability to influence the legislature.

A drawback to this method of organizing a state ELAN is that power in state legislatures is often not distributed just to legislators from the populous regions. Indeed, legislators repeatedly reelected from rural areas are often powerful. Consequently, beginning to organize in populous centers might bring forth a nascent state chapter ELAN whose greatest impact misses the legislature's most powerful members. A related concern is that rural communities are often dominated by different political parties than urban areas are. Both are points to remember, but they are not powerful enough, alone or together, to negate the advantages of organizing the most populous areas in a state first.

As the districts in populous cities become organized, the need for leaders and coordinators develops. In Washington State, leadership and coordinating responsibilities initially corresponded to the territories of the local branches of the state chapter of NASW. This was efficient, but it is now evident that leadership and coordinative responsibilities must correspond geographically to the state's seven congressional districts if ELAN's purposes are to be achieved. There are at least two other reasons for shifting to organization by congressional district instead of maintaining correspondence with the local NASW units: (1) ELAN is a creature of the chapter and is intended to be a statewide mechanism under the direction of the chapter's board, and (2) local units of NASW are "established for the purpose of representing members in the decision-making processes of the state chapter," which is different from the function of a political action network.[9]

ELAN's principal relationship, of course, is to the board of directors of the state chapter, which serves as a political arm for lobbying. The board is ELAN's creator, director, informer, and evaluator; it establishes the network's priorities. ELAN also participates in several other relationships that need to be considered. For example, a relationship exists between ELAN and the state legislature. For many chapter members and some legislators, the only contact each has with the other is through ELAN.

The relationship between ELAN and Congress was discussed earlier in this article, as was the relationship between any state's ELAN and the national ELAN office. Relations between a state ELAN and the national ELAN operation have become cloudier and more ambiguous with the evolution of state chapters. Better lines of communication and a more identifiable national ELAN center are needed.

ELAN can also be affected by extraorganizational relationships. For different reasons, the Washington State Chapter is a member of a reform coalition advocating a graduated state income tax and also the dominant member of a coalition seeking a licensing law for social workers. The state board assigned both issues high priority, but both require extensive outside coordination for effective action.

Difficult Local Problems

A difficult and still unresolved problem in Washington State is how the ELAN network is activated. The problem contains several difficult considerations: Who is vested with authority to trigger the network? Should there be a backup or fail-safe mechanism? What decisions can and should be made in advance by the board and the ELAN committee? Should there be a defined, hierarchical chain of command, or should authority over the network be delegated to a specific group that would be expected to work out the details? This seemingly mechanical problem is difficult in theoretical consideration; it is greatly exacerbated under the pressures of time and distance and in the absence of traditional chapter authority figures such as the president or staff. A further complication is added if the chapter has hired a professional lobbyist to advance its legislative objective.

A related problem concerns deciding precisely which issues will get ELAN's attention. A chapter may have a list of eight or ten important issues, but the network, particularly the telephone tree, can handle no more than two or three issues in a given period. The decisions about priorities are similar to those concerning who can activate the network, in that pressures of time cause confusing and distorted messages to be communicated, with disheartening results.

The scheduling of legislative sessions in Washington State also poses problems. The state's constitution requires only one sixty-day legislative session biennially. There can be special or extraordinary sessions, but only when called by the governor. Thus, an element of predictability is missing that might otherwise facilitate the network's planning and organizing. If there is no special session, how can the network be kept together? For example, the state's legislature was in regular and special session the first six months of 1977, but not in session during 1978. This is a remediable problem, however. After all, ELAN's primary focus is Congress, and its activity is always needed.

Another troubling question has been how to share the master membership list and legislative district files with the coordinators located throughout the state. Both files are kept in the chapter office for maintenance, security, and administrative reasons. Keeping the coordinators informed of the frequent membership changes is difficult, and an efficient, reliable, and inexpensive system for getting information to them has yet to be found.

Making ELAN Effective

The careful meshing of all ELAN's components and elements will make the network effective, but several other measures can be taken to strengthen the network's impact on legislators. One way to increase its impact is through PACE and other electoral activity that the chapter can generate in many legislative districts. Electoral activity may include traditional campaign practices, such as telephoning, ringing doorbells, fund raising, working on mailings, canvassing, and recruiting other volunteers to work for candidates. Issue questionnaires and endorsement procedures for candidates are also valuable in establishing relationships with legislators.

Training also increases ELAN's effectiveness. Coordinators and members both benefit from training, which can help them identify issues, organize meetings with legislators, become familiar with legislative processes, use legislative resources, and understand the state's political environment and specifics of the network's operation, including when to write or call, how to do both, and how to do follow-up. A frequently unnoticed benefit of training is that it involves members in ELAN's activities before the heat of an actual political struggle and gives them a greater acquaintance with and confidence in the whole operation later.

Other useful year-round activities include community legislative forums, coffee meetings with legislators in members' homes, and the distribution to legislators of information that is solidly related to issues and that has been developed through chapter task forces or allied interest groups. It is useful to search the boards of directors of community or private social welfare agencies to learn which legislators may be serving on them. These activities are all aimed at developing good personal contacts with legislators.

Differences between ELAN and PACE

Confusion exists about the differences between ELAN and PACE. Some cannot discern a difference, and others ascribe the functions of ELAN to PACE and vice versa. There are conceptual, organizational, operational, and behavioral differences between the two organizations. ELAN is essentially a network for legislative lobbying, whereas PACE is a political action committee, whose purpose is to influence voters. PACE is usually a legally constituted, registered entity that can endorse candidates, raise and contribute money, and promote political education and lawful political actions among its members.

ELAN is an integral part of a state chapter. PACE has its own membership and is often separate from the state chapter, although it is always controlled by the chapter. PACE is usually made a separate organization to gain advantages unavailable to tax-exempt groups such as NASW and also to comply with election laws requiring certain political and fiscal accountability of organizations that support candidates and contribute to campaigns. PACE's major responsibility is to endorse and to try to elect candidates from any party. ELAN's responsibility is to establish effective working relationships with all legislators regardless of party.

It is prudent to keep ELAN and PACE separate operationally as well as organizationally. Whenever possible, the same person should not carry similar responsibilities in both organizations. This not only increases the involvement of members but also avoids confusion, frustration, overwork, failure, and dropping out. Obviously, however, there is a definite relationship between PACE and ELAN. PACE is the major instrument ensuring that ELAN will have responsive legislators to work with. ELAN can often provide PACE with crucial, time-saving information about legislators, issues, legislative districts, and the like.

Nationwide Political Capability

Although ELAN has existed nationally for a decade, chapters have only recently started the necessary and strenuous work of making the network a reality. The impetus comes mainly from two sources: first, from state chapters, only recently organized themselves, with concentrated resources and permanent staff; second, from NASW's leadership and membership, who recognize the professional association's immediate need to develop an effective political capability.

Washington State's experience in organizing ELAN provides an example of how others might proceed. Many difficulties will be encountered, and the organizing will take time and effort. The relationships and management problems are more complicated in reality than they are in the abstract, but the means are available to accomplish the end.

In a 1972 journal article, Mahaffey wrote that "Political power develops when people are organized, united, and active. Social work organizations should organize their members and be able to mobilize them as necessary" (see the chapter "Lobbying and Social Work," p. 69). ELAN is mobilization for one political purpose, PACE another. NASW's task is the organization of both to develop fully social workers' political power.

Notes and References

1. "ELAN Handbook" (Washington, D.C.: National Association of Social Workers, undated), p. 1. (Mimeographed.)

2. Ibid., pp. 1-4.

3. Kenneth M.. Dolbeare, *Political Change in the United States: A Framework for Analysis* (New York: McGraw-Hill Book Co., 1974), p. 4.

4. Saul D. Alinsky, *Rules for Radicals* (New York: Random House, 1971), p. 127.

5. Dolbeare, op. cit., p. 4.

6. Norm Schut, untitled and unpublished material used in training lobbyists for senior citizens' groups, Seattle, Washington, 1975.

7. Ibid.

8. Alinsky, op. cit., p. 158

9. "Chapter Bylaws" (Seattle, Wash.: Washington State Chapter of the National Association of Social Workers, 1976), Article X, B. 1(a).

A State Chapter's Comprehensive Political Program

HARVEY A. ABRAMS
SHELDON GOLDSTEIN

15

NEARLY twenty-five hundred years ago, Phocion stated that "The good have no need of an advocate." One doubts that this was true in his time; it is certainly untrue now. When a state expects a mother and her three children to exist on $190 a month under Aid to Families with Dependent Children (AFDC), when in one Florida county the infant mortality rate surpasses that in Pakistan, when migrant workers must do the harshest work for the least rewards, the need for the advocate's role in social work is clear.

Advocacy is not new in social work. The early works of Addams describe numerous instances of advocacy in behalf of clients; she clearly conceived advocacy as a central social work role.[1] Briar described the early caseworker as the "client's support-er, his advisor, his champion, and, if need be, his representative in his dealings with the court, the police, the social agency, and other organizations that affect his well-being."[2] Recent commentators have often called attention to political aspects of advocacy. According to Brager,

> the worker as advocate identifies with the plight of the disadvan-taged. He sees as his primary responsibility the tough-minded and partisan representation of their interests, and this supersedes

his fealty to others. This role inevitably requires that the practitioner function as a political tactician.[3]

Although this cloak of social responsibility is an ill-fitting one for many social workers, action to influence social conditions is deeply rooted in fundamental values of the profession. The profession's Code of Ethics enjoins the social worker to "advocate changes in policy and legislation to improve social conditions and to promote social justice."[4] This attention to broad social conditions has traditionally meant advocacy, but as government assumed an increasingly dominant role in the formation of social policy, advocacy came to require sophisticated interventions aimed at influencing government policies. These interventions have included lobbying and the complex policy-level actions described by Specht—identifying social problems, gathering and analyzing data, developing policy goals, building public support for wise policies, and writing corrective legislation.[5]

The increasing complexity of government requires increasingly complex interventions. The lobbyist's efforts, for example, must often extend beyond the legislature and into the executive branch, which presides over the government agencies responsible for interpreting and implementing the programs mandated by the legislature. Only with such oversight advocacy can the lobbyist make sure that legislative intent is carried out.

The complexities of this country's system of government are such that it can only be understood if it is viewed holistically. A corollary of this observation is that only those groups willing to confront that complexity and undertake comprehensive programs of lobbying and political action consistently achieve the government policies they seek. This view is now widely accepted among legislators, the press, the private sector lobbies of business and industry, and lobbies representing public interest groups and professional organizations, such as the National Association of Social Workers (NASW).[6]

It was against this backdrop of professional responsibility and political reality that NASW, in 1976, formed its political action committee—Political Action for Candidate Election (PACE)—and that Florida NASW subsequently elected to establish its own PACE chapter as an important element in a comprehensive program to influence social policy. Florida's NASW had concluded that only such a systematic, holistic approach could avoid Alinsky's criticism that the purpose of many social service agencies was

ABRAMS and GOLDSTEIN

to get their clients to live in hell and like it.[7]

The purpose of this article is to describe the program undertaken by the Florida Chapter of NASW to influence social policy at the state level. This case study is intended to provide data for evaluating and planning the political activities of other NASW state chapters.

Comprehensive Program

Florida's NASW chapter developed a comprehensive, five-part program to strengthen its efforts to obtain effective social policy legislation. First, the chapter's board develops a set of legislative goals each year. Second, the chapter lobbies to achieve these legislative goals. The third and fourth forms of activity help create the two most essential resources for the legislative program—responsive legislators and informed and active social workers. A political action committee helps elect lawmakers favorable to NASW goals, and an organized program educates and motivates members in local social work units to support the lobbying and the political action committee. The fifth part of the program, which involves the oversight and monitoring of laws that have been enacted and that are in the process of being implemented, is the primary subject of the chapter "Monitoring the Bureaucracy: An Extension of Legislative Lobbying." These five activities complement one another, and each is necessary to the success of the total effort to improve the state's social policy legislation.

LEGISLATIVE GOALS

The state board's process of establishing legislative goals each year gives coherence to the statewide program of legislative action. The goals concern both legislation to be authored and supported and legislation NASW wishes to oppose. Formal statements of goals are important because they represent the discussion by the full board and help the lobbyist and chapter executive set priorities for their activities. Clear statements of goals also facilitate understanding by chapter members when their help is sought. In recent years, Florida NASW has pursued, among other goals, (1) increased funding of AFDC grants, (2) legislation to improve housing and health care for migrant workers, (3) state subsidies for adoption of hard-to-place children, (4) a system to keep track of foster children, (5) sweeping reform of archaic adoption laws, (6) the establishment and funding of community care programs for the elderly, (7) passage of a bill of rights for the retarded, (8) passage of legislation extending due process to the mentally ill who are held involuntarily, (9) Medicaid payments for abortions, (10) the defeat of bills calling for a national constitutional convention to ban abortions, (11) statewide school breakfast programs, (12) legislation establishing services for victims of spouse abuse, (13) the defeat of bills that would make it easier to refer juvenile offenders to adult courts, and (14) social work licensure. Of the fourteen goals listed here, nine have been achieved, and several others have become efforts to be pursued over several years. Given the great, coordinated effort needed to pass a bill, three to five goals is the maximum number a chapter can realistically hope to achieve in one year.

LOBBYING

Florida NASW maintained an organized effort to influence state legislation even before NASW established state chapters and gave Florida the funds to hire a director and open an office in the capital. The effort was the work of a skilled volunteer lobbyist, Budd Bell, and of student trainees from a graduate school. (This is also discussed in "Monitoring the Bureaucracy: An Extension of Legislative Lobbying.") Since 1975, the NASW lobbyist has been aided by the executive director of Florida NASW and, for the purposes of passing a licensure bill, by a paid professional lobbyist. Graduate student trainees also remain a part of the lobbying team.

An organized effort to pass state legislation and influence policy in the capital requires at least the following resources, which are coordinated by the state chapter's lobbyist:

- A skilled lobbyist with the authority to represent NASW and to call upon its resources. The lobbyist obtains sponsors for bills, forms coalitions, and manages the entire program of activities.
- Support personnel, including students and clerical workers. Experts are also needed for testimony on specific bills.
- A Wide Area Telephone Service (WATS) line to keep in close touch with activists in local units so that they can be orches-

trated properly to pressure their local legislators. This is a critical function because legislators must know their own voters care about an issue, particularly if the legislator is not well informed or strongly committed on an issue.

- Access to an up-to-date mailing list to keep the members informed and motivated throughout the legislative session. High-speed duplicating equipment is necessary to prepare mailings and send out alerts.

- A telephone tree to generate calls and letters on specific bills to targeted legislators. This system can be built into each local unit of the chapter.

- Authority to work with coalitions to add strength to NASW and to help others. Frequent coalition partners have been the State Federation of Labor, ERAmerica, the Catholic Welfare Conference, the Florida Medical Association, the National Organization for Women, and the American Civil Liberties Union.

- Monetary resources from the chapter sufficient to support the activities cited here. A chapter may devote up to 20 percent of its total budget to influencing legislation.

The subject of social work legislative lobbying has been studied by others and placed in the context of the profession's history, so it is not necessary to discuss its operations here at greater length.[8] It is important to recognize that the primary purpose of NASW's efforts to affect social policy is to achieve success in passing or defeating bills and that this success is closely intertwined with the other four parts of the system for influencing social policy: clear, realistic goals; an educated, motivated membership; political action to elect supportive legislators; and monitoring of the implementation of social legislation. If an NASW chapter is to affect social policy in a state, it must do so by influencing laws and the state budget. Florida's governor recently described the state budget as the central policy document of the society. Laws and public budgets, as Wade pointed out over a decade ago, are the major means by which society sets its goals and priorities.[9]

EDUCATING MEMBERSHIP

An educated, organized, and motivated membership is necessary to provide the resources and strength for the system to influence policy. Five functions require the involvement of significant numbers of members: (1) contributing funds to PACE, (2) doing volunteer work for PACE and for candidates, (3) attending seminars for social workers to express NASW's views to legislators, (4) calling on legislators in person to argue in behalf of NASW's positions, and (5) responding to the NASW lobbyist's requests that legislators and the press be telephoned or sent letters on a particular issue. Without these forms of support, lobbying and political action are a bluff, quickly called by hardened players in the tough game of politics. A chapter program to educate and raise the political consciousness of members must compete with the members' interests in courses to advance their therapy-related skills, with social workers' traditional reticence to become involved in politics, and with the limited hours and funds most social workers have to devote to activities outside their agencies.

In the months before the legislative session begins, Florida NASW attempts to hold an annual educational meeting with each of its local units. In these meetings, the state legislative chairperson shares state priorities with the local members, explains bills, and tries to increase the number of social workers who will call on local legislators and participate in telephone and letter-writing campaigns during the legislative session. The legislative chairperson also meets with each local unit's legislative committee to help build their skills in lobbying and in organizing letter-writing campaigns. As the membership develops an interest in supporting candidates through PACE, seminars are held to train members in campaign skills so that they can assume leadership roles in campaigns.

Legislative seminars involving the unit's members and its legislators are encouraged and occur every year in most local units. These seminars provide a link in the minds of the legislators between the issues to be voted on and a body of voters the legislator needs. The sessions are used to educate legislators about issues and to make members more comfortable and confident in their ability to confront elected leaders.

Personal phone calls and visits to a legislator's office signal high interest by motivated voters and supporters and thus exert more pressure than do letters or wires. Expanding the network of members who know a legislator, a congressional representative, or a senator and who are thus able to personally call on him or her is an important by-product of PACE activities in support of candidates. Members who work in campaigns, whether passing out leaflets or sponsoring fund raisers, often meet officials in contexts that breed warmth and friendship. That friendship can pay off when NASW members feel comfortable in going to see a legislator to press a point and when legislators perceive a friend as an NASW member walks through the door.

A neglected gold mine for NASW is the membership of the myriad of agency boards and advisory committees. In the ranks of these boards are many influential citizens whose support for NASW bills would be invaluable. Solving the organizational barriers to communicating and motivating these citizens is a major challenge.

POLITICAL ACTION COMMITTEE

The fourth component of a systematic approach to influencing social policy at the state level is involvement in organized electoral politics through a political action committee. NASW in 1976 formed a national committee, PACE, to endorse candidates in the presidential elections and in races for the U.S. Senate and House of Representatives. In 1978 Florida became the first state chapter to organize a political action committee under its state laws. Formal social work participation in electoral politics is thus the newest and probably the most experimental component of a comprehensive approach to influencing social policy. The Florida Chapter entered the electoral arena with its political action committee for the specific purpose of gaining more friends and supporters in the state legislature for the chapter's legislative and lobbying program. The chapter viewed the new process of actively helping sympathetic candidates to be elected or reelected as an integral part of the process of gaining policy victories in the capital.

Political action committees are generally empowered by state election laws, which vary greatly from state to state, to raise funds, to donate to campaigns, to endorse candidates, to publicize the committee's support of candidates, and to urge members and the public in various ways to support an endorsed candidate. In addition, political action committees can usually support or oppose specific issues, such as referenda and legislation. Many other established professions operate political action committees in Florida and other states; physicians, osteopaths, and teachers are among the practitioners of dozens of professions and trades in Florida that use political action committees to support their legislative programs. Each has a corresponding national political action committee as well.

Historically in social work, activities to achieve social policy goals have been limited to lobbying, research, advocacy, and, occasionally, demonstrations.[10] Formally supporting candidates or actually running NASW members for office were not seen as components of social action, although in 1966 Wade skated close to the subject when he wrote that active participation in electoral politics was probably central to achieving policy goals in a society whose major policy goals are made by elected bodies.[11] However, Wade did not contemplate a political action committee when he developed his list of social action roles for professional social workers. Thursz, writing on social action in the 1977 *Encyclopedia of Social Work*, urged improved legislative action by the profession but failed to include organized political action among his strategies.[12] This is curious in light of NASW's 1976 innovation in forming PACE. The creation of political action committees by NASW chapters across the country represents a new level of mature involvement in the political system and a recognition that even good politicians realistically expect professions to put their money and their volunteer hours behind their values.

PACE differs in two important ways from the political action committees sponsored by business and industry. First, PACE is much more limited in the amount of money it can raise for electoral activities than are the political action committees of major industries and trade associations. However, a social work political action committee has a unique strength in a membership that includes many who have formal skills and experience in community organization and voluntary action. These capabilities, when put to use in a campaign, can equal larger financial contributions in effectiveness.

The basic assumptions that underlie all political action committees are essentially the same. First, it is presumed that legislators who help an interest group, such as NASW, need and value endorsements and other support when they are up for election. It is also assumed that receiving assistance from a political action committee will lead a legislator to be more supportive of the group in the future. This electoral aid is a legitimate, partial quid pro quo for the help the legislator gives the group. In a society of competing interest groups, helping one's friends is seen as normal and not doing so is considered odd. Second, endorsements and contributions put the entire political community on notice that the group is willing to make a real commitment to legislators and that it is playing the game the way other major interest groups play. Third, endorsements and contributions to candidates put opponents of a social work group's legislation on notice that there are potential consequences to opposing human welfare legislation.

In the long run, the growing number and power of political action committees in American political life is not necessarily healthy for democracy. It is questionable whether proliferating special interest politics is beneficial to society. However, during this phase of political development in America, a political action committee appears to be a necessary part of a complete NASW political program.

Developing a Political Action Committee

Each state will undoubtedly follow a unique pattern in forming its political action committee. The development of Florida's committee is presented as a case study here because certain universal issues were encountered and because Florida's experiences may provide perspective to social workers elsewhere.

As Wade and Mahaffey point out, certain factors have traditionally been arrayed against lobbying and political action in social work, including timidity, fears of violating the Hatch Act, and the belief that helping individuals through casework is the most appropriate method of social intervention for professionals.[13] In addition to having to deal with these forces of opposition, those forming a state political action committee for NASW can also expect to face the criticism that backing one candidate over another can cause problems if NASW's endorsed candidate loses. This argument is countered by the observed tendency of politicians to seek to repair relationships with groups after winning, as long as the groups did not act unethically in their support of the candidate they endorsed. For example, several candidates whom Florida PACE did not endorse wrote to say they regretted losing the endorsement but would be happy to work with PACE after the elections. Timidity is also countered by noting that most other major professions, facing the same risks, nevertheless endorse candidates or contribute funds to their campaigns.

A second argument often heard is that NASW, like Common Cause, has traditionally supported only issues, and not candidates. However, this overlooks the reality that issues, in the form of bills, pass into law and become social policy because some legislators introduced and fought for the bills. Once a legislature is filled with people who will not fight for a particular bill, or even vote for it, it may be too late to seek a legislative remedy for a social ill. Political action is practical action to provide a more favorable legislature. All innovations are subject to resistance in organizations, and NASW's move into political action is no exception.[14]

The most important activity in setting the climate for establishing PACE in a state chapter is developing the commitment of the chapter's board and other leaders. Because organized political action is new and controversial to many social workers, it will not succeed unless opinion leaders are informed about the process, understand the validity of political action committees, and support the political action committee to the board members and the membership as a whole.

Florida PACE took several steps to ensure acceptance by the membership. These steps included earning support within the chapter's executive committee, particularly with the president, the legislative chairperson, and the executive director. Recognition that NASW was fostering PACE nationally was critical in gaining legitimacy. Florida PACE was authorized by the board only after opinion leaders had the time to study the issue and to communicate fully with the board as a whole. All PACE planning meetings were attended by either the president or the executive director. To make sure that PACE would remain under the control of the NASW state chapter and that it would be oriented to NASW's goals and policies, Florida's NASW board approved the first by-laws and appointed the PACE trustees. Florida PACE is registered as a political action committee officially pursuing the goals of NASW. Its bylaws are filed with the state, and they make it clear that it is nominally separate from NASW but substantially under its control. The first Florida PACE trustees included three NASW board members.

After its formation by the state board of NASW, Florida PACE and its activities were presented to the membership through the state NASW newsletter. A feature article pointed to deep support for PACE among the board members and to the legitimacy of

250   ABRAMS and GOLDSTEIN

the new activity. The organizing process took eight months. States contemplating a political action committee would do well to be certain that key opinion leaders are fully committed to the committee so that it is perceived by the membership as legitimate and that it can be defended from expected criticisms.

As soon as the bylaws were approved, the trustees appointed, and the registration papers filed with state election officials, the focus shifted to informing the membership and enlisting their participation. The state newsletter was the main channel of communication, and to raise membership's awareness, it gave prominence to PACE in each issue. Frequent quotes from chapter leaders were used to demonstrate the value and importance of support for PACE among the membership. In addition, officials from NASW's national office met with NASW members in five cities to inform the members and communicate support. Thus, through careful involvement of chapter leaders and extensive efforts to educate members, the climate was established for political action for candidate election.

Key Elements of a PACE Program

During its first years of existence, Florida PACE engaged in four key activities to select and then aid candidates it hoped would support legislation favored by NASW. It endorsed candidates, raised funds for operations and to contribute to candidates, worked to get out the social work vote in behalf of candidates, and trained and motivated members to participate in PACE and in candidates' campaigns.

ENDORSEMENT PROCESS

The major activity of Florida PACE during its first year was to carry out and publicize a process of endorsing candidates running for governor and in key legislative races. The trustees decided on two important policies at the outset—first, that the organization's scarce resources should be focused on a relatively few races important to social work, and not on hundreds of candidates, most of whom were not really known to NASW; second, that endorsement would be awarded only to candidates who asked for it in writing and who submitted their record and positions in writing to Florida PACE. Written application was viewed as essential to allow for a professional review of credentials and to remind candidates of NASW's social welfare goals.

The trustees made an informal agreement not to allow conflict over choosing candidates to destroy the neophyte group. Consensus was always sought, and win-or-lose battles were avoided by such devices as choosing not to endorse in some races where consensus was unattainable, compromising in some races, and endorsing more than one candidate in others.

The trustees selected the gubernatorial election and twenty-five legislative races as opportunities to support people with excellent records in office or others who were talented newcomers. Based on her extensive knowledge of the legislature, of many candidates, and of the priorities of other groups, such as ERAmerica, the legislative chair led the process of selecting races in which to become involved. Only one local race was selected, that of a distinguished commissioner in Dade County who faced a tough re-election campaign.

Each candidate in a targeted race was invited to apply for endorsement in writing and was sent a detailed questionnaire soliciting views on such issues as licensure of social workers (a do-or-die issue for NASW), AFDC payment levels, health care legislation, and other topics.[15] Several candidates wrote to tell PACE that the questionnaire was the most thorough one they had ever confronted. Most took the process seriously. Of course, in this age when taking positions on issues is seen by candidates as dangerous, some declined to complete the questionnaires. Four of the five Democratic candidates for governor sought endorsement, as did one of the two Republicans. Three of the Democrats had social workers help them with the questionnaires, one spent twenty-five dollars on air freight to get the questionnaire in on time, and one had his questionnaire hand delivered to the trustees by a powerful state senator. The trustees made their endorsement in the governor's race at the earliest possible moment to obtain exposure and the status of having been in on the ground floor of the campaign.

The questionnaires were reviewed in detail in three lengthy, hectic meetings. Coordinating meetings without a travel budget and in a tight, three-month period was a major operational problem for PACE and for the NASW state office. Questionnaire data were considered, along with knowledge of the candidates' past records, and the character of candidates was frankly discussed.

Additional factors the trustees took into account were the likelihood of the candidate's winning and the value of supporting women and minority group members when possible. Endorsed candidates included several incumbents who had traditionally supported social welfare measures, several candidates who were running against senators who opposed the Equal Rights Amendment (ERA), and several desirable newcomers running in significant races against incumbents not friendly to issues of concern to NASW.

Endorsed candidates were given permission and encouragement to use the endorsement in their campaigns. Many referred to the PACE endorsement in brochures, speeches, and ads, and this increased PACE's credibility in the political community. Rejected candidates were sent courteous letters aimed at keeping open lines of communication for the future.

PACE issued press releases of its endorsements. Media coverage was uneven, and in future elections, PACE in Florida must step up its attempts to gain coverage through personal contact with reporters and editors. Coverage in the media is essential to increasing PACE's political clout in the eyes of legislators and should be a major focus for every state PACE.

Endorsement-related activities consumed the bulk of the trustees' time. However, the trustees felt that participation in the open, democratic process was an outstanding learning experience for professionals and that it also added to PACE's credibility with candidates.

The PACE-endorsed nominee for governor won a surprising upset victory, and most of the endorsed legislative candidates won as well. In retrospect, no clear win-lose pattern emerges. Nevertheless, it appears that PACE lost most frequently when it endorsed a person who had not yet held public office and who was opposing an entrenched incumbent. This same pattern of incumbent victories occurs nationally in congressional elections. PACE-supported newcomers seeking vacant seats fared better. Only one PACE-endorsed incumbent was defeated.

After the November 1978 election, several successful candidates made it known that they appreciated PACE's support. The governor invited NASW to participate on the inauguration committee, and PACE trustees became involved in advisory committees and served as advisers to legislators. It is still too soon to judge how much added access and support has been gained for

NASW, but the state's NASW lobbyist and executive director perceive a warmer climate and more open doors.

As expected, fund raising was the greatest challenge. A political action committee needs funds for operations (to cover costs for such items as postage, travel, telephones, and the printing of questionnaires) and for donations to candidates it wishes to help. Because PACE was new and innovative, fund raising was difficult the first year. Relatively few NASW members are in the habit of giving political contributions, and many are not able to do so. Florida PACE borrowed cash and raised funds through membership subscriptions, cocktail parties, and even the raffling off of a canoe. A glance at the approach taken by teachers, many of whom have incomes similar to social workers, points to the value of NASW's eventually basing its funding of PACE on the size of each chapter, as the national teachers' association does, or providing members the choice of designating a portion of their annual dues to PACE. Until then, the activities of PACE will probably develop more slowly than is desirable because of the difficulty in raising funds by donation.

PACE in Florida chose to give funds to candidates it endorsed, which was perhaps its most innovative step. Although these donations were generally small, usually twenty-five or fifty dollars, they were large enough to be personally noted by all but statewide candidates. Contributions indicate serious commitment to a candidate. In low-budget state legislative races, donations of twenty-five dollars are eagerly sought and acknowledged. Several worthy candidates genuinely needed PACE's contributions.

Most states and the federal government have strict reporting requirements for all political contributions. Chapters can expect to spend a substantial sum merely to meet the reporting requirements, which include complete enumeration of every dollar raised and spent.

What is the future of PACE's activities if the financial base is not expanded? Even on a shoestring, social work political action committees can have a meaningful impact through endorsements and through efforts to get out the vote. Additional funds would make possible an important extension of these activities. Chapters with greater resources than the Florida Chapter will probably seek to balance spending among maintenance activities for PACE, campaign contributions, and expanded programs to get out the vote and train members.

GETTING OUT THE VOTE

A state PACE must develop the ability to motivate NASW members and their families to go out on election day and vote for the endorsed slate. Middle-class voters are likely to vote anyway, so the challenge is to turn out the highest percentage of members who vote the NASW ticket. Several procedures facilitate this process.

First, all members must know that the endorsement process was done in an open, democratic manner and that it focused on issues of concern to NASW. The chapter's newsletter was the key mechanism for communicating the idea that the Florida PACE ticket deserved the members' vote.

Second, members must know precisely whom PACE wants them to vote for in each race. To accomplish this, Florida PACE published a sample ballot in the newsletter, listing the endorsed candidates, the counties involved, and the number of the seats in the legislature. In the primary election, the endorsed candidate for governor was allowed to supply PACE with his own printed message for PACE to mail at its expense to every member. The printed sample ballots were timed to arrive at homes in the weeks prior to the primary and general elections. In addition, NASW members in several cities called people on the NASW membership list to urge them to vote for the particular candidates in the area. Members who were called in the phone campaign indicated a high degree of acceptance of PACE's activity. Because primary elections have low turnouts, disciplined bloc voting counts heavily. Legislators know this, and when they see the phone lists being used, they know NASW is helping in a significant way.

CAMPAIGN PARTICIPATION

Even at the outset, PACE in Florida was able to motivate members to work in the campaigns of some endorsed candidates, particularly the gubernatorial candidate, several women candidates, and pro-ERA candidates. As indicated earlier, personal involvement in a legislator's struggle builds strong bonds. In each state where PACE develops, a priority should be to carry out training early to enable members to become leaders in campaigns. Each political campaign needs coordinators for telephoning, volunteer organizing, polling, canvassing, speech writing, direct mail work, fund raising, and election day activities. These coordinators, who are usually unpaid volunteers in legislative races, build the closest relationships with the candidate. One key function is to learn to organize NASW members to volunteer. As members of Florida PACE found out, campaign leadership roles are learnable, and when combined with a willingness to volunteer for long hours, undertaking these roles enables an individual to have a rich experience. As a result of voluntary leadership in a campaign, one PACE member joined the staff of a key legislator as an intern for the 1979 legislative year. She is now in a position to interact on an intimate, collegial basis with the chairman of a committee controlling legislation of importance to social welfare. Such are the anticipated results of campaign involvement.

CHALLENGES

Clearly, the undertaking by NASW chapters of activities related to PACE raises important issues. Foremost among them is the challenge to finance PACE's efforts, which are expensive. It has been argued here that NASW per capita funding is necessary. A second challenge is to identify more NASW members with the skills, community identification, and determination to seek public office. The sooner the profession begins to work for social worker candidates in every state, the sooner the profession and its values will have articulate voices in legislative committees and on floors of debate. (In 1978 the national association's PACE assisted eight social workers in their election campaigns.) Social worker candidates should be actively cultivated now so that before the 1980s are over every state legislature will have social workers in its ranks.

A third challenge is educating and motivating membership. For the foreseeable future, PACE committees will be working in an atmosphere in which most members will not be willing to contribute funds or time to political action and only a small percentage will write or call legislators on key votes. Activities by NASW chapters and by schools of social work that provide greater exposure and sanction for political action are necessary foundations for developing a motivated and knowledgeable membership. A fourth challenge will be to establish clear links in the minds of elected officials between the help given by PACE in the autumn of elections and the support and leadership needed in the winter of hard legislative politics.

ABRAMS and GOLDSTEIN

OVERSIGHT OF IMPLEMENTATION

After laws are made out and budgets allocated, bureaucrats must develop rules and programs to implement the purposes of those laws. The Florida Chapter's system of influencing policy has included attendance at rule-making procedures and review of program plans. These are important year-round activities to ensure that a law's purposes are not subverted. Student interns have been successfully used to monitor carefully how programs are implemented. When significant sabotage or misdirection is perceived, the legislative sponsors of the relevant bill are notified so that they can exert corrective pressure on the bureaucracy. In other cases, the media can be informed in the hope that they will publicize the problem.[16]

Administrative oversight completes the circle of policy and social action processes. That is, the idea for a law or a budgetary allocation begins the cycle and is followed by the drafting of a bill and lobbying and marshaling support for it. Finally, if the bill is successful, NASW has the pleasure and responsibility to monitor the implementation of the resulting program.

System Coordination

All complex systems such as the state chapter program described here require coordination if the parts are to work together successfully. Channels of communication that facilitate close coordination between the system's elements are critical to the success of complex coordination in all organizations.[17] As NASW chapters continue to develop their systems for influencing policy, they confront the need to articulate two structures clearly. First, a leadership group is necessary to make decisions concerning broad policy and goals. The state board and key opinion leaders on the board must accept this responsibility if a chapter's program is to attract the involvement of the membership and become organized.

Second, an individual or small group should be clearly delegated the authority to implement plans, use resources, and coordinate the annual effort. For example, in Florida the chapter's full-time executive director and the legislative chairperson, who is also a lobbyist, share this coordinative function. The president of PACE was an integral part of the coordinating group during the year-long election campaigns and continues to help remind legislators of the link between bills and NASW-supported issues and the organization's earlier campaign support through PACE.

It is the responsibility of the executive director and legislative chair to prepare the annual effort and execute it under the board's mandate. Thus, close communication channels that link these functions laterally are important. The simplified communication chart of necessary internal linkages (see Figure 1) illustrates the need for mechanisms to facilitate communication and points to the importance of both technical supports (in the form of WATS lines, frequent face-to-face contact, photocopying, and typing services) and a trusting relationship that leads the key participants to engage in a great deal of task-oriented communication.

The lobbyist is responsible for recommending legislative action, devising tactics, and communicating to NASW's local units. The executive director aids in organizing support from the units, prepares tactics and strategies with the lobbyist, and provides administrative support and is the key link between the board's policies, NASW's resources, and the other actors. In general,

Fig. 1. Channels of Communication among the State Political Units of NASW

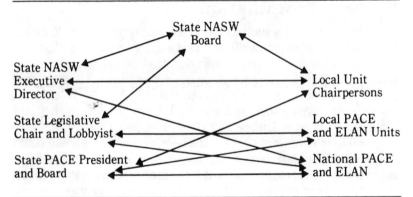

it is worthwhile reemphasizing that successful organization and action require leaders in each role who have most of the following skills: the ability to work on a team and to resolve conflicts in a healthy way, the ability to communicate clearly, the ability to accept the ideas and needs of others on the team, and skills in organizing and motivating volunteers.

ABRAMS and GOLDSTEIN

Summary

As Wade argued a decade ago, a central task of NASW's state chapters is to achieve legislative successes in the formation of social policy.[18] It is recognized that because NASW commands the resources of fewer than one hundred thousand members and represents values upholding social justice and welfare that are frequently opposed by legislative majorities, achieving many legislative victories will require intense organization, a careful use of resources, and the frequent formation of coalitions with other groups. As long as interest groups continue to exert increasing influence in American society, NASW's chapters must accept the responsibility of becoming more potent political interest groups for the profession and for their clients. That responsibility carries with it the need to elaborate a complete system of activities that can mobilize and focus a chapter's scarce resources on legislative targets. The system described in this article is based on the program of the Florida Chapter's twenty-five hundred members, which consists of five key elements that interact to support each other:

- Leadership and the selection of legislative goals by the state board.
- Legislative lobbying, including the development of bills and the use of management and coalition tactics to implement the board's legislative priorities.
- Membership education and motivation to increase local members' contributions to NASW's political activities, letter and telephone communications to legislators when requested, and participation in the campaigns of endorsed candidates.
- PACE to improve access to legislators and to elect social welfare advocates.
- Oversight and monitoring of the bureaucracy's implementation of laws to ensure that rules and procedures do not subvert the intent of legislative programs NASW worked to establish.

Notes and References

1. Jane Addams, *Twenty Years at Hull House* and *The Second Twenty Years at Hull House* (New York: Macmillan Publishing Co., 1911 and 1930, respectively.)

2. Scott Briar, "The Current Crisis in Social Casework," in *Social Work Practice, 1967* (New York: Columbia University Press, 1967), p. 28.

3. George A. Brager, "Advocacy and Political Behavior," *Social Work,* 13 (April 1968), p. 6.

4. *Code of Ethics of the National Association of Social Workers,* NASW Policy Statements, 1 (Washington, D.C.: National Association of Social Workers, 1980), p. 9.

5. Harry Specht, "Casework Practice and Social Policy Formulation," *Social Work,* 13 (January 1968), p. 44. On the history of lobbying in social work, *see* Daniel Thursz, "Social Action," *Encyclopedia of Social Work,* Vol. II (17th issue; Washington, D.C.: National Association of Social Workers, 1977), pp. 1,274–1,280; and Wilbur J. Cohen, "What Every Social Worker Should Know about Political Action," *Social Work,* 11 (July 1966), pp. 3–11.

6. For a discussion of the activities of political action committees in Florida, including a donation of $110,984 by the medical doctors, *see* William R. Amlong and Robert D. Shaw, Jr., "Special Interests Wait for Payoff in Legislative Finale," *Miami Herald,* May 19, 1977, pp. 20A–22A. *See also* Albert R. Hunt, "How Rival Lobbyists Battled to Win Vote on Gas Deregulation," *Wall Street Journal,* July 15, 1977, p. 1.

7. Saul Alinsky, *Reveille for Radicals* (New York: Vantage Books, 1969), p. 212.

8. Thursz, op. cit.; Budd Bell and William G. Bell, "Lobbying as Advocacy," in Bernard Ross and S.K. Khinduka, eds., *Social Work in Practice* (Washington, D.C.: National Association of Social Workers, 1976), pp. 154–167; Cohen, op. cit.; and Maryann Mahaffey, "Lobbying and Social Work," *Social Work,* 17 (January 1972), pp. 3–11. [For a revised version of Mahaffey's article, *see* pp. 69 of this book.]

9. Alan D. Wade, "The Social Worker in the Political Process," *Social Welfare Forum, 1966* (New York: Columbia University Press, 1966), pp. 52–67.

10. Ibid.; Cohen, op. cit.; and Mahaffey, op. cit.

11. Wade, op. cit.

12. Thursz, op. cit.

13. Wade, op. cit.; and Mahaffey, op. cit.

14. *See* Gerald Zaltman, Robert Duncan, and Jonny Holbeck, *Innovations and Organizations* (New York: Wiley-Interscience, 1973).

15. The text of the Florida questionnaire is substantially reprinted in Carol J. Sheffer, *PACE Handbook* (Washington, D.C.: National Association of Social Workers, 1978), pp. 10–13.

16. Bell and Bell, op. cit.

17. Jerald Hage, *Communication and Organizational Control,* (New York: John Wiley & Sons, 1974).

18. Wade, op. cit.